HARLEY GRANVILLE BARKER RECLAIMED

Edited by

JONATHAN BANK

Introduction by Gus Kaikkonen

GRANVILLE PRESS

Inquires regarding individual plays should be made to:

The Society of Authors
84 Drayton Gardens
London SW10 9SB

Inquiries regarding performance rights to *The Voysey Inheritance* adapted by Gus Kaikkonen should be made to:

Gus Kaikkonen
124 MacDougal Street #12
New York, NY 10012
GusKaikkonen@cs.com

ISBN: 9780971826229
Library of Congress Control Number: 2007923697

Book designed by Nita Congress
nita@njccommunications.com

This book is made possible through the generous support of the Gladys Krieble Delmas Foundation.

The Gladys Krieble Delmas Foundation promotes the advancement and perpetuation of humanistic inquiry and artistic creativity by encouraging excellence in scholarship and in the performing arts, and by supporting research libraries and other institutions which transmit our cultural heritage.

Trustees
George Labalme, Jr.
Joseph C. Mitchell
David H. Stam

Foundation Administrator
Shirley A. Lockwood

CONTENTS

INTRODUCTION

Gus Kaikkonen

"The greatest man in the theatre I ever met."
—John Gielgud on Harley Granville Barker

The works of Bernard Shaw first brought me to Granville Barker. I read *The Voysey Inheritance* in 1991, while preparing a production of *Candida*. Shaw chose Barker to play the first Marchbanks—a role the twenty-three-year-old actor performed to great success (he was also the original Edward Voysey)—and Shaw's later letters praise Barker's plays as highly as his acting. From the first scene, *Voysey* leaps off the page as a very great play, Shavian in its cunning dissection of social institutions; but Barker also mines in a very personal way the profoundly dangerous intimacies of his characters' hearts: their secret lives.

I tracked down Barker's other plays—difficult to find in New York in the 1990s—and grew more and more impressed by the subtlety, wit, and detailed observation of his writing, and the splendid opportunities this actor/playwright gives his fellow performers. I was appalled that the plays were so infrequently produced—a complaint Shaw himself registered in his 1946 obituary of Barker. In England, Barker's plays, especially *Voysey*, tend to be rediscovered with great excitement every decade or so. The Shaw Festival in Canada had unearthed them as well. But as of 1999, *Voysey* had never been produced in New York, *Madras House* not since 1921, and the one-act, *Farewell to Theatre*, had never been staged anywhere as far as I could tell. Between 1999 and 2007, Jonathan Bank, Artistic Director of the Mint Theater Company, gave me the opportunity to direct these three works in New York.

The Voysey Inheritance depicts generations of financial fraud put to an end by Edward Voysey's determined personal integrity. But the formerly honest Edward puts things right by doing wrong, flagrantly breaking the letter of the law to save small investors from ruin at the expense of wealthy ones. The thrill, danger, and pleasure of his own financial piracy makes a man of him, wins him his true love, and gives him an intimate appreciation of his father's character and crime. *The Madras House* is an enormous canvas, a serious comedy in four movements: Act One, a comedy of manners; Act Two, a problem play; Act Three, a Shavian board meeting; Act Four, an Ibsen comedy. Twenty-four characters animated, illuminated, and tortured by sex. *Farewell to the Theatre* paints the theater less as a profession than a seductive and incurable disease. Written in 1916, when Barker himself was caught between wives and careers, it depicts the dilemma of an indomitable, but aging and impoverished actress/manager who can neither give up the theater, nor retreat into a comfortable marriage.

Writing a preface to the plays of Harley Granville Barker is daunting. His own *Prefaces to Shakespeare* revitalized modern notions of the Bard's plays in performance. Barker writes in *Prefaces*: "…these books have quite a practical aim. I want to see Shakespeare made fully effective on the English stage. This is the best sort of help I can lend." I respectfully offer these versions of three of his plays, to I hope a similar effect.

A NOTE ON THE TEXTS

Other than an "Americanized" adaptation at the Long Wharf Theatre in 1990, *The Voysey Inheritance* had never been produced in the States. Jonathan challenged me to come up with a version of the Barker which the Mint could afford to present. There are eighteen characters in *Voysey*, including Booth Voysey's wife Emily and son Christopher; Ethel Voysey's fiancé Denis; the Reverend Colpus, and two domestics at Chislehurst. These six characters combined have only forty-two lines. I cut all six and divided their lines among the remaining roles, which made those parts all the more interesting to play. The only major character cut is Hugh Voysey, the artist brother, who does not appear until Act Three. Most of his lines in this adaptation have gone to his wife, Beatrice, whose character originally appeared only in Acts Two and Five. As a result, Beatrice's role doubles in size, and she becomes one of the more intriguing characters of the play.

The original text of *The Madras House* is a long and difficult read for the twenty-first century reader. It is loaded with topical references from 1909 and has twenty-four characters for the audience to keep straight. However, the play's episodic nature allowed our actors to be double cast, and so, without the textual surgery required for *Voysey*, we were able to produce the play with only fourteen actors. The only character missing is the eldest Huxtable daughter, Laura, whose four lines were distributed among her sisters. I then weeded the text down to a running time of 2:45, and occasionally changed or added lines to clarify references. The opening of the play provides an example of the cuts:

PHILIP: About how long?

PARLOURMAID: In just a few minutes now I should say, sir. Oh, I beg pardon, does it appen to be the third Sunday in the month?

PHILIP: I don't know. Tommy, does it?

THOMAS: *(From the window.)* Don't ask me. Well, I suppose I can tell you. *(And he vaguely fishes for his diary.)*

PARLOURMAID: No, I don't think it does, sir. Because then some of them stop for the Oly Communion, and that may make them late for dinner, but I don't think it is, sir.

This becomes:

PHILIP: About how long?

PARLOURMAID: Just a few minutes now, I would say, sir. Oh, I beg pardon, does it appen to be the third Sunday in the month?

PHILIP: I don't know.

PARLOURMAID: Because then some of them stop for the Oly Communion and that may make them late for dinner.

An example of text added for clarity is the following exchange later in Act One:

EMMA: Well, a collar marked Lewis Waller came back from the wash in mistake for one of Father's I don't think he lives near here, but it's one of those big steam laundries…

becomes:

EMMA: Well, a shirt collar marked Lewis Waller came back from the wash in mistake for one of Father's.

PHILIP: The actor?

EMMA: The matinee idol. I don't think he lives near here, but it's one of those big steam laundries…

A Farewell to the Theatre is also slightly edited, with some topical references changed for clarity.

∽ ∾

I must thank my collaborators: the hard-working staff of the Mint and the many fine actors and designers who brought Barker to life, especially the excellent George Morfogen, who played major roles in all three productions. *The Madras House* double-casting could not have succeeded without the skilled performances of Laurie Kennedy, Mary

Bacon, Kraig Swartz, Lisa Bostnar, Angela Reed, and the fine work of costume designer Clint Ramos and the transformative wigs of designer Gerard James Kelly.

Gus Kaikkonen's plays have been produced off Broadway at Playwrights Horizons, the Production Company, and the NYMF; and in London at the New End Theatre and the Theatre Museum. He has been a MacDowell Fellow, the James Thurber Playwriting Fellow at Ohio State, and a visiting artist at Juilliard and NYU. His directing credits in New York include multiple productions at the Pearl Theatre and Riverside Shakespeare. For the Mint Theater, he directed the New York premieres of The Voysey Inheritance, The Charity that Began at Home, *and* Farewell to the Theatre *and revivals of* The Madras House *and* The Flattering Word. *He is the Artistic Director of the Peterborough Players in New Hampshire.*

THE MADRAS HOUSE

BARKER'S "MAHOMMEDAN"

Lana Cable

For this theatergoer, the Mint Theater Company's excellent production of Harley Granville Barker's *The Madras House* provides an opportunity to revisit a puzzle that has lingered in the back of my mind since 1977 when I first saw the play at the National Theatre in London. Along with that audience I had been thrilled by the wit of Barker's social critique, but the character of Constantine Madras baffled me. His exoticism seemed to count for more than was acknowledged by the script. As a student, I had no idea that my ambivalence toward Constantine was not necessarily that of most in the audience, who were more familiar than I with the cultural context of the British empire. By way of comparison, the context of contemporary politics gives today's audiences a special *frisson*, as they gasp at Constantine's offhand remark that Europe ought to be prepared for an "Islamic revival." But even as the performance again captivated me, this time I could understand my ambivalence toward Constantine's exoticism in the context not just of the audience's frame of reference but of English drama history. Playwrights from the sixteenth century onward can be seen utilizing, with a variety of cultural and social objectives, a critical instrument that also informs the character of Constantine Madras.

Barker's Constantine is far more than a critical instrument, of course. The play's every action is influenced by this fascinating character: founder of an exclusive Victorian fashion house; idolized designer for aristocrats of an empire on which the sun never set; an expatriate alienated from his own family as well as from his native culture; a self-styled convert to Islam. This of course is where his critical instrumentality comes into play. Constantine's conversion to Islam is "self-styled" because Barker gives him an understanding of his adopted faith that is neither different from, nor better informed than, the popular notion that happens to prevail in the minds of Barker's non-Muslim audience. Indeed, throughout British drama history, the prevailing European conception of Islam constitutes a versatile trope that playwrights feel free to deploy as they choose. The trope's versatility as an instrument of social critique depends substantially on the fact that neither English audiences in general nor most English playwrights actually knew much about Islam.

The historical reasons for this are clear. As John Tolan shows in *Saracens*,* the European idea of Islam was originally established by medieval Christian writers whose mistrust of the new religion went as deep as did their conviction that only *they* had a purchase on God's truth.

---

*New York: Columbia University Press, 2002.

How could God allow these people of the desert to grow so rich and sophisticated, learned and powerful? they asked. And since revered Christian scholarly tradition offered no answers, they accounted for Islam by pigeonholing perceived cultural differences into time-honored Christian categories of sin. Depending on the polemical occasion, Muslims were defined as heretics, idolaters, or embodiments of deadly sins such as wrath, avarice, pride, and—above all—lechery. Since these medieval Christians' Pauline spirituality demanded scourging of the flesh, they assumed that religious permission for multiple wives could only indicate unbridled lust. Over the ensuing centuries, these ideas were elaborated by other Christians as they chronicled Muslim expansion into the Iberian peninsula, the Crusades, the fall of Constantinople, the Spanish reconquest, and growth of the Ottoman Empire.

Historically balanced readings of those events today lead scholars to cringe over Muslim stereotypes that proliferate in early English plays. But it is worth noting that despite (and partly because of) widespread cultural ignorance about Islam, sixteenth and seventeenth century stage Muslims performed analytical work similar to that performed by Constantine Madras. Between the time of these early stereotypes and Barker's richly delineated character lay three centuries of historical experience that included the fall of the Ottoman Empire and rise of the British one, as well as constant travel to, and trading or colonial relations with, Muslim countries. Yet none of this long and complicated historical experience furnishes Constantine Madras with a religious understanding that is any more complex than the 1910 British trope that reduced Islam to the practice of polygamy.

Sixteenth and seventeenth century playwrights were also known to deploy a single-issue Islam in their critiques, but their issue of choice often dealt with the public debate over free conscience rather than gender relations. At the time, England was a mere apprentice in global trade dominated by Ottoman Muslims. In a rapidly urbanizing mercantile economy, penniless but daring Englishmen often looked abroad for their futures, and their odds of success were better on the pirate-ridden Barbary coast than in the American wilderness. So using popular conceptions of Islam to explore the problem of free conscience seemed perfectly reasonable to early modern theater audiences. Dramatized oriental adventures could put English cultural and spiritual identity to a test that was both alarming and alluring: conversion to Islam was a recognized feature of scenarios in which the risks were high, but the rewards could be great. Yet as with Barker, the early modern playwright's objective was never to explore Muslim religion or culture. It was rather to posit a credible outsider perspective for intervening in cultural debates at home—debates that might otherwise be too elusive, too familiar, or too disturbing of vested interests to attract popular audience attention.

A quick look at how this worked for England's long-running free conscience debate puts Barker's "Mahommedan" strategy into historical
perspective. In Robert Daborne's 1612 *A Christian Turned Turk*, the
Tunisian governor, himself a convert to Islam, offers patronage to the
English adventurer Ward by saying:

> What difference in me as I am a Turk
> And was a Christian? Life, Liberty,
> Wealth, honor–they are common unto all!
> If any odds be, 'tis on Mahomet's side.*

Had the governor's analysis yielded only wealth and honor, Daborne's
audience might have seen his conversion as mere opportunism. But by
adding "Life" and "Liberty"—causes that would one day join "pursuit of
happiness" to declare a new democracy—the Tunisian governor voices
human instincts too deep and universal to be claimed by a single faith
or, as he puts it, by any "fetters of religion" at all. In George Peele's
1588 *The Battle of Alcazar*, Thomas Stukley converts the freedom of
being born English into freedom *from* being English. "As we are Englishmen, so are we men," he says: "I may at libertie make choise/Of all
the continents that bound the world."† Stukley's potentially anarchic
freedom sheds every unchosen aspect of personal identity, including
family bonds. The allure of absolute freedom defines even a terrifying
character like Christopher Marlowe's Tamburlaine, who grounds his
authority on the free choice of men rather than on divine right: the
crown rests "more surer on my head," he says, "Than if the *gods* had
held a parliament/And all pronounced me King of Persia."‡ In Marlowe's
Elizabethan England, such arguments posed risks to the establishment
even greater than that posed by Constantine's Woman Question to
the British Empire. Yet early modern playwrights compulsively and
publicly probed their ideas about free conscience by dramatizing them,
as it were, under protection of Mahomet.

But even the "unsolved problem" that Constantine Madras calls "this
Woman Question" has predecessors in plays that treat Islam as a
critical trope. Early modern English society was troubled by a Woman
Question too: as women learned to read, they demanded new liberties.

A Christian Turned Turk, Scene 7.28–32, in Daniel J. Vitkus, ed., *Three
Turk Plays from Early Modern England* (New York: Columbia University Press,
2000).

†*The Battle of Alcazar*, II.ii.410–415, J. Yoklavich, ed., in *The Life and
Works of George Peele, Vol. II*, Charles Tyler Prouty, gen. ed. (New Haven:
Yale University Press, 1961).

‡*Tamburlaine the Great, Part One*, II.vii.65–67, Revels Student Editions, J.
S. Cunningham and Eithne Henson, eds. (New York: Manchester University
Press, 1998).

Philip Massinger stirs up the Woman Question in *The Renegado* (1624) when beautiful Donusa, niece to the Ottoman emperor, learns that the liberties of English ladies are similar to her own except that, she slyly observes, *"our* religion/Allows all *pleasure."** Donusa's pleasure leads her to unveil in the marketplace just enough to conquer the heart of a Christian. She ultimately redeems herself by converting, which mollifies English orthodoxy, but meanwhile, Massinger has scored a point in the English debate over feminist aspirations. Restless women *might* be accommodated, Donusa's action hints, by adhering to this simple equation: exotic plus erotic equals shopping. Thus Massinger serves the interests of budding English mercantilism while prodding newly literate ladies to indulge in the liberty of spending money. Meanwhile, Massinger's sardonic slant on what motivates English feminists can be blamed on a Muslim woman.

This maneuver is closely related to the one Barker achieves via Constantine Madras. Constantine paves the way toward analysis of the Woman Question with his shocking revelation that he has "settled [his] personal share" in the problem by becoming a "Mahommedan." Constantine's use of the term "Mahommedan" itself demands attention, for it points not to faith in *Islam* (that is, submission to God), but rather, to faith in the religion's founding prophet. This ideologically distorted term, which is not used by Muslims, was invented by the same medieval Christians who had defined Islam by framing it as embodying deadly sins. Yet the term serves Barker by invoking the 1910 version of the Islamic trope, so that his audience will experience the force of his critique. Since "Mahommedan" in British imperial culture conveniently signals "polygamy," the term breaks open to scrutiny Mr. State's ecstatic vision of Middle-Class Women. These are the women whose "Birthright" State has claimed is to "Dazzle and Conquer": the very women he has also admonished his fellow empire builders to "think of…in bulk." Thinking of women "in bulk" would of course have been the foremost charge against "Mahommedans" in the prevailing view of Islam. So Constantine's shocking revelation that he himself is a Mahommedan throws State's actual exploitation of women into harsh relief. The implications of this are played out as *The Madras House* goes on to expose empire's dependence on women not only as conquistador-consumers whose corseting makes them unfit to bear children, but also as mass producers of material goods in the spirit-killing factories of the imperial money machine.

Complacency toward empire is the condition of Barker's audience, hence his merciless focus on empire's ethical blind spots. The playwright

---

The Renegado, I.ii.49–50., in Daniel J. Vitkus, ed., *Three Turk Plays from Early Modern England* (New York: Columbia University Press, 2000); my italics.

could count on his audience to share State's breathless fascination with Constantine: "A *real* Mahommedan?" he exclaims: "But do you indulge in a Harem?" State's word "indulge" opens the whole panoply of his orientalist fantasy, the distinctly *Western* fantasy that was known to sell every commodity from Camel cigarettes to Rudolph Valentino. State's "indulge in a Harem" evokes nubile dancing girls and ornate bath houses, hookahs and opium, danger and decadence, all of the seductive pleasures with which Western imaginations had been filling in the blanks on Islam since the Middle Ages. But correcting State is of no interest to Constantine. He wants rather to make State feel vulgar for raising such a question. So, to elicit an embarrassed apology, he needs only to describe his household as "that of the ordinary Eastern gentleman in my position. We do not speak of our women in public." This rebuke so shatters orientalist fantasies—not only State's but those of Barker's audience—that all are compelled to listen to Constantine's scathing critique of European attitudes toward women.

This does not, of course, mean that Constantine's own attitudes toward women are exonerated by the play. Barker uses the prevailing idea of Islam both for and against his character, exploiting fully the stereotype that treats Muslims as libidinous. No sooner does Constantine wind down his critique of European attitudes than he begins to reveal his own. He makes a logical case for polygamy as a material asset to empire; he demonstrates his actual contempt for women along with his susceptibility to their charms; he proves by referring to "the little baggage" Miss Yates that he has no use for English proprieties; and in the end he is given his comeuppance by the same young woman, whose English virtue turns out to depend neither on sex nor on shopping.

Constantine achieves all of this as a "Mahommedan," but his religious profile warrants review. He claims oriental heritage from his grandfather, a Smyrna Jew whom he has never known. We hear that being raised a Baptist put him through "little hells of temptation and shame and remorse." It is from these torments, and from the claims on his person made by Amelia's intolerable forgiveness, that he escapes under protection of Mahomet. That at least is the conversion story Constantine relates to Amelia. To his business associates, he claims that his conversion enabled him to fit in with community life in the village of Hit. He had been "searching for a religion," he says, "a common need in these times," although he does not at this point elaborate on why *his* particular need has led him in *this* particular direction. But once his high-minded critique of European attitudes toward women shifts to critique of women themselves, he attributes his flight Eastward to Western repudiation of polygamy. At no point does Constantine mention the fundamental tenets of the Islamic faith. In short, Constantine's Mahommedanism is simply what the playwright's fluid argument needs it to be: a malleable trope.

Yet because it enables Barker to provoke his audience and focus their attention on the daring critique that powers *The Madras House*, the Islamic trope provides an indispensable rhetorical asset. "If it weren't for Mahomet," says Constantine about freeing himself from European social constraint, "I should hardly be escaping it now." The same might be said of the penetrating analyses brought to life by Constantine's presence in *The Madras House*: if it were not for the trope that is the popular idea of Islam, Barker's uncomfortable truths about British society would have remained too familiar to be recognized.

Lana Cable teaches in the Department of English at the University at Albany, SUNY. She writes on early modern English literature, and her book Carnal Rhetoric: Milton's Iconoclasm and the Poetics of Desire *(Durham: Duke University Press, 1995) received the James Holly Hanford Award.*

THE "LIVING-IN" SYSTEM

Heather J. Violanti

The Madras House is not only the title of Granville Barker's 1909 play, it is the name the playwright gives to his equivalent of the sprawling Edwardian department store, an amalgamation of drapery shop and fashion house. (Contemporary audiences made the immediate connection to Selfridge's, the London retail mecca established by American entrepreneur H. Gordon Selfridge.)

In Act Two, we meet some of the workers who "live in." A descendant of the pre-industrial apprenticeship, "living in" was a system whereby employees lived in or near their place of work, in dormitory-type housing provided by their employer.

Mint Theater Company audiences might recall another play, *Diana of Dobson's* (written by Cecily Hamilton in 1908, produced by the Mint in 2001, and published in 2002 in *Worthy But Neglected: Plays of the Mint Theater*), whose first act portrays life in a typical drapery shop dormitory. Conditions were brutal. Six to twenty employees shared a room. The room was sparsely furnished—a bed for each employee, some pegs for clothes, a box for storage, and a single stove or gas jet were all the amenities usually provided. "Everything plain and comfortless to the last degree," was how Hamilton described it.

Many employers considered a separate bathroom an unnecessary luxury. Some firms even limited workers to one pint of hot water a week for washing. Food was often stale; week-old bread was not uncommon. In some dormitories, rats scampered across the room at night, and lice infested the bedclothes.

Employees, whose salaries were already reduced to cover the costs of room and board, were charged for any infraction of house rules. These included burning a candle after "lights out," putting on the gas after hours, or coming in after curfew. Behavior at work was also subject to fines. Any employee caught in "unbusinesslike conduct"—such as being rude to a customer or, heaven forbid, not dusting the shelves properly—would see a reduction in salary for the week. Any mistake, such as miscounting inventory or giving the wrong change, was also grounds for salary reduction. Even behavior outside of work was subject to punishment. An employee caught smoking or reading novels could find his or her wages cut.

Conditions were grim, but a shop assistant's workday was "only" fourteen hours, as opposed to the sixteen hours or more expected from a household servant. This made living in a more attractive option than domestic service for an increasing number of workers. In 1891, 450,000 assistants "lived in" their shops. By 1914, five years after Granville Barker wrote *The Madras House*, 400,000 employees still lived in.

Employers argued that living in promoted morality among the work-force, another factor ensuring the system's survival. In the interests of "morality," each dormitory was segregated by gender. A strict fore-woman or foreman, usually an older employee of many years standing, kept watch over the other workers (Miss Chancellor in *The Madras House* and Miss Pringle in *Diana of Dobson's*). Actions deemed "immoral" were grounds for docked wages or, depending upon their severity, dismissal. Unwed pregnancy was one cause for dismissal. Marriage, surprisingly, was another. Workers were expected to remain single. Family life could interfere with obligations to the firm. One employer remarked, "I would rather they go elsewhere and get married; we do not want people in our employ like that...it tends to make them—well, certainly not honest."

In *The Madras House*, Granville Barker exposes the hypocrisy behind such sentiments. By 1910, the year the play premiered, avant-garde audiences had seen many "shopgirl" dramas recounting the horrors of living in. *The Madras House* nevertheless still proved a shock. Not only did Granville Barker present a vibrant shopgirl (Miss Yates) who does not atone for her "wrongdoing," he had the audacity to compare the exploitation of drapery shop workers to the entrapment of middle-class women.

Heather Violanti is a playwright, translator, dramaturge, and critic. She has an MFA in dramaturgy and dramatic criticism from Yale School of Drama. Heather was the dramaturge for Mint Theater Company's produc-tion of Susan and God.

Mint Theater Company's production of *The Madras House,* written by Harley Granville Barker, began performances on January 31, 2007, at the Mint Theater, 311 West 43rd Street, New York City, with the following cast and credits:

Huxtable Parlourmaid ....Mary Bacon/Amy Fitts
Philip Madras.. Thomas M. Hammond
Major Hippisly Thomas ....Mark L. Montgomery/Gareth Saxe
Julia Huxtable .... Angela Reed
Jane Huxtable...Pamela McVeagh
Emma Huxtable ....Allison McLemore
Katherine Huxtable ....Laurie Kennedy
Henry Huxtable ....Jonathan Hogan
Amelia Madras ....Roberta Maxwell
Minnie Huxtable.. Lisa Bostnar
Clara Huxtable.............................Mary Bacon/Amy Fitts
William Brigstock ....Kraig Swartz
Freda Brigstock...Angela Reed
Miss Chancellor ....Laurie Kennedy
Marion Yates ....Mary Bacon/Amy Fitts
Belhaven...Scott Romstadt
Jessica Madras .... Lisa Bostnar
Mr. Windlesham ....Kraig Swartz
Eustace Perrin State.. Ross Bickell
The Mannequins........... Mary Bacon/Amy Fitts, Allison McLemore,
                                                                 Pamela McVeagh
Constantine Madras.............................. George Morfogen
Madras Parlourmaid................................Pamela McVeagh

Directed by: Gus Kaikkonen
Set Design by: Charles Morgan
Costume Design by: Clint Ramos
Lighting Design by: William Armstrong
Sound Design: Ellen Mandel
Properties: Jesse Dreikosen
Wigs and Hair Design: Gerard James Kelly
Production Stage Manager: Allison Deutsch/Melissa M. Spengler
Assistant Stage Manager: Andrea Jo Martin
Dialects and Dramaturgy: Amy Stoller
General Manager: Sherri Kotimsky
Press Representative: David Gersten & Associates
Graphic Design: Jude Dvorak

ACT ONE

The HUXTABLES live at Denmark Hill, for MR. HUXTABLE is the surviving partner in the well-known Peckham drapery establishment of Roberts & Huxtable, and the situation, besides being salubrious, is therefore convenient. It is a new house. MR. HUXTABLE bought it half-finished, so that the interior might be to his liking; its exterior the builder said one might describe as of a Free Queen Anne Treatment; to which MR. HUXTABLE rejoined, after blinking at the red brick spotted with stone ornament, that After all it was inside they were going to live, you know.

Through the stained, grained front door, rattling with coloured glass, one reaches the hall, needlessly narrow, needlessly dark, but with its black and white tessellated pavement making for cleanliness. On the left is the stained and grained staircase, with its Brussels carpet and twisted brass stair rods, on the right the drawing room. The drawing room can hardly be said to express the personality of MR. HUXTABLE. The foundations of its furnishings are in the taste of MRS. HUXTABLE. For fifteen years or so, additions to this family museum have been disputed into their place by the six MISS HUXTABLES: LAURA (aged thirty-nine), MINNIE, CLARA, JULIA, EMMA, JANE (aged twenty-six). The rosewood cabinets, the picture from some Academy of the early Seventies entitled "In Ye Olden Time" (this was a wedding present most likely); the gilt clock, which is a Shakespeare, narrow-headed, but with a masterly pair of legs, propped pensively against a dial and enshrined beneath a dome of glass, another wedding present. These were the treasures of MRS. HUXTABLE's first drawing room, her solace in the dull post-honeymoon days. She was the daughter of a city merchant, wholesale as against her husband's retail; but even in the Seventies retail was lifting its head. It was considered, though, that

Katherine Tombs conferred some distinction upon young Harry Huxtable by marrying him, and even now, as a portly lady nearing sixty, she figures by the rustle of her dress, the measure of her mellow voice, with its carefully chosen phrases, for the dignity of the household.

The difference between one MISS HUXTABLE and another is, to a casual eye, the difference between one lead pencil and another, as these lie upon one's table, after some weeks' use; a matter of length, of sharpening, of wear. MINNIE and CLARA are inclined to religion; not sentimentally; works are a good second with them to faith. They have veered, though, lately, from district visiting to an interest in Missions—missions to Poplar or China (one is almost as far as the other); good works, the results of which they cannot see. Happily they forbear to ask why this proves the more soul-satisfying sort.

JULIA started life—that is to say, left school—as a genius. The headmistress had had two or three years of such dull girls that really she could not resist this excitement. Watercolour sketches were the medium. So JULIA was dressed in brown velveteen and sent to an art school, where they wouldn't let her do watercolour drawing at all. And in two years she learnt enough about the trade of an artist not ever to want to do those watercolour drawings again. JULIA is now over thirty and very unhappy. Three of her watercolours (early masterpieces) hang on the drawing-room wall. They shame her, but her mother won't have them taken down. On a holiday she'll be off now and then for a solitary day's sketching, and as she tears up the vain attempt to put on paper the things she has learnt to see, she sometimes cries. It was JULIA, EMMA, and JANE who, some years ago, conspired to present their mother with that intensely conspicuous cosy corner. A cosy corner is apparently a device for making a corner just what the very nature of a corner should forbid it to be. *They beggared themselves; but one wishes that MR. HUXTABLE were more lavish with his dress allowances, then they might at least have afforded something not quite so hideous.*

EMMA, having JULIA in mind, has run rather to coats and skirts and common sense. She would have been a success in an office, and worth, perhaps, thirty shillings a week. But the HUXTABLES don't want another thirty shillings a week, and this gift, such as it is, has been wasted, so that EMMA runs also to a brusque temper.

JANE is meekly enough a little wild. MRS. HUXTABLE's power of applying the brake of good breeding, strong enough over five daughters, waned at the sixth attempt in twelve years, and JANE has actually got herself proposed to twice by not quite desirable young men. Now the fact that she was old enough to be proposed to at all came as something of a shock to the family. Birthdays pass, their celebration growing less emphatic. No one likes to believe that the years are passing; even the birthday's owner, least able to escape its significance, laughs, and then changes the subject. So the MISS HUXTABLES never openly asked each other what the marriage of the youngest of them might imply; perhaps they never even asked themselves. Besides, JANE didn't marry. But if she does, unless, perhaps, she runs away to do it, there will be heart searchings, at least. MR. HUXTABLE asked, though, and MRS. HUXTABLE's answer—given early one morning, before the hot water came—scarcely satisfied him. "For," said MR. HUXTABLE, "if the girls don't marry some day, what are they to do! It's not as if they had to go into the shop." "No, thank Heaven!" said MRS. HUXTABLE.

Since his illness MR. HUXTABLE has taken to asking questions—of anybody and about anything; of himself oftenest of all. But for that illness he would have been a

conventional enough type of successful shop-keeper, coarsely fed, whiskered, podgy. But eighteen months' nursing and dieting and removal from the world seem to have brought a gentleness to his voice, a spark of humour to his eye, a childishness to his little bursts of temper—they have added, in fact, a wistfulness which makes him rather a lovable old buffer on the whole.

This is a Sunday morning, a bright day in October. The family are still at church, and the drawing room is empty. The door opens, and the PARLOURMAID—much becapped and aproned—shows in PHILIP MADRAS and his friend, MAJOR HIPPISLY THOMAS. THOMAS, long-legged and deliberate, moves across the room to the big French windows, which open onto a balcony and look down on the garden and to many gardens beyond. THOMAS is a good fellow.

PHILIP MADRAS is more complex than that. To begin with, it is obvious he is not wholly English. A certain litheness of figure, the keenness and colour of his voice, and a liking for metaphysical turns of speech show on Eastern origin, perhaps. He is kind in manner, but rather cold, capable of that least English of dispositions—intellectual passion. He is about thirty-five, a year or two younger than his friend. The PARLOURMAID has secured MAJOR THOMAS's hat, and stands clutching it. As PHILIP passes her into the room, he asks…

PHILIP: About how long?

PARLOURMAID: In just a few minutes now, I would say, sir. Oh, I beg pardon, does it appen to be the third Sunday in the month?

PHILIP: I don't know.

PARLOURMAID: Because then some of them stop for the Oly Communion and that may make them late for dinner. (*She backs through the door, entangling the hat in the handle.*)

PHILIP: Is my mother still staying here?

PARLOURMAID: Mrs. Madras, sir? Yes, sir.

(Then, having disentangled the hat, the PARLOURMAID vanishes. PHILIP thereupon plunges swiftly into what must be an interrupted argument.)

PHILIP: Well, my dear Tommy, what are the two best ways to judge a man's character? His attitude towards money and his attitude towards women.

THOMAS: *(Ponderously slowing him up.)* Yes, you're full up with moral precepts. Why behave about money as if it didn't exist? I never said don't stand for County Council.

PHILIP: *(Deliberately, but in a breath.)* It's impossible for any decent man to walk across London on a Sunday morning without wishing to stand for County Council.

THOMAS: *(Entrenches himself on a sofa.)* You've got what I call the Reformer's mind. I shouldn't cultivate it, Phil. It makes a man unhappy, not with himself, but with other people, mark you... so it makes him conceited. Don't imagine you can make this country better by tidying it up.

PHILIP: *(Whimsically.)* But I'm very interested in England, Tommy.

THOMAS: *(Not without some answering humour.)* We all are. But we don't go about saying so. *(He leans back.)*

PHILIP: *(His eyes fix themselves on some great distance.)* I once thought I might give my goods to the poor and go slumming—keep my immortal soul superior still. There's something wrong with a world, Tommy, if it took me this long to find out it's bread people want, and neither cake nor crumbs.

THOMAS: There's something wrong with a man, Philip, who sees other people as ants struggling on an ant heap.

PHILIP: *(Relaxing to a smile.)* Tommy, that's perfectly true. I like having a good talk with you: sooner or later you always say one sensible thing.

THOMAS: Thank you; you're damn polite. Go on six County Councils, if you like. But why chuck twelve hundred a year and a directorship of Madras House, if the buyer wants you to keep 'em? And you could have double or more, and manage the place, if you'd ask for it.

PHILIP: *(Almost venomously.)* Tommy, I loathe the dressmaking business. Your Mr. State may buy it and do what he likes with it.

(JULIA and JANE arrive. They are the first from Church. Sunday frocks, Sunday hats, best gloves, umbrellas, and prayer books.)

JULIA: What a surprise!

PHILIP: Yes, we walked down. Ah, let me introduce Major Hippisly Thomas. My cousin, Miss Julia Huxtable... and Miss Huxtable.

JULIA: How do you do?

THOMAS: How do you do?

JANE: How do you do?

JULIA: Have you come to see Aunt Amy?

PHILIP: No, your father.

JANE: Will you stay for dinner?

PHILIP: No, I think not.

JANE: I'd better tell them you won't. Perhaps they'll be laying for you.

(JANE goes out, decorously avoiding a collision with EMMA, who, panoplied as the others, comes in at the same moment.)

EMMA: Well, what a surprise!

PHILIP: Hullo, Emma!

PHILIP: You don't know…Major Hippisly Thomas…Miss Emma Huxtable.

THOMAS: How do you do?

EMMA: How do you do? Will you stay to dinner?

PHILIP: No, we can't. *(That formula again completed, he varies his explanation.)* I've just brought Thomas to help me tell Uncle Henry a bit of news. My father will be back in England tomorrow.

EMMA: *(With a round mouth.)* Oh!

JULIA: It's a beautiful morning for a walk, isn't it?

THOMAS: Wonderful for October.

(These two look first at each other, and then out of the window. EMMA gazes quizzically at PHILIP.)

EMMA: I think he knows.

PHILIP: He sort of knows.

EMMA: Why are you being odd, Philip?

(PHILIP is more hail-fellow-well-met with EMMA than with the others.)

PHILIP: Emma…I have enticed a comparative stranger to be present so that your father and mother cannot in decency begin the family battle over again with me. I know it's very cunning, but we did want a walk. Besides, there's a meeting tomorrow…

(JANE returns, warning PHILIP.)

JANE: You! Mother! *(She has turned to the hall.)*

MRS. HUXTABLE: *(Rotund voice from the hall.)* Yes, Jane!

JANE: Cousin Philip!

MRS. HUXTABLE: What a surprise! Will you stay to dinner?

EMMA: No, Mother, they can't.

PHILIP: May I introduce my friend…Major Hippisly Thomas…my aunt, Mrs. Huxtable.

MRS. HUXTABLE: *(Stately and gracious.)* How do you do, Major Thomas?

PHILIP: Thomas is Mr. Eustace State's London manager.

THOMAS: How do you do?

(MRS. HUXTABLE takes an armchair with the air of one mounting a throne, and from that vantage point begins polite conversation. Her daughters distribute themselves, so do PHILIP and HIPPISLY THOMAS.)

MRS. HUXTABLE: Not in the Army, then, Major Thomas?

THOMAS: I was in the Army.

EMMA: Jessica quite well, Philip?

PHILIP: Yes, thanks.

EMMA: And Mildred?

PHILIP: I think so. She's back at school.

MRS. HUXTABLE: A wonderfully warm autumn, is it not?

THOMAS: Quite.

MRS. HUXTABLE: Do you know Denmark Hill well?

THOMAS: Not well.

MRS. HUXTABLE: We have always lived here. I consider it healthy. But London is a healthy place, I think. Oh, I beg your pardon…my daughter Jane.

JANE: How do you do?

(They shake hands with ceremony. EMMA, in a mind to liven things up, goes to the window.)

EMMA: We've quite a good garden, that's one thing.

THOMAS: *(Not wholly innocent of an attempt to escape from his hostess, makes for the window, too.)* I noticed it. I am keen on gardens.

(MRS. HUXTABLE's attention is distracted by JULIA's making for the door.)

MRS. HUXTABLE: Julia, where are you going?

JULIA: To take my things off, Mother.

(JULIA departs. When they were quite little girls MRS. HUXTABLE always did ask her daughters where they were going when they left the room and where they had been when they entered it, and she has never dropped the habit. They resent it only by the extreme patience of their replies.)

EMMA: *(Entertainingly.)* That's the Crystal Palace.

THOMAS: Is it?

(They both peer appreciatively at that famous landmark. In the Crystal Palace and the sunset the inhabitants of Denmark Hill have acquired almost proprietary interest. Then MRS. HUXTABLE speaks to her nephew with a sudden severity.)

MRS. HUXTABLE: Philip, I don't consider your mother's health is at all the thing!

PHILIP: *(Amicably.)* It never is, Aunt Kate.

MRS. HUXTABLE: *(Admitting the justice of the retort.)* That's true.

PHILIP: Uncle Henry keeps better, I think.

MRS. HUXTABLE: He's well enough now. I have had a slight cold. Is it true that your father may appear in England again?

PHILIP: Yes. He arrives tomorrow.

MRS. HUXTABLE: I'm sorry.

JANE: Mother!

(MRS. HUXTABLE has launched this with such redoubled severity that JANE had to protest. However, at this moment arrives MR. HUXTABLE himself, one glad smile.)

MR. HUXTABLE: Ah, Phil…I ad an idea you might come over. You'll stay to dinner. Jane, tell your aunt…she's taking er bonnet off.

(JANE obeys. He sights on the balcony MAJOR THOMAS's back.)

MR. HUXTABLE: Who's that outside?

PHILIP: Hippisly Thomas. We wanted a walk; we can't stay.

MR. HUXTABLE: Oh.

MRS. HUXTABLE: Have you come on business?

PHILIP: Well…

MRS. HUXTABLE: On Sunday?

PHILIP: Not exactly.

(MRS. HUXTABLE shakes her head, gravely deprecating. THOMAS comes from the balcony.)

MR. HUXTABLE: Ow are you?

THOMAS: How are *you?*

MR. HUXTABLE: Fine morning, isn't it? Nice prospect this…that's the Crystal Palace.

(While THOMAS turns, with perfect politeness, to view again this phenomenon, PHILIP pacifies his aunt.)

PHILIP: You see, Aunt Katherine, tomorrow afternoon we have the first real conference with this American, Mr. State, about buying the firm, and my father is passing through England again to attend it.

MRS. HUXTABLE: Of course, Philip, if it's business, I know nothing about it. But is it suggested that your uncle should attend, too?

(Her voice has found a new gravity. PHILIP becomes very airy; so does MR. HUXTABLE, who comes back to rejoin the conversation.)

PHILIP: My dear Aunt, naturally.

MR. HUXTABLE: What's this?

MRS. HUXTABLE: *(The one word expressing volumes.)* Constantine.

MR. HUXTABLE: *(With elaborate innocence.)* That's definite now, is it?

MRS. HUXTABLE: You dropped a hint last night, Henry.

MR. HUXTABLE: I dessay. I dessay I did. *(His eye shifts guiltily.)*

MRS. HUXTABLE: Quite out of the question it seems to me.

(JANE comes back.)

JANE: Aunt Amy's coming.

MR. HUXTABLE: *(Genial again.)* Oh. My daughter Jane…Major Thomas, Major Hippisly Thomas.

JANE: *(With discretion.)* Yes, Father.

MRS. HUXTABLE: *(Tactfully.)* You are naturally not aware, Major Thomas, that for family reasons, into which we need not go, Mr. Huxtable has not spoken a word to his brother-in-law for a number of years.

(PHILIP's eye meets THOMAS's in comic agony. But MR. HUXTABLE, too, plunges delightedly into the forbidden subject.)

MR. HUXTABLE: Thirty years, very near. Wonderful, isn't it? Partners in the same business. Wasn't easy to keep it up.

THOMAS: I had heard.

MR. HUXTABLE: Oh yes, notorious.

MRS. HUXTABLE: *(In reprobation.)* And well it may be, Henry.

(MRS. MADRAS comes in. It is evident that PHILIP is his father's son. He would seem so wholly, but for that touch of "self-worship" which is often self-mistrust"; his mother's gift, appearing nowadays less lovably in her as a sort of querulous assertion of her rights and wrongs against the troubles which have been too strong for her. She is a pale old lady, shrunk a little, the life gone out of her.)

MRS. HUXTABLE: *(Some severity remaining.)* Amy, your husband is in England again.

(PHILIP presents a filial cheek. It is kissed.)

PHILIP: How are you, Mother?

MR. HUXTABLE: *(Sotto voce.)* Oh tact, Katherine, tact!

PHILIP: Perhaps you remember Reggie Thomas?

THOMAS: I was at Marlborough with Philip, Mrs. Madras.

MRS. MADRAS: Yes. Is he, Katherine?

(Having given THOMAS a limp hand, and her sister this coldest of responses, she finds her way to a sofa, where she sits silent, thinking to herself. MRS. HUXTABLE keeps majestic hold upon her subject.)

MRS. HUXTABLE: I am utterly unable to see, Philip, why your uncle should break his rule now.

MR. HUXTABLE: There you are, Phil!

PHILIP: Of course it is for Uncle Henry to decide.

MR. HUXTABLE: Naturally…naturally.

(Still he has an appealing eye on PHILIP, who obliges him.)

PHILIP: But Mr. State's offer is not yet secured and...if the two principal proprietors can't meet him round a table to settle the matter...

THOMAS: *(Ponderously diplomatic.)* Yes...a little awkward...if I may say so...as Mr. State's representative, Mrs. Huxtable.

MRS. HUXTABLE: You don't think, do you, Major Thomas, that any amount of awkwardness should induce us to pass over wicked conduct?

(This reduces the assembly to such a shamed silence that poor MR. HUXTABLE can only add—)

MR. HUXTABLE: Oh, talk of something else...talk of something else.

(After a moment MRS. MADRAS's pale voice steals in, as she turns to her son.)

MRS. MADRAS: When did you hear from your father?

PHILIP: A letter from Marienbad two or three days ago, and a telegram yesterday morning.

MRS. HUXTABLE: *(With a hostess's authority, now restores a polite and easy tone to the conversation.)* And have you left the Army long, Major Thomas?

THOMAS: Four years.

MRS. HUXTABLE: And you've taken to Dressmaking?

PHILIP: *(Very explanatory.)* Tommy represents an American financier, Aunt Kitty, who has bought up Burrow's, the big ready-made dress shop in the city, and is about to buy us up, too, perhaps.

MRS. HUXTABLE: We are not in difficulties, I hope.

PHILIP: Oh, no.

MRS. HUXTABLE: No. No doubt Henry would have told me if we had been.

(As she thus gracefully dismisses the subject there appear up the steps and along the balcony the last arrivals from Church, MINNIE and CLARA. The male part of the company unsettles itself.)

MR. HUXTABLE: Ullo! Where have you been?

MINNIE: We went for a walk.

MRS. HUXTABLE: *(In apparently deep surprise.)* A walk, Minnie! Where to?

MINNIE: Just the long way home. We thought we'd have time.

CLARA: Did you notice what a short sermon?

MR. HUXTABLE: Oh, may I...My daughter Clara...Major Ippisly Thomas. My daughter Minnie...Major Thomas.

MINNIE: How d'you do?

THOMAS: How d'you do?

CLARA: How d'you do?

MINNIE: How d'you do, Philip?

PHILIP: How d'you do?

CLARA: How d'you do?

PHILIP: How d'you do?

(The chant over, the company resettles; MR. HUXTABLE buttonholing PHILIP in the process with an air of some mystery.)

MR. HUXTABLE: By the way, Phil, remind me to ask you something before you go...rather important.

PHILIP: I shall be at your shop in the morning. Thomas is coming to go through some figures.

MR. HUXTABLE: *(With a regular snap.)* Yes...I shan't.

PHILIP: The State meeting is in Bond Street, three o'clock.

MR. HUXTABLE: I know, I know. *(Then, finding himself prominent, he captures the conversation.)* I'm slacking off, Major Thomas, slacking. Ever since I was ill I've been slacking off.

MRS. HUXTABLE: You are perfectly well now, Henry.

MR. HUXTABLE: Not the point. I want leisure, you know, leisure. Time for reading…time to think a bit.

MRS. HUXTABLE: Nonsense! *(She adds, with correctness.)* Major Thomas will excuse me.

THOMAS: Quite. I got most of my reading done early.

MRS. HUXTABLE: The natural time for it.

MR. HUXTABLE: Ah lucky feller! Educated, I suppose. Well, I wasn't. I've been getting the books for years—good editions. I'd like you to see my library. But these geniuses want settling down to…if a man's to keep pace with the thought of the world, y'know. Macaulay, Erbert Spencer, Grote's *Istory of Greece*! I've got em all there.

(He finds no further response. MRS. HUXTABLE fills the gap.)

MRS. HUXTABLE: I thought the sermon dull this morning, Amy, didn't you?

MRS. MADRAS: *(Unexpectedly.)* No, I didn't.

MINNIE: *(To do her share of the entertaining.)* Mother, somebody ought to speak about those boys…it's disgraceful. Mr. Vivian had actually to turn round from the organ at them during the last hymn.

(JULIA, her things taken off, reappears. MR. HUXTABLE is on the spot.)

MR. HUXTABLE: Ah, my daughter Julia…Major—

JULIA: We've been introduced, Father.

(She says this with a hauteur which really is pure nervousness, but MR. HUXTABLE is sufficiently crushed.)

MR. HUXTABLE: Oh, I beg pardon.

(But MRS. HUXTABLE disapproves of any self-assertion, and descends upon the culprit; who is, for some obscure reason—or for none—more often disapproved of than the others.)

MRS. HUXTABLE: Close the door, please, Julia.

JULIA: I'm sorry, Mother.

(PHILIP closes the offending door. JULIA obliterates herself in a chair, and the conversation, hardly encouraged by this little affray, comes to an intolerable standstill. At last CLARA makes an effort.)

CLARA: Is Jessica quite well, Philip?

PHILIP: Yes, thank you, Clara.

MRS. HUXTABLE: And dear little Mildred?

PHILIP: Yes, thank you, Aunt Kate.

(Further standstill. Then MINNIE contrives a remark.)

MINNIE: Do you still like that school for her?

PHILIP: *(With finesse.)* It seems to provide every accomplishment that money can buy.

MRS. HUXTABLE: *(Discovers a sure opening.)* Have you been away for the summer, Major Thomas?

THOMAS: *(Vaguely—he is getting sympathetically tongue-tied.)* Oh…yes…

PHILIP: Tommy and Jessica and I took our holidays motoring around Munich and into it for the operas.

MRS. HUXTABLE: Was that pleasant?

PHILIP: Very.

MRS. HUXTABLE: And where was dear Mildred?

PHILIP: With her aunt most of the time…Jessica's sister-in-law, you know.

MINNIE: Lady Ames?

PHILIP: Yes.

MRS. HUXTABLE: *(Innocently, genuinely snobbish.)* Very nice for her.

MR. HUXTABLE: We take a ouse at Weymouth as a rule.

MRS. HUXTABLE: Do you know Weymouth, Major Thomas?

THOMAS: No, I don't.

MRS. HUXTABLE: George III used to stay there, but that is a hotel now.

MR. HUXTABLE: Keep your spare money in the country, y'know.

MRS. HUXTABLE: Oh, there is everything one wants at Weymouth.

(They have made their last effort. The conversation is dead. MR. HUXTABLE's discomfort suddenly becomes physical.)

MR. HUXTABLE: I'm going to change my coat.

PHILIP: I think perhaps we ought to be off.

MR. HUXTABLE: No, no, no, no, no! I shan't be a minute. Don't go, Phil; there's a good fellow.

(And he has left them all to it. The HUXTABLE conversation, it will be noticed, consists mainly of asking questions. Visitors, after a time, fall into the habit, too.)

MRS. HUXTABLE: Do you live in London, Major Thomas?

THOMAS: No, I live at Woking. I come up and down every day.

MRS. HUXTABLE: Not a cheerful place, is it?

THOMAS: Oh, very cheerful!

MRS. HUXTABLE: I had thought not, for some reason.

EMMA: The cemetery, Mother.

MRS. HUXTABLE: *(Accepting the suggestion with dignity.)* Perhaps.

MINNIE: It is the largest one in the world.

CLARA: We have a very large garden. We have the garden of the next house as well.

JANE: Not all the garden of the next house.

CLARA: Well, most of it.

(This stimulating difference of opinion takes them to the balcony. PHILIP follows. JULIA follows PHILIP. MINNIE departs to take her things off.)

JULIA: That's the Crystal Palace. Do you notice how near it seems? That means rain.

PHILIP: Of course…Tommy, you can see the Crystal Palace.

MRS. HUXTABLE: Julia, do you think you won't catch cold on the balcony without a hat?

JULIA: *(Meek, but before the visitor, determined.)* I don't think so, Mother.

MRS. HUXTABLE: *(Turns with added politeness, to MAJOR THOMAS.)* We used to live not so far along the hill; a smaller house.

(PHILIP is now on the balcony, receiving more information.)

PHILIP: That's Ruskin's house, is it? Yes, I see the chimney pots.

MRS. HUXTABLE: I should not have moved, myself, but I was overruled.

EMMA: Mother, we had outgrown Hollybank.

MRS. HUXTABLE: I was overruled. Things are done on a larger scale than they used to be. My father's practice was to live on half his income. He lost the greater part of his money by unwise investments in lead, I think it was. I was at school at the time in Brighton. And he educated me above my station in life.

(At this moment CLARA breaks out of the conservatory. Something has happened.)

CLARA: Jane, the Agapanthus is out at last!

JANE: Oh!

(They crowd in to see it. PHILIP crowds in, too. MRS. HUXTABLE is unmoved.)

MRS. HUXTABLE: We are told that riches are a snare, Major Thomas.

THOMAS: It is one I have always found easy to avoid, Mrs. Huxtable.

MRS. HUXTABLE: *(Oblivious of the joke, which indeed she would not have expected on such a subject.)* And I have noticed that their acquisition seldom improves the character of people.

THOMAS: *(Forestalling a yawn.)* Quite so. Quite so.

MRS. HUXTABLE: *(Takes a breath.)* A family of daughters, Major Thomas…

EMMA: *(A little agonised.)* Mother!

MRS. HUXTABLE: What is it, Emma?

EMMA: *(Thinks better of it and goes to join the Agapanthus party.)* Nothing, Mother, I beg your pardon.

MRS. HUXTABLE: *(Retakes her breath.)* I find that people look differently on family life to what they used. A man no longer seems prepared to marry and support a wife and family by his unaided exertions. I consider that a pity.

THOMAS: *(Near another yawn.)* Quite… quite so.

MRS. HUXTABLE: I have always determined that my daughters should be sought after for themselves alone. That should ensure their happiness. Any eligible gentleman who visits here constantly is always given to understand, delicately, that nothing need be expected from Mr. Huxtable beyond his approval. Are you married, Major Thomas?

(This quite wakes him up, though MRS. HUXTABLE is really innocent of her implication.)

THOMAS: Huh? Yes, oh, dear me, yes.

MRS. HUXTABLE: And a family?

THOMAS: Four children… the youngest is only three.

MRS. HUXTABLE: Pretty dear!

THOMAS: No, ugly little beggar, but has character.

MRS. HUXTABLE: I must take off my things before dinner. You'll excuse me. If one is not punctual oneself…

THOMAS: Quite.

MRS. HUXTABLE: We cannot induce you to join us?

THOMAS: Many thanks, but we have to meet Mrs. Phil for lunch at two.

MRS. HUXTABLE: I am sorry.

(THOMAS opens the door for her with his best bow, and she graciously departs, conscious of having properly impressed him. CLARA crosses the room; PHILIP follows her from the balcony.)

CLARA: You haven't had a chance to see Laura yet. She went straight upstairs after church. I'll tell her you are here.

(All this time there has been MRS. MADRAS upon her sofa, silent, as forgotten as any other piece of furniture for which there is no immediate use. PHILIP now goes to her. When she does speak it is unresponsively.)

PHILIP: How long do you stay in town, Mother?

MRS. MADRAS: I have been here a fortnight. I generally stay three weeks.

PHILIP: Jessica has been meaning to ask you to Phillimore Gardens again.

MRS. MADRAS: Has she?

PHILIP: *(A little guiltily.)* Her time's very much occupied...with one thing and another.

MRS. MADRAS: *(Suddenly rouses herself.)* I wish to see your father, Philip.

PHILIP: *(In doubt.)* He won't be here long, Mother.

MRS. MADRAS: No, I'm sure he won't.

(With three delicate strides THOMAS lands himself onto the balcony.)

PHILIP: Tommy being tactful! Well, I'll say that you want to see him.

MRS. MADRAS: No, please don't. Tell him that I think he ought to come and see me.

PHILIP: He won't come, Mother.

MRS. MADRAS: No, I know he won't. He came to England in May, didn't he? He was here till July, wasn't he? Did he so much as send me a message?

PHILIP: *(With unkind patience.)* No, Mother.

MRS. MADRAS: What was he doing all the while, Philip?

PHILIP: I didn't see much of him. I really don't know. I don't think there's much to be gained by your seeing him.

MRS. MADRAS: You are a little heartless, Philip.

PHILIP: *(This being a little true, PHILIP a little resents it.)* My dear Mother, you and he have been separated for...how long is it?

MRS. MADRAS: *(With withered force.)* I am his wife still, I should hope. He went away from me when he was young. But I have never forgotten my duty. And now that he is an old man, and past such sin, and I am an old woman, I am still ready to be a comfort to his declining years, and it's right that I should be allowed to tell him so. And you should not let your wife put you against your own mother, Philip.

PHILIP: *(Bewildered.)* Really!

MRS. MADRAS: I know what Jessica thinks of me. Jessica is very clever, and has no patience with people whose best is simply to be good...I can understand that. Well, it isn't her duty to love me...at least it may not be, I don't say. But it is your duty. I sometimes think, Philip, you don't love me any longer, though you're afraid to say so.

(The appeal ends so pathetically that PHILIP is very gently equivocal.)

PHILIP: If I didn't love you, my dear Mother, I should be afraid to say so.

MRS. MADRAS: When are you to see your father?

PHILIP: We've asked him to dinner tomorrow night.

(At this moment EMMA comes in with a briskness so jarring to MRS. MADRAS's already wrought nerves, that she turns on her.)

MRS. MADRAS: Emma, why do you come bouncing in like that when I'm trying to get a private word with Philip?

EMMA: Really, Aunt Amy, the drawing room belongs to everyone.

MRS. MADRAS: I'm sure I don't know why I come and stay here at all. I dislike your mother intensely.

EMMA: Then kindly don't tell me so. I've no wish not to be polite to you.

PHILIP: *(Pacifically.)* Emma, I think Uncle Henry ought to attend this meeting tomorrow.

MRS. MADRAS: *(Beginning to cry.)* Of course my brother ought. Who is he to go on like this about Constantine! My handkerchief's upstairs.

EMMA: *(Contritely.)* Shall I fetch it for you, Aunt Amy?

MRS. MADRAS: No, I'll be a trouble to no one. *(She retires, injured.)*

PHILIP: *(Continues, purposely placid.)* What's more, he really wants to attend it.

EMMA: I'm sorry I was rude…but she does get on our nerves, you know.

PHILIP: Why do you invite her?

EMMA: *(Quite jolly with him.)* Oh, we're all very fond of Aunt Amy, and anyhow Mother would think it our duty.

PHILIP: *(Quizzically.)* You're all too good, Emma.

EMMA: Yes. But if one stopped doing one's duty how upside-down the world would be! *(Her voice now takes that tone which is the well-bred substitute for a wink.)* Did you hear us making fun of Julia in the conservatory? I suppose I oughtn't tell you, but it is rather a joke. You know Julia gets hysterical sometimes, when she has her headaches.

PHILIP: Does she?

EMMA: Well, a shirt collar came back from the wash in mistake for one of Father's: It was marked Lewis Waller.

PHILIP: The actor?

EMMA: The matinee idol. I don't think he lives near here, but it's one of these big steam laundries. And Morgan the cook got it, and she gave it to Julia…and Julia kept it. And when Mother found out she cried for a whole day. She said it showed a wanton mind.

PHILIP: *(His mocking face becomes grave.)* I don't think that's at all amusing, Emma.

EMMA: *(In genuine surprise.)* Don't you?

PHILIP: How old is Julia?

EMMA: She's thirty-four. *(Her face falls too.)* No…it is rather dreadful, isn't it? *(Then wrinkling her forehead, as at a puzzle.)* It isn't exactly that one wants to get married. I daresay Mother is right about that.

PHILIP: About what?

EMMA: Well, some time ago a gentleman proposed to Jane. And Mother said it would have been more honourable if he had spoken to Father first, and that Jane was the youngest, and too young to know her own mind. Well, you know, she's twenty-six. And then they heard of something he'd once done, and it was put a stop to. And Jane was very rebellious, and Mother cried…

PHILIP: Does she always cry?

EMMA: Yes, she does cry, if she's upset about us. And I think she was right. One ought not to risk being unhappy for life, ought one?

PHILIP: Are you all happy now, then?

EMMA: Oh, deep down, I think we are. It would be so ungrateful not to be. When one has a good home and…! But of course living together, and going away together, and being together all the time, one does get a little irritable now and then. There wasn't a bigger house to be got here or I suppose we could have had it.

PHILIP: But what occupations have you girls?

EMMA: We're always busy. I mean there's lots to be done about the house, and there's calling and classes and things. Julia used to sketch quite well. You mustn't think I'm grumbling, Philip. I know I talk too much. They tell me so.

PHILIP: *(Half-serious.)* Why don't you go away, all six of you, or say five of you?

EMMA: *(Wide-eyed.)* Go away!

PHILIP: *(Comprehensively.)* Out of it.

EMMA: *(Wider eyed.)* Where to?

PHILIP: *(With a sigh—for her.)* Ah, that's just it.

EMMA: How could one! And it would upset them dreadfully.

(MR. HUXTABLE returns, at ease in a jacket. He pats his daughter kindly on the shoulder.)

MR. HUXTABLE: Now run along, Jane…I mean Emma…I want a word with your cousin.

EMMA: Yes, Father. *(Obediently disappears into the garden.)*

PHILIP: *(Looks sideways at his uncle.)* I've come over, as you asked me to.

MR. HUXTABLE: I didn't ask you.

PHILIP: You dropped a hint.

MR. HUXTABLE: *(Almost with a blush.)* Did I? I dessay I did.

PHILIP: But you must hurry up and decide about the meeting tomorrow. Thomas and I have got to go.

MR. HUXTABLE: Phil, I suppose you're set on selling.

PHILIP: Quite.

MR. HUXTABLE: You young men! The Madras Ouse means nothing to you.

PHILIP: *(Anti-sentimental.)* Nothing unsalable, Uncle.

MR. HUXTABLE: Well, well, well! *(Then in a furtive fuss.)* Well, just a minute, my boy, before your aunt comes down… she's been going on at me upstairs, y'know! Something you must do for me tomorrow, like a good feller, at the shop in the morning. *(He suddenly becomes portentous.)* Have you heard this yet about Miss Yates?

PHILIP: No.

MR. HUXTABLE: Disgraceful! Disgraceful!

PHILIP: She's an excellent employee. We sent her to our couture showroom in Bond Street for training and she got on very well…learnt a good deal.

MR. HUXTABLE: *(Snorting derisively.)* Learnt a good deal! *(Then he sights THOMAS on the balcony, and hails him.)* Oh, come in, Major Thomas. *(And dropping his voice again ominously.)* Shut the window, if you don't mind; we don't want the ladies to hear this.

(THOMAS shuts the window, and MR. HUXTABLE spreads himself to the awful enjoyment of the imparting scandal.)

MR. HUXTABLE: I tell you, my boy, when she was up training with you in Bond Street, got hold of she's been by some feller…some West End Club feller, I dessay…and he's put her in the…well, I tell you!! Major Thomas will excuse me. Not a simple chit of a girl, mind you, but first hand in our high fashion room. Buyer we were going to make her, and all!

PHILIP: *(Frowns, both at the news and at his uncle's manner of giving it.)* What do you want me to do?

MR. HUXTABLE: *(More portentous than ever.)* You wait; that's not what's the worst of it. You know Brigstock.

PHILIP: Do I?

MR. HUXTABLE: Oh, yes; third man in the osiery.

PHILIP: True.

MR. HUXTABLE: Well…it seems that more than a week ago Miss Chancellor caught them kissing.

PHILIP: *(His impatience of the display growing.)* Caught *who* kissing?

MR. HUXTABLE: I know it ain't clear. Let's go back to the beginning…Major Thomas will excuse me.

THOMAS: *(Showing the properest feeling.)* Not at all.

MR. HUXTABLE: Wednesday afternoon, Willoughby, that's our company doctor, comes up to the shop as usual, Miss Yates goes in to see him. Miss Chancellor—that's our housekeeper, Major Thomas—over'ears, quite by accident, so she says, and afterwards confronts her with it.

PHILIP: Unwise.

MR. HUXTABLE: No, no, her plain duty…she knows my principle about such things. But then she remembers about the kissing and somehow that gets about among our young ladies. Somebody stupid there, I grant you, but you know what these things are. And then it gets about about Miss Yates…all over the shop. And then it turns out that Brigstock's a married man…been married two years…secret from us, you know, because it's not allowed, Major Thomas, you see—he's

living in the company dormitory…God knows where his wife lives…and he's up for promotion and all the rest. And yesterday morning his wife turns up in my office, and has hysterics, and says her husband's been slandered.

PHILIP: I don't see how Miss Yates could have come to harm in Bond Street. We sleep them ten to a room—a girl's only out of sight on weekend afternoons, and even then we're supposed to know where she is.

MR. HUXTABLE: *(Still instinctively spreading himself, but with that wistful look creeping on him now.)* Well…I had Miss Yates in my office the day before. And I don't know what's coming over me. I scolded her well. I was in the right in all I said…but…! Have you ever suddenly eard your own voice saying a thing? Well, I did…and it sounded more like a dog barking than me. And I went funny all over. So before I finished the business I told her to leave the room. *(He grows distressed and appealing.)* And you must take it on, Phil…it ought to be settled tomorrow. Miss Yates must have the sack, and I'm not sure Brigstock hadn't better have the sack. We don't want to lose Miss Chancellor, but really if she can't hold er tongue at her age…well, she'd better have, too.

PHILIP: *(Out of patience.)* Oh, nonsense, Uncle!

MR. HUXTABLE: *(His old unquestioning self asserted for a moment.)* No, I will not have these scandals in the shop. We've always been free of em…almost always. I don't want to be overly hard on the girl. If the father's in our employ and you can find im out…give him the sack as well. *(That breath exhausted, he continues, quite pathetically, to THOMAS.)* I don't know what's come over me. Before I got ill I'd have tackled this business like winking. But when you're a long time in bed, you get thinking…and things which used to be quite clear don't seem nearly so clear as they did and that puts you off everything…

(This is interrupted by the reappearance of MRS. HUXTABLE, lace-capped and ready for dinner. She is at the pitch to which the upstairs dispute with her husband evidently brought her. It would seem he bolted in the middle of it.)

MRS. HUXTABLE: Is it the fact, Philip, that if your uncle does not attend the meeting tomorrow that this business transaction with Mr.—I forget his name—the American gentleman…

MR. HUXTABLE, PHILIP, and THOMAS: *(Together.)* State.

MRS. HUXTABLE: …And which I, of course, know nothing about, will be seriously upset?

MR. HUXTABLE: *(Joining battle.)* Kitty, I don't see why I shouldn't go. If Constantine chooses to turn up…that is his business. I needn't speak directly to him…so to say.

MRS. HUXTABLE: *(Hurling this choice bolt from her vocabulary.)* A quibble, Henry.

MR. HUXTABLE: If he's leaving England now for good…

MRS. HUXTABLE: But you do as you like, of course.

MR. HUXTABLE: *(Wistful again.)* I should so like you to be convinced.

MRS. HUXTABLE: Don't prevaricate, Henry. And your sister is just coming into the room. We had better drop the subject.

(And in MRS. MADRAS does come, but what with one thing and another MR.

HUXTABLE is now getting what he would call thoroughly put out.)

MR. HUXTABLE: Now if Amelia here was to propose seeing im—

MRS. HUXTABLE: Henry…a little consideration!

MR. HUXTABLE: *(Goaded to the truth.)* Well, I want to go, Kitty, and that's all about it. And I dropped a int, I did, to Phil to come over and help me through it with you. I thought he'd make it seem as if it was most pressing business so as to hurt your feelings less…only he hasn't… Goodness gracious me, here's the Madras House, which I've sunk enough money in these last ten years to build a battleship, very nearly…a small battleship, y'know…it's to be sold because Phil won't stand by me, and his father don't care a button now. Not but what that's Constantine all over! Marries you, Amelia, behaves like a duke and an archangel, mixed, for eighteen months and then—

MRS. HUXTABLE: *(Scandalised "Before visitors too!")* Henry!

MR. HUXTABLE: All right, all right. And I'm not to attend this meeting, if you please!

(The little storm subsides.)

MRS. MADRAS: It's to be sold, is it?

PHILIP: Yes, Mother.

MRS. MADRAS: *(At her brother.)* It was started with my money as well as yours.

(MR. HUXTABLE is recovering and takes no notice.)

PHILIP: Yes, Mother, we know.

MRS. MADRAS: And if that's all you've lost by Constantine, I don't see you've a right to be so bitter against him.

(She is still ignored. MR. HUXTABLE, quite cheery again, goes on affably.)

MR. HUXTABLE: D'you know, Major Thomas, that twenty years ago when that shop began to be the talk of London, Duchesses were known to go on their knees to him to design them a dress. And he wouldn't do it unless he pleased—not unless he approved their figure. Ad Society under his thumb.

MRS. HUXTABLE: *(From the height of respectability.)* No doubt he knew his business.

MR. HUXTABLE: *(In an ecstasy.)* Knew his business! Knew his business!! My boy, in the old days...your father was asked everywhere like one of themselves very nearly! First of his sort to break that barrier. D'you know, it's my belief that if Mrs. Gladstone had been thirty years younger, and a fashionable woman...he could have had a knighthood.

MRS. HUXTABLE: *(Explicitly.)* He was untrue to his wife, Henry.

(At this MR. HUXTABLE is the moral man again. These sudden changes are so like him. They are genuine; he is just half-conscious of their suddenness.)

MR. HUXTABLE: Yes, I know, and Amy did what she should have done. You see, it wasn't an ordinary case, Major Thomas. It was girls in the shop. And even though he took em out of the shop...that's a slur on the whole trade. A man in his position...you can't overlook that.

MRS. MADRAS: *(Palely asserting herself.)* I could have overlooked it if I had chosen.

PHILIP: *(To whom this is all so futile and foolish.)* My dear Mother, you were unhappy with my father, and you left him...the matter is very simple.

MRS. MADRAS: I beg your pardon, Philip...I was not unhappy with him.

MRS. HUXTABLE: Amy, how could you be happy with a man who was unfaithful to you? What nonsense!

(EMMA and JULIA, from the balcony, finding the window locked, tap with their fingernails upon the pane. The very sharpness of the sound begins to put out MR. HUXTABLE again.)

MR. HUXTABLE: No, no, they can't come in. *(He mouths at them through the window.)* You can't come in.

(EMMA mouths back.)

MR. HUXTABLE: What? *(Then the sense of it coming to him, he looks at his watch.)* No, it isn't...two minutes yet.

(And he turns away, having excluded the innocent mind from this unseemly discussion. But at the very moment JANE comes in by the door. His patience flies.)

MR. HUXTABLE: Oh, damn! Well, I beg pardon. *(Then in desperate politeness.)* Let me introduce...my daughter Jane...Major Thomas.

JANE: *(Collectedly.)* We have met, Father.

MR. HUXTABLE: *(Giving it all up.)* Well...how can I tell...there are so many of you!

MRS. HUXTABLE: *(Severely.)* I think, Henry, you had better go to this meeting tomorrow.

MR. HUXTABLE: *(Wistful for a moment.)* You think I ought?

MRS. HUXTABLE: You know you ought not.

MR. HUXTABLE: *(Disputing it manfully.)* No...I don't know I ought not. It isn't so easy to know what ought and ought not to be done as you always make out, Kitty. And suppose I just do something wrong for once, and see what happens.

MRS. HUXTABLE: Henry, don't say such things.

MR. HUXTABLE: *(Very reasonably to MAJOR THOMAS.)* Well, since I've been ill—

(But MINNIE has come in now and EMMA and JULIA, finding their exile a little unreasonable, rattle hard at the window. MR. HUXTABLE gives it all up again.)

MR. HUXTABLE: Oh, let em in, Phil… there's a good feller.

THOMAS: Allow me. *(And he does so.)*

JANE: *(Crisply.)* Oh, what's it all been about?

MRS. HUXTABLE: Never mind, Jane.

(She says this to JANE as she would have said it to her at the age of four. Meanwhile, MR. HUXTABLE has recovered.)

MR. HUXTABLE: You know, Major Thomas, Constantine could always get the better of me in little things.

JANE: *(Has sighted MINNIE and, callously, across the breadth of the room, imparts a tragedy.)* Minnie, your frog's dead…in the conservatory.

MINNIE: *(Pales.)* Oh, dear.

MR. HUXTABLE: …After the difference I began to write to him as Dear Sir; to his day he'll send me business letters beginning Dear Arry.

(MINNIE is hurrying to the glass house of death.)

JANE: I buried it.

MR. HUXTABLE: …Always at his ease, you know.

(THOMAS escapes from him. PHILIP is bending over his mother a little kindlier.)

PHILIP: I'll try to see you again before you go back to Sussex, Mother.

(At this moment the gong rings. A tremendous gong, beloved of the English middle class, which makes any house seem small. A hollow sound: the dinner hour striking its own empty stomach. JANE, whose things are not taken off, gives a mitigated yelp and dashes for the door. MRS. HUXTABLE shakes a finger.)

JANE: Dinner time already?

MRS. HUXTABLE: Late again, Jane.

PHILIP: We'll be off, Aunt Katherine.

MRS. HUXTABLE: *(With a common humanity she has not shown before.)* Philip…never think I mean to be self-righteous about your father. But he made your mother most unhappy when you were too young to know of it…and there is the example to others, isn't there?

PHILIP: Yes…of course, Aunt Kate. I know just how you feel about it…I'm not fond of him, either.

(PHILIP must be a little mischievous with his aunt. She responds by returning at once to her own apparent self again.)

MRS. HUXTABLE: My dear boy…and your own father! *(Exits.)*

(From the balcony one hears the tag of JULIA's entertaining of MAJOR THOMAS. They have been peering at the horizon.)

JULIA: Yes, it means rain…when you see it so clearly.

(A general post of leave-taking now begins. JULIA exits. JANE returns.)

PHILIP: Well, see you tomorrow, Uncle Henry.

MR. HUXTABLE: Yes, I suppose so. Oh, and about that other matter…

PHILIP: What can I do?

MR. HUXTABLE: I'll telephone you in the morning.

PHILIP: Goodbye, Mother.

THOMAS: Goodbye, Mr. Huxtable.

MR. HUXTABLE: *(With a final flourish of politeness.)* You've excused this domestic discussion, I ope, Major Thomas…it will appen sometimes.

THOMAS: I've been most interested.

(MINNIE comes back sadly from the frog's grave.)

PHILIP: Goodbye, Minnie.

MINNIE: Goodbye, Philip.

MR. HUXTABLE: You really won't stay to dinner?

PHILIP: Goodbye, Jane.

THOMAS: Thanks, no. We meet tomorrow.

(The general post quickens, the chorus grows confused.)

JANE: Goodbye.

THOMAS: Goodbye.

MINNIE: Goodbye.

THOMAS: Goodbye.

PHILIP: Goodbye, Emma—oh, pardon.

(There has been the confusion of crossed hands. Apologies, withdrawals, a treading on toes, more apologies.)

EMMA: Goodbye, Major Thomas.

PHILIP: Now goodbye, Emma.

THOMAS: Goodbye, Mrs. Madras.

PHILIP: Goodbye.

THOMAS: Goodbye.

(The chorus and the general post continue, until at last PHILIP and THOMAS escape to a tram and a tube and their lunch, while the HUXTABLES sit down in all ceremony to Sunday dinner: roast beef, horseradish, Yorkshire pudding, brown potatoes, Brussels sprouts, apple tart, custard and cream, Stilton cheese, dessert.)

ACT TWO

The business offices of Roberts & Huxtable are tucked away upon the first floor somewhere at the back of that large drapery establishment. The waiting room—the one in which employee sits in shivering preparation for interviews with employer—besides thus having been the silent scene of more misery than most places on earth, is one of the very ugliest rooms that ever entered into the mind of a builder and decorator. Four plain walls of brick or plaster, with seats round them, would have left it a waiting room pure and simple. But the ugly hand of the money-maker was upon it. In the person of a contractor he thrust upon the unfortunate room—as on all the others—everything that could excuse his price and disguise his profit. The walls, to start with, were distempered an unobjectionable green, but as that might seem too plain and cheap, a dado of nice stone colour was added, topped with stencilling in dirty red of a pattern that once was Greek.

The hand of the money-maker that has wrenched awry the Greek pattern on the wall has been laid also on all the four people who sit waiting for MR. PHILIP at noon on this Monday; and to the warping more or less of them all.

MRS. BRIGSTOCK, sitting stiffly on the plush bench, in brown quilled hat and coat and skirt, is, one would guess, a clerk of some sort. She lacks colour; she lacks repose; she lacks—one stops to consider that she might possibly be a beautiful woman were it not for the things she lacks. But she is the product of fifteen years or so of long hours and little lunch. Certainly at this moment she is not seen at her best. She sits twisting her gloved hands, pulling at a loose thread, now and then biting it. Otherwise she bites her lips; her face is drawn, and she stares in front of her with only a twist of the eye now and then towards her husband, who is uncomfortable upon a chair a few feet away.

If one were asked to size up MR. BRIG-STOCK, one would say: Nothing against him. The position of Third Man in the Hosiery does not require any special talents, and it doesn't get them; or if it does, they don't stay there. And MR. BRIGSTOCK stays there—just stays there. It sums him up—sums up millions of him—to say that in their youth they have energy enough to get into a position; afterwards, in their terror—or sometimes only because their employers have not the heart to dismiss them—they stay there. Sometimes, though, the employers have the heart, and do. And then what happens? Considered as a man rather than a wage earner—not that it is usual for us so to consider him—he is one of those who, happily for themselves, get married by women whom apparently no other man much wants to marry. Subdued to what he works in, he is dressed as a Third Man in the Hosiery should be. He is, at the moment, as agitated as his wife, and as he has no nervous force to be agitated with, is in a state of greater wretchedness.

On the other side of the room sits MISS CHANCELLOR. Every large living-in draper's should have as housekeeper a lady of a certain age, who can embody in her own person the virtues she will expect in the young ladies under her. Decorum, sobriety of thought, tidiness, respect of persons—these are the qualities generally necessary to a shop-assistant's salvation. MISS CHANCELLOR radiates them. They are genuine in her, too. She is now planted squarely on her chair, as it might be, in easy authority, but looking closely, one may see that it is a dignified resentment keeping her there unmovable.

In the middle of the room, by the table, sits MISS YATES. While they wait this long time the other three try hard to keep their eyes off her. It isn't easy; partly because she is in the middle of the room and they are not. But anyhow and anywhere MISS YATES is a person that you look at, though you may ignorantly wonder why. She is by no means pretty, nor does she try to attract you. But you look at her as you look at a fire or a light in an otherwise empty room. She is not a lady, nor is she well educated, and ten years' shop-assisting has left its marks on her. But there it is. To the seeing eye she glows in that room like a live coal. She has genius—she has life, to however low a use she—or the world for her—may put it. And commoner people are lustreless beside her.

They wait silently, and the tension increases. At last it is slightly relieved by PHILIP's arrival. He comes in briskly, his hat on, a number of unopened letters in his hand. They get up to receive him with varying degrees of respect and apprehension.

PHILIP: Good morning, Miss Chancellor. Good morning, Miss Yates. Good morning, Mr. Brigstock.

MR. BRIGSTOCK: (Introducing her.) Mrs. Brigstock.

(PHILIP nods pleasantly to MRS. BRIG-STOCK, who purses her lips in a half-frightened, half-vengeful way, and sits down again. Then he puts his hat on the mantelpiece and settles himself in the master position at the table.)

PHILIP: I'm afraid I've kept you waiting a little. Well, now—

(There is a sharp knock at the door.)

PHILIP: Come.

(It is BELHAVEN. BELHAVEN is seventeen, perhaps, on the climb from office boy to clerk, of the usual pattern. PHILIP greets him pleasantly.)

PHILIP: Oh, good morning, Belhaven.

BELHAVEN: I've put Major Thomas in your room, sir, as the papers were there, but Mr. Huxtable's is empty, if you'd like…

PHILIP: No, this'll do.

BELHAVEN: Major Thomas said would you speak to him for a minute, as soon as you came.

PHILIP: I'll go in now.

BELHAVEN: Thank you, sir.

PHILIP: *(To the waiting four.)* Excuse me one minute, please.

(BELHAVEN bolts back to his outer office by one door—his way of opening and getting through it is a labour-saving invention; and PHILIP goes to find THOMAS through the other. There is silence again, held by these four at a greater tension than ever. At last MRS. BRIGSTOCK, least able to bear it, gives one desperate wriggle-fidget. BRIGSTOCK looks at her deprecatingly and says…)

MR. BRIGSTOCK: Will you sit here, Freda, if you feel the draught?

MRS. BRIGSTOCK: *(Just trusting herself to answer.)* No, thank you.

(Silence again, but soon broken by PHILIP, who comes from the other room, throwing over his shoulder the last of his few words with THOMAS.)

PHILIP: All right, Tommy. *(TOMMY, even at the dullest business, always pleasantly amuses him. Then he settles himself at the table for the second time, conciliatory, kind.)* Well, now…

MRS. BRIGSTOCK: *(Determined to be first heard, lets slip the torrent of her wrath.)* It's slander, Mr. Madras, and I request that it shall be retracted immediately…before everybody…in the public press…by advertisement.

MR. BRIGSTOCK: *(In an agonised whisper.)* Oh, Freda…not so eadstrong.

PHILIP: *(Elaborately cool and good tempered.)* Miss Chancellor.

MISS CHANCELLOR: *(Even more elaborately cold and dignified.)* Yes, sir.

PHILIP: I think we might inform Mrs. Brigstock that we're sorry the accusation has become so public…It has naturally caused her some pain.

MRS. BRIGSTOCK: *(Ascending the scale.)* I don't believe it…I didn't believe it…if I'd have believed it—

MR. BRIGSTOCK: *(Interposing.)* Oh, Freda!

MISS CHANCELLOR: *(Very definitely.)* I saw them kissing. I didn't know Mr. Brigstock was a married man. And even if I had known it…I saw them kissing.

MISS YATES: *(Opening her mouth for the first time, shows an easy impatience of their anger and their attitudes, too.)* Oh…what sort of kiss?

MISS CHANCELLOR: Are there different sorts of kisses, Miss Yates?

MISS YATES: Well…aren't there?

MRS. BRIGSTOCK: *(Growing shrill now.)* He owns he did that, and he knows he shouldn't have, and he asked my pardon…and whose business is it, but mine…?

MR. BRIGSTOCK: *(Vainly interposing this time.)* Oh, Freda!

MRS. BRIGSTOCK: *(Climbing to hysterics.)* Hussy to let him...hussy...hussy!

PHILIP: *(Adds a little severity to his coolness.)* Mrs. Brigstock.

MISS YATES: *(As pleasant as possible.)* All right...Mr. Madras, I don't mind.

PHILIP: But I do. Mrs. Brigstock, I shall not attempt to clear up this business unless we can all manage to keep our tempers.

MISS YATES: I've been friends with Mr. Brigstock these twelve years. We both came into the firm together...and I knew he was married...p'raps I'm the only one that did. And when I told him...all I chose to tell him as to what had happened to me...I asked him to kiss me just to show he didn't think so much the worse of me. And he gave me one kiss...here. *(She dabs with one finger the left top corner of her forehead.)* And that is the truth of that.

PHILIP: You might have given this explanation to Miss Chancellor.

MISS YATES: She wouldn't have believed it.

MISS CHANCELLOR: I don't believe it.

MRS. BRIGSTOCK: *(With gathering force.)* William! William!! William!!!

BRIGSTOCK: *(Desperately musters a little authority.)* Freda, be quiet...haven't I sworn it to you on the Bible?

MISS CHANCELLOR: I may say I have known other young ladies in trouble and whether they behaved properly or improperly under the circumstances...and I've known them behave both...they did not confide in their gentlemen friends...without the best of reasons.

PHILIP: There is no reason that they shouldn't, Miss Chancellor.

MISS CHANCELLOR: They didn't.

MISS YATES: Well...I did.

MISS CHANCELLOR: I had no wish for the scandal to get about. I don't know how it happened.

MISS YATES: Ask your little favourite, Miss Jordan, how it happened.

MISS CHANCELLOR: Mr. Madras, if I am to be accused of favouritism—

PHILIP: Yes, yes...we'll keep to the point, I think.

MISS CHANCELLOR: If Mr. Brigstock wasn't the man—

MRS. BRIGSTOCK: *(The spring touched.)* William!

MISS CHANCELLOR: Why shouldn't she tell me who it was?

MISS YATES: Why should I?

MISS CHANCELLOR: Am I here to look after the morals of these young ladies, or am I not?

MRS. BRIGSTOCK: A set of hussies.

MR. BRIGSTOCK: *(In agony.)* Freda, you'll get me the sack.

PHILIP: Brigstock, if I wished to give anyone the sack, I should not be taking the trouble to discuss this with you all in—I hope—a reasonable way.

MRS. BRIGSTOCK: *(Much resenting reasonableness, stands up now to give battle.)* Oh, give him the sack, if you please, Mr. Madras. It's time he had it for his own sake.

MR. BRIGSTOCK: No, Freda!

MRS. BRIGSTOCK: You've got your way to make in the world, haven't you? He's got to start on his own like other people, hasn't he?

MR. BRIGSTOCK: *(Feeling safety and his situation slipping.)* In time, Freda.

MRS. BRIGSTOCK: Now's the time. If you're not sick of the life you lead…seeing me once a week for an hour or two…then I am. And this libel and slander makes about the last straw, I should think.

PHILIP: How long have you been married, Mrs. Brigstock?

MRS. BRIGSTOCK: Four years.

PHILIP: Four years!

MRS. BRIGSTOCK: *(A little quelled by his equable courtesy.)* Four years!

PHILIP: *(In amazed impatience.)* My dear Brigstock, why not have come to the firm and told them? It could have been arranged for you to live out with your wife.

MR. BRIGSTOCK: Well, I have been thinking of it lately, sir, but I never seem to happen on a really likely moment. I'm afraid I'm not a favourite in my department.

MRS. BRIGSTOCK: No fault of his!

MR. BRIGSTOCK: And it's sometimes a very little thing makes the difference between a feller's going and staying…when all those that aren't wanted are cleared out after sale time, I mean, for instance. And, of course, the thirty pound a year they allow you to live out on does not keep you…it's no use my saying it does. And when you're married…

MRS. BRIGSTOCK: *(Who has gathered her grievances again.)* I agreed to it. I have my profession too. We've been saving quicker. It's three hundred pounds now, all but a bit…that's enough to start on. I've got my eye on the premises. It's near here, I don't mind telling you. Why shouldn't we do as well as others…and ride in our carriages when we're fifty!

MR. BRIGSTOCK: *(Deprecating such great optimism.)* Well, I've asked advice…

MRS. BRIGSTOCK: You think too much of advice. If you'd value yourself higher! Give him the sack, if you please, Mr. Madras, and I'll say thank you.

(She finishes, and suddenly MISS YATES takes up this part of the tale quite otherwise.)

MISS YATES: He has asked my advice, and I've told him to stay where he is.

MRS. BRIGSTOCK: Oh, indeed!

MISS YATES: He's as steady as can be. But his appearance is against him.

MRS. BRIGSTOCK: Well, I never!

MR. BRIGSTOCK: A feller does think of the future, Marion.

MISS YATES: I wouldn't if I were you. I don't know where we all get to when we're fifty, and I've never met anyone who did. We're not in the shop any longer, most of us, are we? And we're not all in our carriages.

MR. BRIGSTOCK: *(Meekly.)* I suppose it can be done.

MISS YATES: Oh…premises near here and three hundred pounds. Perfect foolery, and William ought to know it is. This firm'll undersell you and eat you up and a dozen more like you…and the place you're in debt to for your stock will repossess and sell off every stick you own, and there you'll be in the gutter. I advised him to own up to *you* and live out and do the best he could.

MRS. BRIGSTOCK: *(More drenched with the cold water than she'll own.)* I'm much obliged, I'm sure…I've my own opinion…

PHILIP: *(Who has been studying her rather anxiously.)* You've no children, Mrs. Brigstock?

MRS. BRIGSTOCK: *(Goes white.)* No, I've no children. How can you save when you have children? But if it was his child this hussy was going to have, and I thought God wouldn't strike him dead on the spot, I'd do it myself, so I would...and he knows I would.

MR. BRIGSTOCK: Haven't I taken my oath to you, Freda?

MRS. BRIGSTOCK: How can I tell if he's speaking the truth...I ask you how can I tell? I lie awake at night away from him till I could scream with thinking about it.

(Only MISS YATES is ready with her bit of practical comfort.)

MISS YATES: Look here, don't you worry. I could have married William if I'd wanted to. That ought to be proof enough.

MR. BRIGSTOCK: There you are, Freda.

MISS YATES: Before he knew you.

MRS. BRIGSTOCK: *(Opening her eyes.)* Did you ask her?

MISS YATES: No, he never asked me... but you know what I mean. *(MISS YATES give emphasis to this with what one fears must be described as a wink.)*

(MRS. BRIGSTOCK looks at the acquiescent BRIGSTOCK and acknowledges the implication.)

MISS CHANCELLOR: *(Who has been sitting all this while still, silent, and scornful, inquires in her politest voice.)* Do you wish me still to remain, Mr. Madras?

PHILIP: One moment. I don't think I need detain you any longer, Mr. and Mrs. Brigstock. Your character is now quite clear in the firm's eyes, Brigstock, and I shall see that arrangements are made for you to live out in the future. I apologise to you both for all this unpleasantness.

(They have both risen at this.)

MR. BRIGSTOCK: *(Hesitatingly.)* Well...thank you...sir...and...

MRS. BRIGSTOCK: No, William.

MR. BRIGSTOCK: All right, Freda! *(He struggles into his prepared speech.)* We are very much obliged to you, sir, but I do not see how I can remain with the firm unless there has been, with regard to the accusation, some definite retraction.

PHILIP: *(Near the end of his patience.)* My good man, it is retracted.

MRS. BRIGSTOCK: Publicly.

PHILIP: Nonsense, Mrs. Brigstock.

MRS. BRIGSTOCK: *(Quite herself again.)* Is it indeed...how would you like it? *(Then becoming self-conscious.)* Well, I beg pardon. I'm sure we're very sorry for Miss Yates, and I wish she were married.

MISS YATES: *(With some gusto.)* So do I!!

MISS CHANCELLOR: *(Bursts out.)* Then you wicked girl, why didn't you say so before...when I wished to be kind to you? And we shouldn't all be talking in this outrageous, indecent way. I don't know how I manage to sit here. Didn't I try to be kind to you?

MISS YATES: *(Unconquerable.)* Yes, and you tried to cry over me. No, I don't wish I were married.

MR. BRIGSTOCK: Of course, it's not for me to say, Marion, but will the way you're going on now stop the other young ladies tattling?

(The tone of the dispute now sharpens rather dangerously.)

MRS. BRIGSTOCK: How's Mr. Brigstock to remain in the firm if Miss Chancellor does?

PHILIP: That is my business, Mrs. Brigstock.

MISS CHANCELLOR: What...when I saw him kissing her...kissing her!

MRS. BRIGSTOCK: William!

PHILIP: That has been explained.

MISS CHANCELLOR: No, Mr. Madras, while I'm housekeeper here I will not countenance loose behaviour. I don't believe one word of these excuses.

PHILIP: This is just obstinacy, Miss Chancellor.

MISS CHANCELLOR: And personally I wish to reiterate every single thing I said.

MRS. BRIGSTOCK: Then the law shall deal with you.

MISS CHANCELLOR: You can dismiss me at once, if you like, Mr. Madras.

MRS. BRIGSTOCK: It's libellous...it's slander...!

MR. BRIGSTOCK: Oh, Freda, don't!

MRS. BRIGSTOCK: Yes, and she can be put in prison for it.

MISS CHANCELLOR: If Miss Yates and Mr. Brigstock stay with this firm, I go.

MRS. BRIGSTOCK: And she shall be put in prison...the cat!

MR. BRIGSTOCK: Don't, Freda!

MRS. BRIGSTOCK: The heartless cat! Do you swear it's true, William?

PHILIP: (Sudden vehemence.) Take your wife away, Brigstock.

MRS. BRIGSTOCK: (At the edge of her self-control—and over it.) Yes, and he takes himself away...leaves the firm, I should think so, and sorry enough you'll be before we've done. I'll see what the law will

say to her...the police are not a hundred yards off...and on the better side of the street, too!

MR. BRIGSTOCK: Do be quiet, Freda!

MRS. BRIGSTOCK: (In hysterics now.) Three hundred pounds and how much did Harrod have when he started...or Marks and Spencer...and damages what's more...And me putting up with the life I've led...!

(They wait till the fit subsides—PHILIP with kindly impatience, BRIGSTOCK in mute apology—MRS. BRIGSTOCK is a mass of sobs. Then BRIGSTOCK edges her towards the door.)

PHILIP: Wait...wait...wait. You can't go into the passage making that noise.

MR. BRIGSTOCK: Oh, Freda, you don't mean it.

MRS. BRIGSTOCK: (Relieved and contrite.) I'm sure I hope I've said nothing unbecoming a lady...I didn't mean to.

PHILIP: Not at all...it's natural you should be upset.

MRS. BRIGSTOCK: And we're very much obliged for your kind intentions to us...

PHILIP: Wait till you're quite calm.

MRS. BRIGSTOCK: Thank you.

(With a final touch of injury, resentment, dignity, she shakes off BRIGSTOCK's timid hold.)

MRS. BRIGSTOCK: You needn't hold me, William.

(WILLIAM follows her out to forget and make her forget it all as best he can. PHILIP comes back to his chair, still good-humoured, but not altogether pleased with his own part in the business so far.)

PHILIP: I'm afraid you've put yourself in the wrong, Miss Chancellor.

MISS CHANCELLOR: One often does, sir, in doing one's duty. *(Then her voice rises to a sort of swan song.)* Thirty years have I been with the firm…only thirty years. I will leave tomorrow.

PHILIP: I hope you recognise it will not be my fault if you have to.

MISS CHANCELLOR: Miss Yates can obviate it. She has only to speak the truth.

PHILIP: Miss Chancellor, are we quite appreciating the situation from Miss Yates's point of view? Suppose she were married?

MISS YATES: I'm not married.

PHILIP: But if you told us you were, we should have to believe you.

MISS CHANCELLOR: Why, Mr. Madras?

PHILIP: *(With a smile.)* It would be good manners to believe her. We must believe so much of what we're told in this world.

MISS YATES: *(Who has quite caught on.)* Well, I did mean to stick that up on you…if anyone wants to know. I bought a wedding ring, and I had it on when I saw Dr. Willoughby. But when she came in with her long face and her What can I do for you, my poor child?…well, I just couldn't…I suppose the Devil tempted me and I told her the truth.

PHILIP: That's as I thought, so far. Miss Yates, have you that wedding ring with you?

MISS YATES: Yes, I have…it's not real gold.

PHILIP: Put it on.

(MISS YATES, having fished it out of a petticoat pocket, rather wonderingly does so, *and PHILIP turns, maliciously humourous, to MISS CHANCELLOR.)*

PHILIP: Now where are we, Miss Chancellor?

MISS CHANCELLOR: I think we're mocking at a very sacred thing, Mr. Madras.

MISS YATES: Yes…and I won't now.

(With sudden emotion she slams the ring upon the table. PHILIP meditates for a moment on the fact that there are some things in life still inaccessible to his light-hearted logic.)

PHILIP: True…true…I beg both your pardons. But suppose the affair had not got about, Miss Yates?

MISS YATES: Well…I should have had a nice long illness. It'd all depend on whether you wanted me enough to keep my place open.

PHILIP: You are an employee of some value to the firm.

MISS YATES: I reckoned you would. And Miss McIntyre'd be pleased to stay on a bit and hold my place now she's quarrelled with her fiancé. But, of course, if I could just work behind the counter…

MISS CHANCELLOR: *(Who has drawn the longest of breaths at this calculated immodesty.)* This is how she brazened it out to me, Mr. Madras. This is just what she told Mr. Huxtable…and you'll pardon my saying he took a very different view of the matter to what you seem to be taking.

MISS YATES: Oh, I've got to go, now I'm found out…I'm not arguing about it.

MISS CHANCELLOR: *(Severely.)* Mr. Madras. What sort of notions are you fostering in this wretched girl's mind?

PHILIP: *(Gently enough.)* I was trying for a moment to put myself in her place.

MISS CHANCELLOR: You will excuse me saying, sir, that you are a man…

PHILIP: Thank you, I was aware of that.

MISS CHANCELLOR: *(Unconscious of his joke.)* Because a woman is independent and earning her living, she's not to think she can go on as she pleases. If she wishes to have children, Providence has provided a way in the institution of marriage. Miss Yates would have found little difficulty in getting married, I gather.

MISS YATES: Living in here for twelve years!

MISS CHANCELLOR: Have you been a prisoner, Miss Yates? Not to mention that there are two hundred and thirty-five gentlemen employed here.

MISS YATES: Supposing I don't like any of em?

MISS CHANCELLOR: My dear Miss Yates, if you're merely looking for a husband as such… well…we're all God's creatures, I suppose. Personally, I don't notice much difference in men, anyway.

MISS YATES: Nor did I.

MISS CHANCELLOR: Lack of self-control…

MISS YATES: *Is* it!

MISS CHANCELLOR: …And self-respect. Are we beasts of the field, I should like to know? Is there nothing for a woman to do but to run after men? I simply do not understand this unlady-like attitude towards the facts of life. I am fifty-eight…and I have passed, thank God, a busy and a happy and I hope a useful life…and I have never thought any more or less of men than I have of any other human beings. I look upon spinsterhood as an honourable state, as my Bible teaches me to. Men are differ-ent. But some women marry happily and well…and some can't marry at all. These facts have to be faced.

PHILIP: We may take it that Miss Yates has been facing them.

MISS CHANCELLOR: Yes sir, but in what spirit? I have always endeavoured to influence the young ladies under my control towards the virtues of modesty and decorum…If I can no longer do that, I prefer to resign my charge. I will say before this young person that I regret the story should have got about. But when anyone has committed a fault, it seems to me immaterial who knows of it.

PHILIP: *(Reduced to irony.)* Do you really think so?

MISS CHANCELLOR: Do you require me anymore now?

PHILIP: I am glad to have had your explanation. We'll have a private talk tomorrow.

MISS CHANCELLOR: Thank you, sir. I think that will be more in order. Good morning.

PHILIP: Good morning.

(MISS CHANCELLOR has expressed her-self to her entire satisfaction and retires in good order. MISS YATES, conscientiously brazen until the enemy has quite disap-peared, collapses pathetically. And PHILIP, at his ease at last, begins to scold her in a most brotherly manner.)

MISS YATES: I'm sure she's quite right in all she says.

PHILIP: She may not be. But are you the sort of woman to have got yourself into a scrape of this kind, Miss Yates?

MISS YATES: I'm glad you think I'm not, sir.

PHILIP: Then what on earth did you go and do it for?

MISS YATES: I don't know. I didn't mean to.

PHILIP: Why aren't you married?

MISS YATES: That's my business. *(Then, as if making amends for the sudden snap.)* Oh...I've thought of getting married any time these twelve years. But look what happens...look at the Brigstocks...

PHILIP: No, no, no...that's not what I mean. Why aren't you to be married even now?

MISS YATES: I'd rather not say.

(MISS YATES assumes an air of reticence natural enough; but there is something a little peculiar in the manner of it, so PHILIP thinks.)

PHILIP: Very well.

MISS YATES: I'd rather not talk about that part of it, sir, with you, if you don't mind. *(Then she bursts out again.)* I took the risk. I knew what I was about. I wanted to have my fling. And it was fun for a bit. That sounds horrid, I know, but it was.

PHILIP: Miss Yates, I've been standing up for you, haven't I?

MISS YATES: Yes.

PHILIP: That's because I have unconventional opinions. But I don't do unconventional things.

MISS YATES: *(Naïvely.)* Why don't you?

PHILIP: I shouldn't do them well. But I'm not happy about you. As man to man, Miss Yates...were you in a position to run this risk?

MISS YATES: *(Honestly thinks before she speaks.)* Yes... I'd planned it all. I thought when I came back you'd give me a hundred

and forty a year and let me live out. There's a maisonette at Raynes Park and I can get a cheap girl to look after...I shall call him my nephew, like the Popes of Rome used to...or why can't I be a widow? I can bring him up and do him well. Insurance'll be a bit stiff in case anything happens to me. But I've got nearly two hundred saved to see me through till next summer.

PHILIP: Where are you going when you leave here? What relations have you?

MISS YATES: I have an aunt. I hate her.

PHILIP: Where are you going for the winter?

MISS YATES: Evercreech.

PHILIP: Where's that?

MISS YATES: I don't know. You get to it from Waterloo Station. I found it in the A.B.C.

PHILIP: *(In protest.)* But my dear girl...!

MISS YATES: Well, I want a place where nobody knows me, so I'd better go to one I don't know, hadn't I? I always make friends. I'm not afraid of people. Never been in the country in the winter. I want to see what it's like.

PHILIP: Well...granted that you don't want a husband...it's your obvious duty to make the man help you support his child.

MISS YATES: *(Ready for it; serious, too.)* I daresay. But I won't. I've known other girls in this sort of mess—with everybody being kind to them and sneering at them. And there they sat and cried, and were ashamed of themselves! What's the good of that? And the fellows hating them. Well, I don't want him to hate me. He can forget all about it if he likes...and of course he will. I started by crying my eyes out. Then I thought that if I couldn't buck up and anyway pretend to be pleased and jolly well proud, I might as well die. And d'you know when I'd been pretending a bit I found that I really was pleased and proud...And I am really proud and happy about it now, sir...I am not pretending. I daresay I've done wrong...perhaps I ought to come to grief altogether, but—

(At this moment a telephone on the table rings violently, and MISS YATES apologises—to it apparently.)

MISS YATES: Oh, I beg pardon.

PHILIP: Excuse me. *(Then answering.)* Yes. Who? No, no, no...State. Mr. State. Put him through. Morning! Who? My father...not yet. Yes, from Marienbad.

MISS YATES: *(Gets up, apparently to withdraw tactfully, but looking a little startled, too.)* Shall I...

PHILIP: No, no; it's all right.

(BELHAVEN knocks, comes in, and stands waiting by PHILIP, who telephones on.)

PHILIP: Yes? Well?...Who...Mark who?...Aurelius. No. I've not been reading him recently. Certainly I will...Thomas is here doing figures...d'you want him...Tommy!

BELHAVEN: Major Thomas is in the counting house, sir.

PHILIP: Oh. *(Then through the telephone.)* If you'll hold the line I can get him in a minute. Say Mr. State's on the telephone for him, Belhaven.

BELHAVEN: Yes, sir...and Mrs. Madras is below in a taxicab, sir, and would like to speak to you. Shall she come up or, if you're too busy to be interrupted, will you come down to her?

PHILIP: My mother?

BELHAVEN: No, not Mrs. Madras...your Mrs. Madras, sir.

PHILIP: Bring her up. And tell Major Thomas.

BELHAVEN: Yes, sir.

(BELHAVEN achieves a greased departure, and PHILIP turns back to MISS YATES.)

PHILIP: Where were we?

MISS YATES: *(Inconsequently.)* It is hot in here, isn't it?

(She turns and goes up to the window; one would say to run away from him. PHILIP watches her steadily.)

PHILIP: What's the matter, Miss Yates?

MISS YATES: *(More collectedly.)* Oh, I'm sure Miss Chancellor can't expect me to marry one like that now...can she?

PHILIP: Marry who?

MISS YATES: Not that I say anything against Mr. Belhaven...a very nice young man. And, indeed, I rather think he did try to propose last Christmas. The fact is, y'know, it's only the very young men that ever do ask you to marry them here. When they get older they seem to lose heart...or they think it'll cost too much...or...but anyway, I'm sure it's not important.

(The very out-of-place chatter dies away under PHILIP's sternly enquiring gaze.)

PHILIP: There's one more thing I'm afraid I ought to ask you. This trouble hasn't come about in any way by our sending you up to train at the Bond Street store, has it?

MISS YATES: *(Diving into many words again.)* Oh, of course it was most kind of you to send me there to get a polish on my manners...but I tell you...I couldn't have stood it for long. Those society ladies that you get coming in there...well, it does just break your nerve. What with following them about, and the things they say you've got to hear, and the things they'll say...about you half the time...that you've got not to hear...and keep your voice low and sweet, and let your arms hang down straight. You may work more hours in Huxtables, and I daresay it's commoner than the Madras House, but the customers are friendly with you.

PHILIP: ...Because, you see, Mr. Huxtable and I would feel responsible if it was anyone connected with us at either shop who...

MISS YATES: *(Quite desperately.)* No, you needn't...indeed you needn't...I will say there's something in that other place that does set your mind going about men. What he saw in me I never could think...honestly, I couldn't, though I think a good deal of myself, I can assure you. But it was my own fault, and so's all the rest of it going to be...my very own...

(MAJOR THOMAS's arrival is to MISS YATES a very welcome interruption, as she seems, perhaps by the hypnotism of PHILIP's steady look, to be getting nearer and nearer to saying just what she means not to. He comes in at a good speed, glancing back along the passage, and saying...)

THOMAS: Here's Jessica.

PHILIP: State on the telephone.

THOMAS: Thank you.

(And he makes for it as JESSICA comes to the open door. PHILIP's wife is an epitome of all that aesthetic culture can do for a woman. More: She is the result—not of thirty-three years—but of three or four generations of cumulative refinement. She might be a racehorse! Come to think of it, it is a very wonderful thing to have raised this crop of ladyhood. Creatures dainty in mind and body, gentle in thought and word, charming, delicate, sensitive, graceful, chaste, credulous of all good, shaming the world's ugliness and strife by the very ease and delightsomeness of their existence; fastidious—fastidious—fastidious; also in these latter years with their attractions more generally salted by the addition of learning and humour. Is not the perfect lady perhaps the most wonderful achievement of civilisation, and worth the cost of her breeding, worth the toil and the helotage of—all the others? JESSICA MADRAS is even something more than a lady, for she is conscious of her ladyhood. She values her virtue and her charm; she is proud of her culture, and fosters it. It is her weapon; it justifies her. As she floats now into the ugly room, exquisite from her eyelashes to her shoes, it is a great relief—just the sight of her.)

JESSICA: Am I interrupting?

PHILIP: No, come in, my dear.

THOMAS: *(Into the telephone.)* Hullo!

PHILIP: Well, Miss Yates, I want to see if I can that you are not more unfairly treated than people with the courage of their opinions always are.

THOMAS: Hullo!

PHILIP: Oh, you don't know my wife. Jessica, this is Miss Yates, who is in our made-to-order room. You're not actually working in your department now, I suppose?

MISS YATES: *(As defiant of all scandal.)* I am.

THOMAS: *(Still to the unresponsive telephone.)* Hullo! Hullo!

PHILIP: *(Finding MISS YATES beyond—possibly above him.)* Very well. That'll do now.

(But MISS YATES, by the presence of JESSICA, is now brought to her best made-to-order department manner. She can assume at will, it seems, a new face, a new voice; can become, indeed, a black-silk being of another species.)

MISS YATES: Thank you, sir. I'm sure I hope I've not talked too much. I always was a chatterbox, madam.

PHILIP: You had some important things to say, Miss Yates.

MISS YATES: Not at all, sir. Good morning, madam.

JESSICA: Good morning.

(And there is an end of MISS YATES. Meanwhile, the telephone is reducing THOMAS to impotent fury.)

THOMAS: They've cut him off.

(While he turns the handle fit to break it, JESSICA produces an opened telegram, which she hands to PHILIP.)

JESSICA: This…just after you left.

PHILIP: My dear, coming all this way with it! Why didn't you telephone?

THOMAS: *(Hearing something at last.)* Hullo…is that Mr. State's office? No! Well…Counting house, can you not get through to it?

JESSICA: I hate the telephone, especially the one here. Look at Tommy, poor wretch! They put you through from office to office…six different clerks…all stupid, and all with hideous voices.

PHILIP: *(Has now read his telegram and is making a face.)* Well, I suppose Mother must come if she wants to.

JESSICA: What'll your father say?

PHILIP: My dear girl…she has a right to see him if she insists…it's very foolish. Here, Tommy!

(He ousts him from the telephone and deals expertly with it.)

PHILIP: I want a telegram sent. Get double three double O Central, and plug through to my room…not here…my room.

THOMAS: *(Fervently.)* Thank yer.

JESSICA: Got over your anger at the play last night?

THOMAS: Oh, sort of play you must expect if you go to the theatre on a Sunday. Scuse me.

(Having admiringly sized up JESSICA and her costume, he bolts. PHILIP sits down to compose his telegram in reply. JESSICA, discovering that there is nothing attractive to sit on, hovers.)

PHILIP: Can you put her up for the night?

JESSICA: Yes.

PHILIP: Shall I ask her to dinner?

JESSICA: She'll cry into the soup…but I suppose it doesn't matter.

PHILIP: Dinner at eight?

JESSICA: I sound inhospitable.

PHILIP: Well, I've only said we shall be delighted.

JESSICA: But your mother dislikes me so. It's difficult to see much of her.

PHILIP: You haven't much patience with her, have you, Jessica?

JESSICA: Have you?

PHILIP: *(Whimsically.)* I've known her longer than you have.

JESSICA: *(With the nicest humour.)* I only wish she wouldn't write Mildred silly letters about God.

PHILIP: A grandmother's privilege.

(BELHAVEN slides in.)

BELHAVEN: Yessir.

PHILIP: Send this at once, please.

BELHAVEN: Yessir.

(Belhaven slides out. Then PHILIP starts attending to the little pile of letters he brought in with him. JESSICA, neglected, hovers more widely.)

JESSICA: Will you come out to lunch, Phil?

PHILIP: Lord, is it lunch time?

JESSICA: It will be soon. I'm lunching with Margaret Inman and Walter Muirhead at the Dieudonné.

PHILIP: Then you won't be lonely.

JESSICA: *(Mischievous.)* Margaret may be if you don't come.

PHILIP: I can't, Jessica. I'm not nearly through.

JESSICA: *(Comes to rest by his table and starts to play with the things on it, finding at last a blotting roller that gives satisfaction.)* Phil, you might come out with me a little more than you do.

PHILIP: *(Humourously final.)* My dear, not at lunch time.

JESSICA: Ugly little woman you'd been scolding when I came in.

PHILIP: I didn't think so.

JESSICA: Are ugly women as attractive as ugly men?

PHILIP: D'you know…I don't find that women attract me.

JESSICA: What a husband!

PHILIP: D'you want them to?

JESSICA: Yes…in theory.

PHILIP: Why, Jessica?

JESSICA: *(With charming finesse.)* For my own sake. Last day of Walter's pictures. He has sold all but five…and there's one I wish you'd buy.

PHILIP: Can't afford it.

JESSICA: I suppose, Phil, you're not altogether sorry you married me?

PHILIP: *(Although used enough to her charming and reasoned inconsequence, he really jumps.)* Good heavens, Jessica! Well, we've got through eleven years, haven't we?

JESSICA: *(Puts her head on one side and is quite half-serious.)* Are you in the least glad you married me?

PHILIP: My dear…I don't think about it. Jessica, I cannot keep up this game of repartee.

JESSICA: *(Floats away at once, half-seriously snubbed and hurt.)* I'm sorry, I know I'm interrupting.

PHILIP: *(Remorseful at once, for she is so pretty.)* No, no; I didn't mean that. These aren't important.

(But he goes on with his letters, and JESSICA stands looking at him, her face hardening just a little.)

JESSICA: But there are times when I get tired of waiting for you to finish your letters.

PHILIP: I know… Shall we hire a motorcar for the weekend?

(THOMAS bundles into the tête-à-tête, saying as he comes…)

THOMAS: He'll make you an offer for the place here, Phil.

PHILIP: Good.

JESSICA: Tommy, come out and lunch… Phil won't.

THOMAS: I'm afraid I can't.

JESSICA: I've got to meet Maggie Inman and young Muirhead. He'll flirt with her all the time. If there isn't a fourth I shall be fearfully in the cold.

PHILIP: *(Overcome by such tergiversation.)* Oh, Jessica!

THOMAS: *(Nervous, apparently; at least he is neither ready nor gallant.)* Yes, of course you will. But I'm afraid I can't.

JESSICA: *(In cheerful despair.)* Well, I won't drive to Peckham again of a morning. See you Wednesday, then, Tommy.

THOMAS: Wednesday?

JESSICA: Symphony Concert.

THOMAS: *(With sudden seriousness.)* D'you know, I'm afraid I can't on Wednesday either.

JESSICA: Why not?

THOMAS: *(Though the pretence withers before a certain sharpness in her question.)* Well…I'm afraid I can't.

JESSICA: *(It is evident that JESSICA has a temper bred to a point of control which makes it the nastier, perhaps. She now becomes very cold, very civil, very swift.)* We settled it only last night. What's the time?

PHILIP: Five to one.

JESSICA: I must go. I shall be late.

THOMAS: *(With great concern.)* Have you got a cab?

JESSICA: I think so.

THOMAS: We might do the next, perhaps.

JESSICA: All right, Tommy…don't be conscience-stricken. But when you change your mind about going out with me, it's pleasanter if you'll find some excuse. Goodbye, you two.

PHILIP: I shall be in by seven, my dear.

(JESSICA exits. THOMAS looks a little relieved, and then considerably worried; in fact, he frowns portentously. PHILIP disposes of his last letter.)

PHILIP: We've organised the world's work to make companionship between men and women a very artificial thing.

THOMAS: *(Without interest.)* Have we? I want three minutes' talk with you, old man.

PHILIP: Oh!

THOMAS: D'you mind if I say something caddish?

PHILIP: No.

THOMAS: Put your foot down and don't have me asked to your house quite so much.

PHILIP: *(Looks at him for half a puzzled minute.)* Why not?

THOMAS: I'm seeing too much of your wife.

(He is so intensely solemn about it that PHILIP can hardly even pretend to be shocked.)

PHILIP: My dear Tommy!

THOMAS: I don't mean one single word more than I say.

PHILIP: *(Good-naturedly.)* Tommy, you always have flirted with Jessica.

THOMAS: I don't want you to think that I'm the least bit in love with her.

PHILIP: Naturally not…you've got a wife of your own.

THOMAS: *(In intense brotherly agreement.)* Right. That's good horse sense.

PHILIP: And though, as her husband, I'm naturally obtuse in the matter…I really don't think that Jessica is in love with you.

THOMAS: *(Most generously.)* Not for a single minute.

PHILIP: Then what's the worry, you silly old ass?

THOMAS: *(A little tortuously.)* Well, Phil, this is such a damned subtle world. I don't pretend to understand it, but in my old age I have got a sort of rule of thumb experience to go by...which, mark you, I've paid for.

PHILIP: Well?

THOMAS: Phil, I don't like women, and I never did...but I'm hardly exaggerating when I say I married simply to get out of the habit of finding myself once every six months in such a position with one of them that I was supposed to be making love to her.

PHILIP: *(Enjoying himself.)* What do they see in you, Tommy?

THOMAS: God knows, old man...I don't. And the time it took up! Of course I was as much in love with Mary as you like, or I couldn't have asked her to marry me. And I wouldn't be without her and the children now for all I ever saw. But I don't believe I'd have gone out of my way to get them if I hadn't been driven to it, old man...driven to it. I'm not going to start the old game again now.

PHILIP: What's the accusation against Jessica? Let's have it in so many words.

THOMAS: *(Gathers himself up to launch the vindicating compliment effectively.)* She's a very accomplished and a very charming and a very sweet-natured woman. I consider she's an ornament to society.

PHILIP: *(With equal fervour.)* You're quite right, Tommy...what are we to do with them?

THOMAS: *(It's his favourite phrase.)* What d'you mean?

PHILIP: Well...what's your trouble with her?

THOMAS: *(Tortuously still.)* There ain't any yet...but...well...I've been dreading for the last three weeks that Jessica would begin to talk to me about you. That's why I'm talking to you about her. *(Then, with a certain enjoyment of his shocking looseness of behaviour.)* I'm a cad!

PHILIP: *(Still amused—but now rather sub-acidly.)* My standing for the County Council must be a most dangerous topic.

THOMAS: But that's just how it begins. Then there's hints...quite nice ones...about how you get on with each other. Last night in the cab she was talking about when she was a girl...

PHILIP: I walked home. Tactful husband!

THOMAS: Phil...don't you be French.

PHILIP: *(Suddenly serious.)* But, Tommy, do you imagine that she is unhappy with me?

THOMAS: No, I don't. But she thinks a lot...when she's bored with calling on people, and her music and her pictures. And once you begin putting your feelings into words...why, they grow.

PHILIP: But if she were unhappy, I'd rather that she did confide in you.

THOMAS: *(Shakes his head vehemently.)* No.

PHILIP: Why shouldn't she? You're friends.

THOMAS: Yes...there's no reason...but I tell you, it always begins that way.

PHILIP: You silly ass...can't you let a woman talk seriously to you without making love to her?

THOMAS: Damn it, that's what they say…but it never made any difference. I remember when I was twenty-four…there was one woman…years older than me…had a grown-up son. She took to scolding me for wasting my time flirting. I kept off kissing her for six weeks, and, I'll swear she never wanted me to kiss her. But I did.

PHILIP: Did she box your ears?

THOMAS: No…she said she couldn't take me seriously. If I'd gone away that would have been priggish. If I stayed I'd have done it again.

PHILIP: *(Mischievously.)* Which do you do?

THOMAS: Oh…never you mind.

PHILIP: *(With the utmost geniality.)* Well…you have my permission to kiss Jessica, if you think she wants you to.

THOMAS: Thanks, old man…that's very clever and up to date, and all the rest of it…but I asked you to chuck me out of the house to some extent.

PHILIP: I'm not going to.

THOMAS: Then you're no friend of mine.

PHILIP: Let us put it quite brutally. If Jessica chooses to be unfaithful to me how am I to stop her…even if I've the right to stop her?

THOMAS: If you're not prepared to be-have like a decent married man you've no right to be married…you're a danger.

PHILIP: Also, Tommy, if you caught me making love to your wife you might talk to me…but you wouldn't talk to her about it.

THOMAS: *(With a touch of sentiment.)* Mary's different. *(Then protesting again.)* And I'm not making love to your wife. I told you so.

PHILIP: Then if she's making love to you, run away for yourself.

THOMAS: She isn't making love to me. But if you can't take a hint—

PHILIP: A *hint!* Well…I'm dashed!

THOMAS: Well, old man, I give you fair warning of the sort of fool I am…and I'll take no more responsibility in the matter.

PHILIP: *(In comic exasperation.)* Don't warn me…warn Jessica. Tell her you're afraid of making a fool of yourself with her…

THOMAS: *(His eyebrows up.)* But that'd be as good as doing it. Good Lord, you can't behave towards women as if they were men!

PHILIP: Why not?

THOMAS: You try it!

PHILIP: I always do.

THOMAS: No wonder she wants to grumble about you to me.

PHILIP: *(Takes him seriously again.)* Look here, Tommy, I know Jessica pretty well. She doesn't want to be made love to.

THOMAS: *(Positively and finally.)* Yes, she does. *(Then with real chivalry.)* I don't mean that unpleasantly…but all women do. Some of em want to be kissed and some want you to talk politics…but the principle's the same.

PHILIP: *(Finely contemptuous.)* What a world you live in!

THOMAS: …And the difficulty with me is that if I try to talk politics I find they don't know enough about it…or else that they know too much about it…and it's simpler to kiss em and have it done.

PHILIP: Oh, much *simpler!*

THOMAS: *(Back to his starting point— pathetic.)* But I'm married now and I want a quiet life…

(A knock at the door interrupts him.)

PHILIP: Come in.

(It is BELHAVEN.)

BELHAVEN: Will you lunch, sir?

PHILIP: What is there?

BELHAVEN: I'm afraid only the Usual, sir.

PHILIP: Can you manage the Usual, Tommy? What is it, Belhaven?

BELHAVEN: Boiled mutton and a jam pudding, I think, sir. *(Then as confessing to a vulgarity.)* Rolypoly.

THOMAS: *(With great approval.)* Right. I hope it's strawberry jam.

PHILIP: Sure to be. Put it in Mr. Huxtable's room, will you…that's airy.

BELHAVEN: Yessir. *(Vanishes.)*

THOMAS: *(As on reflection.)* Not plum, y'know…plum's no use.

PHILIP: *(Gathers up his papers.)* I'll give the wicked woman your message.

THOMAS: *(Stares at him. Then, reflectively.)* Phil, d'you ever thank God you're not a woman?

PHILIP: No.

THOMAS: When I think what most of em have to choose between is soft-hearted idiots like me and hard-headed devils like you…I wonder they put up with us as they do.

PHILIP: *(Stares at him in turn with a queer smile. Then, as he turns to go…)* You've made it again, Tommy.

THOMAS: What?

PHILIP: Your one sensible remark. Come along.

(And he is gone. THOMAS follows, protesting.)

THOMAS: Look here…what d'you mean by One Sensible Remark? It's like your infernal…

(He pulls the door to after him. The room is alone with its ugliness.)

ACT THREE

In 1884 the Madras House was moved to its present premises in Bond Street. In those days decoration was mostly a matter of paint and wallpaper, but MR. CONSTANTINE MADRAS, ever daring, proceeded to beautify the home of his professional triumphs. He could neither draw nor colour, but he designed and saw to it all himself, and being a man of great force of character, produced something which, though extraordinarily wrong, was yet, since it was sincere, in a way effective. It added to his reputation and to the attractiveness of the Madras House.

In twenty-six years there have been changes, but one room remains untouched from then till now. This is the rotunda, a large, lofty, skylighted place, done in the Moorish style. The walls are black marble to the height of a man, and from there to the ceiling the darkest red. The ceiling is of a cerulean blue, and in the middle of the skylight a golden sun, with spiked rays proceeding from its pleasant human countenance, takes credit for some of the light it intercepts. An archway with fretted top leads from the rest of the establishment. Another has behind it a platform, a few steps high, hung with black velvet. The necessary fireplace (were there hot-water pipes in 1884?) is disguised by a heavy multicoloured canopy, whose fellow hangs over a small door opposite. On the floor is a Persian carpet of some real beauty. On the walls are gas brackets (1884 again!), the oriental touch achieved in their crescent shape. Round the wall are divans, many cushioned; in front of them little coffee stools. It is all about as Moorish as Baker Street Station, but the general effect is humourous, pleasant, and even not undignified.

In the old, grand days of the Madras House the rotunda was the happy preserve of very special customers, those on whom the great man himself would keep an eye. If you had been there you spoke of it casually; indeed, to be free of the rotunda was to be a well-dressed woman and recognised by all society as such. Ichabod! Since MR. CONSTANTINE MADRAS retired, the Madras House is on the way to becoming almost like any other shop; the special customers are nobody in particular, and the rotunda is where a degenerate management meet to consider the choice of ready-made models from Paris. A large oval table had to be imported and half a dozen Moorish chairs. It seemed, to the surprise of the gentleman who went innocently ordering such things, that there were only that number in existence. Scene of its former glories, this is now to be the scene, perhaps, of the passing of the Madras House into alien hands.

Three o'clock on the Monday afternoon is when the deal is to be put through, if possible, and it is now five minutes to. MAJOR THOMAS is there, sitting at the table; papers spread before him, racking his brains at a few final figures. PHILIP is there, in rather a schoolboyish mood. He is sitting on the table, swinging his legs. MR. HUXTABLE is there, too, dressed in his best, important and nervous, and he is talking to MR. EUSTACE PERRIN STATE.

MR. STATE is an American, and if American magazine literature is anything to go by, no American is altogether unlike him. He has a rugged, blood and iron sort of face, utterly belied by his soft, smiling eyes; rightly belied, too, for he has made his thirty

or forty millions in the gentlest way—as far as he knows. You would not think of him as a money-maker. As a matter of fact, he has no love of money and little use for it, for his tastes are simple. But moneymaking is the honourable career in his own country, and he has the instinct for turning money over and the knack of doing so on a big scale. His shock of grey hair makes him look older than he probably is; his voice is almost childlike in its sweetness. He has the dignity and aptitude for command that power can give.

From the little canopied door comes MR. WINDLESHAM, present manager of the establishment. He is a tailor-made man; for his clothes are too perfect to be worn by anything but a dummy, and his hair and complexion are far from human. Not that he dyes or paints them; no, they were made like that. His voice is a little inhuman, too, and as he prefers the French language, with which he has a most unripe acquaintance, to his own, and so speaks English as much like French as his French is like English, his conversation seems as unreal as the rest of him. Impossible to think of him in any of the ordinary relations of life. He is a functionary. Nature, the great inventor, will evolve, however roughly, what is necessary for her uses. Millinery has evolved the man-milliner. As he comes in—and he has the gait of a water-wagtail—MR. HUXTABLE is making conversation.

MR. HUXTABLE: A perfect barometer, as you might say—when your eye gets used to it.

MR. STATE: *(Smiling benevolently at MR. HUXTABLE.)* Is it really? The Crystal Palace! But what a sound that has.

MR. HUXTABLE: *(With modest pride.)* And a very ealthy locality!

WINDLESHAM: *(To PHILIP, and with a wag of his head back to the other room.)* They're just ready.

PHILIP: Come along and meet State.

(He jumps off the table, capturing WINDLE-SHAM's arm.)

MR. STATE: *(Enthusiastic.)* Denmark Hill. Name was changed as a compliment to Queen Alexandra.

MR. HUXTABLE: *(Struck by the information.)* Was it, now?

MR. STATE: Used to be Dulwich Hill. That's the charm of London to an American. Association. Every spot speaks.

PHILIP: *(As he joins them.)* This is Mr. Windlesham...our manager. He's going to show us some new models.

MR. STATE: *(Impressively extends a hand and repeats the name.)* Mr. Windlesham.

WINDLESHAM: Most happy. I thought you'd like to see the very latest...brought them from Paris only yesterday.

MR. STATE: Most opportune! *(Then with a sweeping gesture.)* Mr. Philip, this room inspires me. Your father's design?

PHILIP: Yes.

MR. STATE: I thought so.

PHILIP: It used to be his private office.

MR. STATE: *(Reverently.)* Indeed! Where the Duchess went on her knees! A historic spot. Interesting to me!

PHILIP: Something of a legend that.

MR. STATE: *(Intensely solemn, seems now to ascend some philosophic pulpit.)* I believe in legends, sir...they are the spiritual side of facts. They go to form tradition. That is why our eyes turn eastward to you from America, Mr. Huxtable.

MR. HUXTABLE: *(In some awe.)* Do they, now?

MR. STATE: Has it never struck you that while the progress of man has been in the path of the sun, his thoughts continually go back to the place of its rising? I have at times found it a very illuminating idea.

PHILIP: *(Not indecently commonplace.)* Well, have them in now, Windlesham, while we're waiting.

WINDLESHAM: You might cast your eyes over these new girls, Mr. Philip...the very best I could find, I do assure you. Faces are hard enough to get, but figures...well, there! *(Reaching the little door, he calls through.)* Allons Mes'moiselles! Non...non...par l'autre porte et à la gauche. *(Then back again.)* You get the best effect through a big doorway. One, two, and four first. *(He exhibits some costume drawings he has been carrying, distributes one or two, and then vanishes into the other room, from which his voice vibrates.)*

WINDLESHAM: En avant s'il vous plaît. Numéro un! Eh bien...numéro trois. Non Ma'moiselle, ce n'est pas commode...regardez ce corsage—la...

MR. HUXTABLE: *(Making a face.)* What I'm always thinking is, why not have a manly chap in charge of the place up here.

MR. STATE: *(With perfect justice.)* Mr. Windlesham may be said to strike a note. Whether it is a right note...?

(Through the big doorway, WINDLE-SHAM ushers in a costume from Paris, the very last word in discreet and costly finery, delicate in colour, fragile in texture; a creation. This is hung upon a YOUNG LADY of pleasing appearance, preoccupied with its exhibition, which she achieves by slow and sinuous, never-ceasing movements. She glides into the room. She wears a smile also.)

WINDLESHAM: One and two are both Larguillière, Mr. Philip. He can't get in the Soupçon Anglais, can he? Won't...I tell him. Promenez et sortez Ma'moiselle.

(The YOUNG LADY, still smiling and sinuous, begins to circle the room. She seems to be unconscious of its inhabitants, and they, in return, rather dreadfully pretend not to notice her, but only the costume.)

WINDLESHAM: Numéro deux.

(Another costume, rakishly inclined, with a hat deliberately hideous. The YOUNG LADY contained in them is again slow and sinuous and vacantly smiling.)

WINDLESHAM: But this is chic, isn't it? Promenez.

MR. STATE: *(In grave enquiry.)* What is the Soupçon Anglais?

PHILIP: A Frenchman will tell you that for England you must first make a design and then spoil it.

THOMAS: *(Whose attention has been riveted.)* Don't they speak English?

WINDLESHAM: Oh, pas un mot…I mean, not a word. Only came over with me yesterday…these three. Numéro trois.

(A third costume, calculated to have an innocent effect. The accompanying YOUNG LADY, with a sense of fitness, wears a pout instead of a smile.)

PHILIP: What's this? *(His eye is on the surmounting hat of straw.)*

WINDLESHAM: *(With a little crow of delight.)* That's the new hat. La belle Hélène again!

MR. STATE: *(Interested, still grave.)* La belle Hélène. A Parisian firm?

WINDLESHAM: *(Turning this to waggish account.)* Well…dear me…you can almost call her that, can't you?

(Suddenly he dashes at the costume and brings it to a standstill.)

WINDLESHAM: Oh, mon Dieu, Ma'moiselle! La gorgette…vous l'avez dérangé.

(He proceeds to arrange la gorgette to his satisfaction, also some other matters which seem to involve a partial evisceration of the underclothing. The YOUNG LADY, passive, pouts perseveringly. He is quite unconscious of her separate existence.)

THOMAS: *(Shocked, whispering violently to PHILIP.)* I say, he shouldn't pull her about like that.

WINDLESHAM: Là…comme ça.

(The costume continues its round; the others are still circling, veering and tacking, while WINDLESHAM trips admiringly around and about them. It all looks like some dance of modish dervishes.)

PHILIP: La belle Hélène, Mr. State, is a well-known Parisian courtesan…who sets many of the fashions which our wives and daughters afterwards assume.

MR. HUXTABLE: *(Scandalised.)* Don't say that, Phil; it's not nice.

PHILIP: Why?

MR. HUXTABLE: I'm sure no ladies are aware of it.

PHILIP: But what can be more natural than for the professional charmer to set the pace for the amateur!

WINDLESHAM: Quite la haute coquetterie, of course.

MR. STATE: Do you infer, Mr. Madras, a difference in degree, but not in kind?

PHILIP: I do.

MR. STATE: That is a very far-reaching observation, sir.

PHILIP: Do you know the lady personally, Mr. Windlesham?

(WINDLESHAM turns, with some tag of a costume in his hand, thus unconsciously detaining the occupier.)

WINDLESHAM: Oh, no…oh, dear me, no…quite the reverse, I do assure you. There's nothing gay in Paris to me. I was blasé long ago.

MR. STATE: But touching that hat, Mr. Windlesham.

WINDLESHAM: Oh, to be sure. Attendez, Ma'moiselle. *(Tiptoeing, he dexterously tilts the straw hat from the elaborate head it is perched on.)*

WINDLESHAM: It's not a bad story. Sortez.

(By this two costumes have glided out. The third follows. STATE, who has found it hard to keep his eyes off them, gives something of a sigh.)

MR. STATE: If they'd only just smile or wink, I might get over the extraordinary feeling it gives me.

WINDLESHAM: *(Caressing the hat.)* Well…it appears that a while ago out at the Pré Catalan, you know the restaurant in the Bois du Boulogne…there was Hélène, taking her afternoon cup of buttermilk. What should she see but Madame Erlancourt…one knows enough about that lady, of course…in a hat the very twin of Hélène's…the very twin. Well…you can imagine! Someone had blundered.

MR. STATE: *(Absorbed.)* No, I don't follow.

PHILIP: Some spy in the service of that foreign power had procured and parted with the plans of the hat.

MR. STATE: Madame…What's-her-name might have seen it on her before and copied it.

PHILIP: Mr. State, Hélène doesn't wear a hat twice.

MR. STATE: My mistake!

WINDLESHAM: So there was a terrible scene…

THOMAS: With madame…?

WINDLESHAM: *(Repudiating any such vulgarity.)* Oh, no. Hélène just let fly at her chaperone, she being at hand, so to speak.

MR. STATE: *(Dazzled.)* Her *what!* *(Then with humourous awe.)* No, I beg your pardon…go on…go on.

WINDLESHAM: She took off her own hat…pinned it on the head of the ugliest little gamine she could find, and sent the child out into the Bois. Then she sent to the kitchens for one of those baskets they bring the fish in… *(He twirls the hat.)* …you see. Then she ripped a yard of lace off her underskirt and twisted it round. Then she took off both her…well…La Belle France, you know…there is something in the atmosphere! It was her garters she took off…blue silk.

MR. STATE: In public?

WINDLESHAM: *(Professional.)* Oh,…it can be done. Hooked them together and fastened the bit of lace round the basket this way. Très simple! That's what she wore the rest of the afternoon and back to Paris. This is what's going to be the rage!

(Having deftly pantomimed this creation of a fashion, he hands the hat, with an air, to MR. STATE, who examines it.)

PHILIP: *(Smilingly caustic.)* La belle Hélène has imagination, Mr. State. She is also, I am told, thrifty, inclined to religion, a vegetarian, Vichy water her only beverage; in fact, a credit to her profession and externally…to ours.

MR. STATE: *(Hands back the hat, with the solemnest humour.)* Mr. Windlesham,

I am much obliged to you for this illuminating anecdote.

WINDLESHAM: Not at all…Will you see the other three?

MR. STATE: By all means.

WINDLESHAM: They won't be long in changing…but there's one I must just pin on.

MR. STATE: No hurry…sir.

(He has acquired a new joy in WINDLE-SHAM, whom he watches dance away. Then a song is heard from the next room…)

WINDLESHAM: Allons…numéro cinq…numéro sept…numéro dix. Ma'moiselle Ollivier…vous vous mettrez…

(And the door closes.)

PHILIP: *(Looks at his watch.)* But it's ten past three. We'd better not wait for my father.

(They surround the table and sit down.)

MR. STATE: Major Thomas, have you my memoranda?

THOMAS: Here.

(He hands them to STATE, who clears his throat, refrains from spitting, and begins the customary American oration.)

MR. STATE: The reason, gentlemen, I desire to purchase the Madras House and add it to the interest of my Burrows enterprise is—this: The Burrows provincial scheme—you are aware of its purpose—and it goes well enough as far as bringing local stores into our syndicate. It has been interesting to discover which aspects of the Burrows scheme suit which cities…and why. An absorbing problem in the psychology of local conditions! We have, by opening new stores, eliminated a considerable number of competitors, cases where the local people would not join with

us. But in your larger cities, your Leicesters and Norwiches and Plymouths and Coventrys…there the unknown name, the uninspiring name of Burrows, upon a brand-new establishment next door might anyhow be ineffective. It is in these provincial centres that we look to establish our Madras Houses…New Edition. Is that clear so far? Beyond that I have a reason…and I hope a not uninteresting reason to put before you gentlemen…

(During this MR. CONSTANTINE MADRAS has arrived. He turned aside for a moment to the door that the models came from, now he joins the group. A man of sixty, to whom sixty is the prime of life. Tall, quite dramatically dignified, suave, a little remote; he is one of those to whom life is an art of which they have determined to be master. It is a handsome face, Eastern in type, the long beard only streaked with grey. He does not dress like the ruck of men, because he is not of them. The velvet coat, brick-red tie, shepherd's-plaid trousers, white spats, and patent boots both suit him and express him subtly and well—the mixture of sensuous originality and tradition which is the man. PHILIP is purposely casual in greeting him; he has sighted him first. But MR. STATE gets up, impressed. It is part of his creed to recognise greatness; he insists on recognising it.)

PHILIP: Hullo, Father!

MR. STATE: Mr. Madras! Proud to meet you again.

CONSTANTINE: *(Graciously, without emotion.)* How do you do, Mr. State?

PHILIP: You know everyone, Father. Oh…Hippisly Thomas.

CONSTANTINE: *(Just as graciously.)* How do you do, sir? *(Then, with a mischievous smile, he pats HUXTABLE on the shoulder.)* How are you, my dear Harry?

(MR. HUXTABLE had heard him coming, and felt himself turn purple. This was the great meeting after thirty years! He had let it come upon him unawares; purposely let it, for indeed he had not known what to say or do. He had dreaded having the inspiration to say or do anything. Now, alas, and thank goodness! it is too late. He is at a suitable disadvantage.)

MR. HUXTABLE: *(Grunts out sulkily.)* I'm quite well, thank you.

(CONSTANTINE, with one more pat in pardon for the rudeness, goes to his chair.)

MR. STATE: A pleasant trip on the continent?

CONSTANTINE: Instructive. Don't let me interrupt business. I shall pick up the thread.

MR. STATE: I was just placing on the tablecloth some preliminary details of the scheme you and I discussed at our meeting in June to consolidate your name and fame in some of the most important cities of England. We had not got far. *(He consults his notes.)*

CONSTANTINE: *(Produces from a case a pipe and tobacco.)* You've some new models, Phil.

PHILIP: Yes.

CONSTANTINE: The tall girl looks well enough. May I smoke? *(He proceeds to make and light a pipe.)*

MR. STATE: I did not enter upon the finance of the matter because I entertain no doubt that…possibly with a little adjustment of shares and cash…that can be fixed. And I suspect that you are no more interested in money than I am, Mr. Madras. Anyone can make money, if he has capital enough. The little that I have came from lumber and canned peaches. Now, there was poetry in lumber.

The virgin forest…There was poetry in peaches…before they were canned. Do you wonder why I bought a clothing establishment?

PHILIP: *(Who is only sorry that sometime he must stop.)* Why, Mr. State?

MR. STATE: Because, Mr. Philip, I found myself a lonely man. I felt the need of getting into touch with what Goethe refers to as the woman spirit…drawing us ever upward and on. That opportunity occurred, and it seemed a businesslike way of doing the trick.

CONSTANTINE: And satisfying?

MR. STATE: I beg your pardon?

CONSTANTINE: Has the ready-made skirt business satisfied your craving for the eternal feminine?

MR. STATE: Mr. Madras…that sarcasm is deserved…No, sir, it has not. The Burrows business, I discover, lacks all inner meaning…it has no soul. A business can no more exist without a soul than a human being can. I'm sure I have you with me there, Mr. Huxtable.

MR. HUXTABLE: *(Quite chokes at the suddenness of this summons, but shines his best.)* I should say so, quite.

MR. STATE: *(Glowing.)* There was fun, mind you…there still is…in making these provincial milliners hop…putting a pistol to their heads…saying Buy our Goods or be Froze Out. That keeps me lively and it wakes them up…does them good. But Burrows isn't in the Movement. The Great Modern Woman's Movement. It has come home to me that the man, who has as much to do with Woman as manufacturing the bones of her corsets and yet is not consciously in that Movement is Outside History. Shovelling goods over a counter and adding up profits…that's no excuse for obstructing the earth's progress…nothing personal, Mr. Huxtable.

MR. HUXTABLE: No, no…I'm listening to you. I'm not too old to learn.

MR. STATE: Mind, I don't say I haven't taken pleasure in Burrows. We've had Notions…caused Ideas to spring. There was Nottingham.

MR. HUXTABLE: I know Nottingham…got a shop there?

MR. STATE: (With wholesome pride.) In two years Burrows in Nottingham has smashed the competition. I've not visited the city myself. The notion was our local manager's. Simple. The Ladies' department served by gentlemen… the Gentlemen's by ladies. Always, of course, within the bounds of delicacy. Do you think there is nothing in that, Mr. Huxtable?

MR. HUXTABLE: (Round-eyed and open-mouthed.) Oh…well…

MR. STATE: (With a gesture toward TOMMY.) Imagine the Mean Sensual Man surrounded by pretty girls…good girls, mind you…high class. Pay them well…let them live out…pay for their mothers and chaperones, if necessary. Well…Surrounded by Gracious Womanhood, does the Sensual Man forget how much money he is spending or does he not? Does he come again? Is it a little Oasis in the desert of his business day? Is it a better attraction than Alcohol, or is it not?

PHILIP: (Bitingly.) Is it?

MR. STATE: Then, sir…Audi Alteram Partem. I should like you to see our Ladies' Fancy Department at its best…just before the football season.

PHILIP: I think I do!

MR. STATE: Athletes everyone of em…not a man under six foot…bronzed,

noble fellows! And no flirting allowed…no making eyes…no pandering to anything Depraved. Just the Ordinary Courtesies of our Modern Civilisation from Pure Clean-Minded Gentlemen towards any of the Fair Sex who step in to buy a shilling sachet or the like. And pay, sir…the women come in flocks!

MR. HUXTABLE: (Bereft of breath.) Is this how you mean to run your new Madras Houses?

MR. STATE: Patience, Mr. Huxtable. It's but six months ago that I started to study the Woman Question from the point of view of Burrows and Co. I attended women's meetings in London, in Manchester, and in one-horse places as well. Political claims were but the drabbest aspect of the matter as I saw it. The Woman's Movement is Woman expressing herself. And what are a Woman's chief means…often her only means of expressing herself? Anyway…what's the first thing she spends her money on? Clothes, gentlemen, clothes. Therefore, I say…though Burrows may palp with good ideas…the ready-made skirt is out of date…

(WINDLESHAM, pins in his mouth, fashion plates under his arm, and the fish-basket hat in his hand, shoots out of the other room.)

WINDLESHAM: Will you have the others in now? (Then back through the door.) Allons, Mes'moiselles s'il vous plaît. Numéro cinq le premier. (Then he turns the hat upside down on the table.) I thought you'd like to see that they've actually left the handles on. But I don't think we can do that here, do you?

(There comes in as before the most elaborate gown that ever was.)

WINDLESHAM: Numéro cinq…number five.

THOMAS: I say...by Jove!

(*But the cold, searching light seems to separate from the glittering pink affair the poor, pretty, smiling creature exhibiting it, until, indeed, she seems half-naked. MR. WINDLESHAM's aesthetic sense is outraged.*)

WINDLESHAM: Mais non, mais non... pas en plein jour. Mettez vous par là dans le...dans l'alcove.

(*The costume undulates towards the black velvet platform.*)

THOMAS: (*Lost in admiration.*) That gives her a chance, don't it? Damn pretty girl!

PHILIP: (*His eye twinkling.*) She'll understand that, Tommy.

THOMAS: (*In good faith.*) She won't mind.

MR. STATE: How they learn to walk like it...that's what beats me!

(*MR. WINDLESHAM turns on the frame of lights which bear upon the velvet platform. The vision of female loveliness is now complete.*)

WINDLESHAM: There...that's the coup d'oeil.

(*The vision turns this way and that to show what curves of loveliness there may be. They watch, all but CONSTANTINE, who has sat silent and indifferent. He now smokes serenely. At last PHILIP's voice breaks in, at its coolest, its most ironic.*)

PHILIP: And are we to assume, Mr. State, that this piece of self-decoration really expresses the nature of any woman? Rather an awful thought!

THOMAS: Why?

PHILIP: Or if it expresses a man's opinion of her...that's rather worse.

THOMAS: It's damned smart. Ain't it, Mr. Huxtable?

MR. HUXTABLE: (*Who is examining closely.*) No use to us, of course. We couldn't imitate that under fifteen guineas. Look at the...what d'you call it?

WINDLESHAM: (*Loving the very word.*) Diamanté.

THOMAS: (*With discretion.*) Just for England, of course, you might have the shiny stuff marking a bit more definitely where the pink silk ends and she begins.

MR. HUXTABLE: (*Not to be sordid.*) But it's a beautiful thing!

MR. STATE: Fitted to adorn the presiding genius of some intellectual and artistic salon. More artistic than intellectual, perhaps...

WINDLESHAM: Assez, Ma'moiselle... sortez.

(*He turns off the light. The vision becomes once more a ridiculously expensive dress, with a rather thin and shivering YOUNG PERSON half inside it, who is thus unceremoniously got rid of.*)

WINDLESHAM: Numéro sept.

(*Another costume.*)

MR. STATE: Now here again. Green velvet. Is it velvet?

WINDLESHAM: Panne velvet. Promenez, s'il vous plaît.

MR. HUXTABLE: Good Lord...more buttons!

MR. STATE: The very thing, in which some Peeress might take the chair at a drawing-room meeting.

PHILIP: Of the Anti-Sweating League, no doubt.

MR. STATE: (*In gentle reproof.*) Sarcasm, Mr. Philip.

PHILIP: *(Won by such sweetness.)* I really beg your pardon.

WINDLESHAM: Numéro dix.

(A third costume enters.)

PHILIP: What about this?

MR. STATE: Grey with a touch of pink…severely soft. An Anti-Suffrage Platform.

PHILIP: *(In tune with him.)* No…it's cut square in the neck. Suffrage, I should say.

MR. STATE: *(Rubbing his hands.)* Good! Woman allures us along many paths. Be it ours to attend her, doing what service we may.

CONSTANTINE: You are a poet, Mr. State.

MR. STATE: I never wrote one in my life, sir.

CONSTANTINE: How many poets should cease scribbling and try to live such perfect epics as seems likely to be this purchase of yours of the Madras House.

MR. STATE: *(Much gratified.)* I shall be proud to be your successor. *(Then he soars.)* But it is the Middle-Class Woman of England that is waiting for me. She must have *her* chance to Dazzle and Conquer. That is every woman's birthright…be she a Duchess or a doctor's wife in the suburbs. And remember, gentlemen, that the Middle-Class Women of England…think of them in bulk… form one of the greatest Money-Spending Machines the world has ever seen.

MR. HUXTABLE: *(With a wag of the head; he is more at his ease now.)* Yes…their husbands' money.

MR. STATE: *(Taking a long breath and a high tone.)* The economic independence of women is the next step in the march of civilisation.

MR. HUXTABLE: *(Overwhelmed.)* Oh…I beg pardon.

MR. STATE: And now that the Seed of Freedom is sown in their Sweet Natures…what Mighty Forest…what a Luxuriant, Scented growth of Womanhood may spring up around us. For we live in an Ugly World. *(His eye searches for those costumes, and finds one.)* This is all the Living Beauty that there is. We want more of it. I want to see that Poor Provincial Lady Clad in Colours of the Rainbow.

(WINDLESHAM has indeed detained the severely soft costume and its YOUNG LADY, and there she has stood for a while, still smiling, but wondering, perhaps, behind the smile, into what peculiar company of milliners she has fallen. THOMAS, suddenly noticing that she is standing there, with the utmost politeness jumps up to hand his chair.)

THOMAS: I say, though…allow me.

WINDLESHAM: Thank you…but she can't. Not in that corset.

MR. STATE: Dear me, I had not meant to detain Mademoiselle. *(Then to amend his manners, and rather as if it were an incantation warranted to achieve his purpose.)* Bon jour.

(The YOUNG LADY departs, a real smile quite shaming the unreal.)

MR. STATE: You clean forget they're there. You approve of corsets, Mr. Windlesham?

WINDLESHAM: Oh, yes…the figure is the woman, as we say. Can I do any more for you?

PHILIP: See me before I go, will you?

WINDLESHAM: Then it's au'voir.

(He flutters away. There is a pause as if they had to recollect where they were. It is broken by PHILIP meditatively.)

PHILIP: I sometimes wonder if we realise what women's clothes are like...or our own, for that matter.

MR. HUXTABLE: What's that?

PHILIP: Have you ever tried to describe evening dress as it would appear to a strange eye? Can you think of this last? A conspiracy to persuade you that the creature can neither walk, digest her food, nor bear children. Now...can that be beautiful?

MR. STATE: That notion is a lever thrust beneath the very foundations of Society.

MR. HUXTABLE: *(Showing off a little.)* Trying to upset people's ideas. For the sake of doing it!

THOMAS: *(With solid sense.)* I think a crowd of well-dressed women is one of the most beautiful things in the world.

CONSTANTINE: Ah. *(With one long meditative exhalation he sends a little column of smoke into the air.)*

MR. STATE: *(To CONSTANTINE, deferentially.)* We are boring you, Mr. Madras, I'm afraid.

CONSTANTINE: *(In the smoothest of voices.)* No, I am not bored, Mr. State...only a little horrified.

MR. STATE: Why so?

CONSTANTINE: You see...I am a Mahommedan...and this attitude towards the other sex has become loathsome to me.

(This bombshell, so delicately exploded, affects the company very variously. It will be some time before MR. HUXTABLE grasps its meaning at all. THOMAS simply opens his mouth. MR. STATE has evidently found a new joy in life.)

PHILIP: My dear Father!

MR. STATE: *(As he beams round.)* A real Mahommedan?

CONSTANTINE: I have become a Mahommedan. If you were not, it would be inconvenient to live permanently at Hit...a village upon the borders of Southern Arabia...that is my home. Besides, I was converted.

THOMAS: *(Having recovered enough breath.)* I didn't know you could become a Mahommedan.

CONSTANTINE: *(With some severity.)* You can become a Christian, sir.

THOMAS: *(A little shocked.)* Ah...not quite the same sort of thing.

MR. STATE: But how extraordinarily interesting! Was it a sudden conversion?

CONSTANTINE: No...I had been searching for a religion...a common need in these times...and this is a very fine one, Mr. State.

MR. STATE: Is it? I must look it up. The Koran! Yes, I've never read the Koran...an oversight.

(He makes a mental note. And slowly, slowly, the full iniquity of it has sunk into MR. HUXTABLE. His face has gone from red to white and back again to red. He becomes articulate and vehement. He thumps the table.)

MR. HUXTABLE: And what about Amelia?

MR. STATE: Who is Amelia?

PHILIP: Afterwards, Uncle.

MR. HUXTABLE: *(Thumping again.)* What about your wife? No, I won't be quiet, Phil! It's illegal.

CONSTANTINE: *(With a half-cold, half-kindly eye on him.)* Harry...I dislike to see you make yourself ridiculous.

MR. HUXTABLE: (*Only this was needed.*) Who cares if I'm ridiculous? I've not spoken to you for thirty years...have I? And I come here today full of forgiveness...and curiosity...to see what you're really like now...and whether I've changed my mind...or whether I never really felt all that about you at all...and damned if you don't go and put up a fresh game on me! What about Amelia? Religion this time! Mahommedan, indeed...at your age! Can't you ever settle down? I beg your pardon, Mr. State. All right, Phil, afterwards! I've not done...but you're quite right...afterwards.

MR. STATE: (*Partly with a peacemaking intention, partly in curiosity...*) Do you indulge in a Harem?

MR. HUXTABLE: (*On his feet, righteously strepitant.*) If you insult my sister by answering that question...!

(*With a look and a gesture CONSTANTINE can silence him. Then with the coldest dignity he replies...*)

CONSTANTINE: My household, sir, is that of the ordinary Eastern gentleman of my position. We do not speak of our women in public.

MR. STATE: I'm sure I beg your pardon.

CONSTANTINE: Not at all. It is five years since I retired from business and decided to consummate my affection for the East by settling there. This final visit to Europe...partly to see you, Mr. State...was otherwise only to confirm my judgment on the question.

MR. STATE: Has it?

CONSTANTINE: It has. I was always out of place amongst you. I was sometimes tempted to regret my scandalous conduct...

(*A slight stir from MR. HUXTABLE.*)

CONSTANTINE: Hush, Harry...hush! But I never could persuade myself to amend it. It is some slight personal satisfaction to me to discover...with a stranger's eye...that Europe in its attitude towards women is mad.

MR. STATE: Mad!

CONSTANTINE: Mad.

THOMAS: (*Who is all ears.*) I say!

CONSTANTINE: You possibly agree with me, Major Thomas.

THOMAS: (*Much taken aback.*) No...I don't think so.

CONSTANTINE: Many men do, but—poor fellows—they dare not say so. For instance, Mr. State, what can be said of a community in which five men of some ability and dignity are met together to traffic in...what was the Numéro of that aphrodisiac that so particularly attracted Major Thomas?

THOMAS: (*Shocked even to violence.*) No...really. I protest—

MR. STATE: Easy, Major Thomas. Let us consider the accusation philosophically. (*Then with the sweetest smile.*) Surely that is a gross construction to put on the instinct of every beautiful woman to adorn herself.

CONSTANTINE: Why gross? I delight in pretty women, prettily adorned. To come home after a day's work to the welcome of one's women folk...to find them unharassed by notions of business or politics...ready to refresh one's spirit by attuning it to the gentler, sweeter side of life...

THOMAS: (*Making hearty atonement.*) Oh! Quite so...quite so.

CONSTANTINE: I thought you would agree with me, Major Thomas. That is the Mahommedan gentleman's domestic ideal.

THOMAS: Is it?

CONSTANTINE: But you don't expect to find your wife dressed like that...the diamanté and the...

THOMAS: *(Mental discomfort growing on him.)* No...that was a going-out dress.

PHILIP: *(Greatly enjoying this contest.)* Oh...Tommy! Tommy!

THOMAS: But I tell you if my wife would...that is, if any chap's wife will...I mean...*(Then he gets it out.)* if a woman always kept herself smart and attractive at home then a man would have no excuse for gadding about after other women.

MR. HUXTABLE: *(Joins the fray, suddenly, snappily.)* She sits looking after his children...what more does he want of her?

CONSTANTINE: Harry is a born husband, Major Thomas.

MR. HUXTABLE: I'm not a born libertine, I hope.

THOMAS: Libertine be damned!

MR. STATE: Gentlemen, gentlemen... these are abstract propositions.

MR. HUXTABLE: Gadding after another man's wife, perhaps! Though I don't think you ever did that, Constantine...I'll do you justice...I don't think you ever did.

CONSTANTINE: I never did.

PHILIP: *(With intense mischief.)* Oh, Tommy, Tommy...can you say the same?

THOMAS: *(Flabbergasted at the indecency.)* Phil, that ain't nice...that ain't gentlemanly. And I wasn't thinking of that, and

you know I wasn't. And...we ain't all so unattractive to women as you are.

MR. STATE: Ah, Sour Grapes, Mr. Philip. We mustn't be personal, but is it Sour Grapes?

PHILIP: *(Very coolly on his defence.)* Thank you, Tommy...I can attract just the sort of woman I want to attract. But as long as it's Numéro Cinq, Six, or Sept that attracts you...well...so long will Madras House be an excellent investment for Mr. State.

CONSTANTINE: Phil is a cold-blooded egotist and if women like him that is their misfortune. I know his way with a woman...coax her on to the intellectual plane where he thinks he can better her. You have my sympathy, Major Thomas. I also am as susceptible as Nature means a man to be. And I referred to these going-out dresses because—candidly—I found myself obliged to leave a country where women are let loose with money to spend and time to waste. Encouraged to flaunt their charms on the very streets...proud to see the busmen wink...

MR. HUXTABLE: Not busmen. *(He is only gently deprecating now.)*

CONSTANTINE: Proud, my dear Harry, if they see a cabman smile.

MR. HUXTABLE: *(Looks round and then nods solemnly and thoughtfully.)* Yes, it's true. I'd deny it any other time, but I've been thinking a bit lately...and the things you think of once you start to think! It's true. Only they don't know they do it. They don't know they do it. *(Then a doubt occurring.)* D'you think they know they do it, Phil?

PHILIP: Some of them suspect, Uncle.

MR. HUXTABLE: No, what I say is it's Instinct...and we've just got to be as nice-minded about it as we can. There was Julia, this summer at Weymouth... that's one of my daughters. Bought herself a dress...not one of the Numéro sort, of course...but very pretty...orange colour, it was...stripes. But you could see it a mile off on the parade...and her sisters all with their noses out of joint. I said to myself... Instinct...

MR. STATE: *(Suddenly rescues the discussion.)* Yes, sir...the noblest Instinct of all...the Instinct to Perpetuate our Race. Let us take High Ground in this matter, gentlemen.

CONSTANTINE: *(Unstirred.)* The very highest, Mr. State. If you think that to turn Weymouth for a month a year into a cockpit of haphazard lovemaking is the best way of perpetuating your race...well, it's a point of view. What I ask is why Major Thomas and myself...already in a state of marital perpetuation...should have our busy London lives obsessed by...What is this thing?

PHILIP: La belle Hélène's new hat, Father.

CONSTANTINE: Now, that may be ugly...I hope I never made anything quite so ugly myself...but it's attractive.

PHILIP: *(With a wry face.)* No, Father.

CONSTANTINE: Isn't it, Major Thomas?

THOMAS: *(Honestly.)* Well, it makes you look at em when you might not otherwise.

CONSTANTINE: Yes...it's provocative. Its intention is that none of the world's work shall be done while it's about. And when it's always about I honestly confess again that I cannot do my share. It's a terrible thing to be constantly conscious of women. They have their uses to the world...as you so happily phrased it, Mr. State...their perpetual use...and the

world's interest is best served by keeping them strictly to it. Are these provocative ladies *(He fingers the hat again.)* noted for perpetuation nowadays?

MR. STATE: *(Bursts in—this time almost heartbrokenly.)* I can't bear this, sir...no man of feeling could. Besides, it's Reactionary...You must come back to us, sir. You gave us Joy and Pleasure...can we do without them? When you find yourself once more among the Loveliness you helped us to Worship you'll change your mind. What was the end of that little story of the Duchess? How, on the appointed night, attired in her Madras Creation, she swept into the Ballroom, her younger rivals Pale before the Intoxication of her Beauty and every man in the room...young and old...struggled for a Glimpse...a Word...a Look. A Ballroom, sir...isn't it one of the Sweetest Sights in the World?

(At the end of this recitation, MR. HUXTABLE barely refrains from applauding.)

CONSTANTINE: Mr. State, that is my case. The whole of our upper class life, which everyone with a say in the government of the country tries to lead...is now run as a ballroom is run. Men swaggering before women...women ogling the men. Once a lad got some training in manliness. But now from the very start...! In your own progressive country...mixed education...oh, my dear sir...

MR. STATE: A softening influence.

CONSTANTINE: *(Unexpectedly.)* Of course it is. And what has it sunk to, moreover...all education nowadays? Book learning. Because a woman's good at that.

THOMAS: That's so.

CONSTANTINE: From seventeen to thirty-four...the years which a man should consecrate to acquiring political virtue...wherever he turns he is distracted, provoked, tantalised by the barefaced presence of women. How's he to keep a clear brain for the larger issues of life? Why do you soldiers, Major Thomas, volunteer with such alacrity for foreign service?

THOMAS: *(With a jump.)* Good God...I never thought of that.

CONSTANTINE: What's the result? Every great public question...politics, religion, economy brought down to the level of women's emotion. Charming in its place. But softening, sentimentalising, lapping the world, if you let it, in the cotton wool of prettiness and pettiness. Men don't realise how far rotted by the process they are...that's what's so fatal. Getting used to the thought that it's naughty to be angry, Justice degenerates into kindness. You four unfortunates might own the truth just for once...you needn't tell your wives.

MR. STATE: I am not married.

CONSTANTINE: I might have known it.

MR. STATE: *(A little astonished.)* But no matter.

CONSTANTINE: *(With full appreciation of what he says.)* Women haven't morals or intellect in our sense of the words. They have other incompatible qualities quite as important, no doubt. But shut them away from public life and public exhibition. It's degrading to compete with them. It's as degrading to compete for them.

THOMAS: Are you advocating polygamy in England?

CONSTANTINE: That is what it should come to.

THOMAS: Well...I call that rather shocking. *(Then with some hopeful interest.)* And is it practical?

CONSTANTINE: I did not anticipate the reform in my lifetime...so I left for the East.

PHILIP: *(Finely.)* You did quite right, Father. I wish everyone of your way of thinking would do the same.

CONSTANTINE: *(Ready for him.)* Are you prepared for so much depopulation? Think of the women who'd be off tomorrow.

MR. HUXTABLE: *(Wakes from stupefaction to say with tremendous emphasis.)* Never!

CONSTANTINE: Wrong, Harry.

MR. HUXTABLE: No, I'm not wrong just because you say so! You ought to listen to me a bit sometimes. I always listened to you.

CONSTANTINE: Bless your quick temper.

(Who could resist CONSTANTINE's smile?...Well, not HUXTABLE.)

MR. HUXTABLE: Oh...go on...tell me why I'm wrong...I daresay I am.

CONSTANTINE: Even if you have liked bringing up six daughters and not getting them married...how have they liked it? You should have drowned them at birth, Harry...

MR. HUXTABLE: You must have your joke, mustn't you?

CONSTANTINE: Therefore, how much pleasanter for you...how much better for them...if you'd only to find one man ready, for a small consideration, to marry the lot.

MR. HUXTABLE: *(With intense delight.)* Now if I was to tell my wife that she wouldn't see the umour of it.

CONSTANTINE: ...And apart from the prisoners in that chaste little fortress on Denmark Hill...we used to employ, Harry, between us...what?...two or three hundred free and independent women...making clothes for the others, the ladies. They are as free as you like...free to go...free to starve. How much do they rejoice in their freedom to earn their living by ruining their health and stifling their instincts? Answer me, Harry, you monster of good-natured wickedness.

MR. HUXTABLE: What's that?

CONSTANTINE: You keep an industrial seraglio.

MR. HUXTABLE: A what!

CONSTANTINE: What else is your shop but a harem of industry? Do you know that it would sicken with horror a good Mahommedan? You buy these girls in the open market...you keep them under lock and key...

MR. HUXTABLE: I do?

CONSTANTINE: Quite right, Harry, no harm done. *(Then his voice sinks to the utmost seriousness.)* But you coin your profits out of them by putting on exhibition for ten hours a day...their good looks, their good manners, their womanhood. And when you've worn them out you turn them out...wouldn't know their faces if you met them selling matches at your door. For such treatment of potential motherhood, my Prophet condemns a man to Hell.

MR. HUXTABLE: Well, I never did in all my born days! They can marry respectably, can't they? We like em to marry.

PHILIP: Yes, Uncle...I went into that question with Miss Yates and the Brigstocks this morning.

CONSTANTINE: Where are your future generations coming from? What with the well-kept women you aestheticise till they won't give you children, and the free women you work till they can't give you children...

MR. HUXTABLE: Miss Yates has obliged us anyhow.

PHILIP: And we're going to dismiss her.

MR. HUXTABLE: What else can we do? But I said you weren't to be hard on the girl. And I won't be upset like this. I want to take things as I find em ...that is as I used to find em...before there was any of these ideas going around...and I'm sure we were happier without em. Stifling their instincts...it's a horrid way to talk. And I don't believe it. Not that that proves anything, does it? I'm a fool. It's a beastly world. But I don't make it so, do I?

PHILIP: Who does?

MR. HUXTABLE: Other people. Oh, I see it coming. You're going to say we're all the other people or something. I'm getting up to you.

CONSTANTINE: *(Very carefully.)* What is this about a Miss Yates?

PHILIP: A little bother at the Peckham shop. I can tell you afterwards if you like.

CONSTANTINE: No...there is no need.

(Something in the tone of this last makes PHILIP look up quickly. But MR. STATE, with a sudden thought, has first dived for his watch, and then, at the sight of it, gets up from the table.)

MR. STATE: Gentleman, are you aware of the time? I have a City appointment at four o'clock.

CONSTANTINE: Are we detaining you, Mr. State? Not universal or compulsory polygamy, Major Thomas. That would be nonsense. The very distribution of the sexes forbids it. Women will find, I hope, some intellectual companions like my son who will, besides, take a gentle interest in the County Council. There will be single-hearted men like Harry, content with old-fashioned domesticity. There will be poets like you, Mr. State, to dream about women and to dress them…their bodies in silks and their virtues in phrases. But there must also be such men as Major Thomas and myself…

THOMAS: No, no, I'm not like that…not in the least. Because a fellow has been in the Army! Don't drag me in.

MR. STATE: As stimulating a conversation as I remember. A little hard to follow at times…but worth far more than the sacrifice of any mere business doings.

CONSTANTINE: *(Takes the hint graciously and is apt for business at once.)* My fault! Shall we agree, Mr. State, to accept as much of your offer as you have no intention of altering? We are dealing for both the shops?

MR. STATE: Yes. What are we proposing to knock off their valuation, Major Thomas?

THOMAS: Eight thousand six hundred.

CONSTANTINE: Phil, what were we prepared to come down?

PHILIP: Nine thousand.

CONSTANTINE: A very creditable margin. Your offer is accepted, Mr. State.

MR. STATE: *(Feeling he must play up to such magnificent conducting of business.)* I should prefer to knock you down only eight thousand.

CONSTANTINE: *(Keeping the advantage.)* Isn't that merely romantic of you, Mr. State?

THOMAS: But do you know the conditions?

CONSTANTINE: We accept your conditions. If they won't work you'll be only too anxious to alter them. So the business is done.

MR. HUXTABLE: *(Eyes are wide.)* But look here.

PHILIP: Uncle Harry has something to say…

MR. HUXTABLE: *(Assertively.)* Yes.

CONSTANTINE: Something *different* to say, Harry?

MR. HUXTABLE: *(After thinking it over.)* No.

CONSTANTINE: *(Returns happily to his subject.)* What interests me about this Woman Question…now that I've settled my personal share in it…is to wonder how Europe, hampered by such an unsolved problem, can hope to stand up against the Islamic revival.

THOMAS: What's that?

CONSTANTINE: You'll hear of it shortly.

MR. STATE: Mr. Madras, I am proud to have met you again. If I say another word, I may be so interested in your reply that I shall miss my appointment. My coat? Thank you, Mr. Philip. I have to meet a man about a new septic system he wants me to finance. I can hardly hope for another Transcendental Discussion upon that.

CONSTANTINE: Why not?

MR. STATE: If you were he! Goodbye sir. Good day, Mr. Huxtable. Till tomorrow, Major Thomas. No, Mr. Philip, don't you see me down.

(He is off for his next deal. PHILIP civilly takes him past the door.)

PHILIP: Your car's at the Bond Street entrance, I expect.

THOMAS: That's how he settles business. But leaves us all the papers to do. I shall take mine home.

MR. HUXTABLE: I must be getting back, I think.

CONSTANTINE: Harry…you're running away from me.

MR. HUXTABLE: (In frank, amused confession.) Yes…I was. Habit y'know…habit.

CONSTANTINE: (With the most friendly condescension.) Suppose I go with you…part of the way. How do you go?

MR. HUXTABLE: On a bus.

CONSTANTINE: Suppose we go together…on a bus.

MR. HUXTABLE: (Desperately cunning.) It's all right…they won't see me with you. We don't close till seven.

CONSTANTINE: (His face sours.) No, to be sure. Phil, I can't come to dinner, I'm afraid.

PHILIP: Oh, I was going to tell you. Mother will be there. Tommy?

THOMAS: (All tact.) Oh, quite! (Departs.)

CONSTANTINE: (Indifferently.) Then I'll come in after dinner.

PHILIP: You don't mind?

CONSTANTINE: No.

(There stands MR. HUXTABLE, first on one foot and then on the other, desperately nervous. CONSTANTINE smiling at him.)

PHILIP: It's afterwards now, Uncle. Fire away…

(And is off. CONSTANTINE still smiles. Poor MR. HUXTABLE makes a desperate effort to do the proper thing by this reprobate. He forms his face into a frown. It's no use; an answering smile will come. He surrenders.)

MR. HUXTABLE: Look here…don't let's talk about Amelia.

CONSTANTINE: No…never rake up the past.

MR. HUXTABLE: Lord! What else has a chap got to think of?

CONSTANTINE: That's why you look so old.

MR. HUXTABLE: Do I, now?

CONSTANTINE: What age are you?

MR. HUXTABLE: Sixty.

CONSTANTINE: You should come and stay with me at Hit…not far from the ruins of Babylon, Harry.

MR. HUXTABLE: (Curious.) What's it like there?

CONSTANTINE: The house is white, and there are palm trees about it…and not far off flows the Euphrates.

MR. HUXTABLE: Just like in the Bible. (His face is wistful.) Constantine.

CONSTANTINE: Yes, Harry.

MR. HUXTABLE: You've said odder things this afternoon than I've ever heard you say before.

CONSTANTINE: Probably not.

MR. HUXTABLE: (Wondering.) And I haven't really minded em. But I believe it's the first time I've ever understood you…and p'raps that's just as well for me.

CONSTANTINE: Oh…why, Harry?

MR. HUXTABLE: Because...d'you think it's only not being very clever keeps us...well behaved?

CONSTANTINE: Has it kept you happy?

MR. HUXTABLE: (Impatient at the petty word.) Anyone can be happy. What worries me is having got to my age and only just beginning to understand anything at all. And you can't learn it out of books, old man. Books don't tell you the truth...at least not any that I can find. I wonder if I'd been a bit of a dog like you...? But there it is...you can't do things on purpose. And what's more, don't you go to think I'd have done them if I could...knowing them to be wrong. (Then comes a discovery.) But I was always jealous of you, Constantine, for you seemed to get the best of everything...and I know people couldn't help being fond of you...for I was fond of you myself, whatever you did. And now here we are, both of us old chaps...

CONSTANTINE: (As he throws back his head.) I am not old.

MR. HUXTABLE: (With sudden misgiving.) You don't repent, do you?

CONSTANTINE: What of?

MR. HUXTABLE: Katherine said this morning that you might have...but I wasn't afraid of that. (Now he wags his head wisely.) You know...you evil-doers...you upset us all and you hurt our feelings, and of course you ought to be ashamed of yourself. But...well...it's like the only time I went abroad. I was sick going...I was orribly uncomfortable...I ated the cooking...I was sick coming back. But I wouldn't have missed it...!

CONSTANTINE: (In affectionate good fellowship.) Come to Arabia, Harry.

MR. HUXTABLE: Don't you make game of me. My time's over. What have I done with it, now? Married. Brought up a family. Been master to a few hundred girls and fellows who never really cared a bit for me. I've been made a convenience of...that's my life. That's where I envy you. You've had your own way...and you don't look now as if you'd be damned for it either.

CONSTANTINE: I shan't be.

MR. HUXTABLE: (Shakes a fist, somewhat, though unconsciously, in the direction of the ceiling.) It's not fair, and I don't care who hears me say so.

CONSTANTINE: Suppose we shout it from the top of the bus.

(As they start, MR. HUXTABLE returns to his mundane, responsible self.)

MR. HUXTABLE: But you know, old man...you'll excuse me, I'm sure...and it's all very well having those theories and being able to talk...still, you did treat Amelia very badly...and those other ones, too...say what you like! Let go my arm, will you!

CONSTANTINE: Why?

MR. HUXTABLE: (His scruples less strong than the soft touch of CONSTANTINE's hand.) Well...p'raps you needn't. (A thought strikes him.) Are you really going away for good this time?

CONSTANTINE: Tomorrow.

MR. HUXTABLE: (Beaming on him.) Then come home and see Mother and the girls.

CONSTANTINE: It will make them feel very uncomfortable.

MR. HUXTABLE: D'you think so? Won't it do em good...broaden their minds?

(PHILIP comes back, too, his overcoat on.)

MR. HUXTABLE: Phil...shall I take your father ome to call?

PHILIP: (*After one gasp at the prospect, says with great cheerfulness…*) Certainly.

CONSTANTINE: I'll be with you by nine, Phil.

MR. HUXTABLE: I say…better not be too friendly through the shop.

(*CONSTANTINE smiles still, but does not loose his arm. Off they go.*)

ACT FOUR

PHILIP, his mother, and JESSICA are sitting, after dinner, round the drawing-room fire in Phillimore Gardens. JESSICA, rather, is away upon the bench of her long, black piano, sorting bound books of music, and the firelight hardly reaches her. But it flickers over MRS. MADRAS, and though it marks more deeply the little bitter lines on her face, it leaves a glow there in recompense. She sits, poor, anxious old lady, gazing, not into the fire, but at the shining copper fender, her hands on her lap, as usual. Every now and then she lifts her head to listen. PHILIP is comfortable upon the sofa opposite; he is smoking and is deep besides in some weighty volume, the Longman Edition of the Minority Report of the Poor Law Commission, perhaps.

It is a charming room. The walls are grey, the paint is a darker grey. The curtains to the two long windows are of the gentlest pink brocade; the lights that hang on plain little brackets from the walls are a soft pink, too, and there is no other colour in the room, but the maziness of some Persian rugs on the floor and the mellowed brilliancy of the Arundel prints on the walls. There is no more furniture than there need be; there is no more light than there need be; yet it is not empty or dreary. There is just nothing to jar, nothing to prevent a sensitive soul finding rest there.

The PARLOURMAID comes in; she is dressed in grey, too, capless, some black rib-bons about her. (Really, JESSICA's home inclines to be a little precious!) She brings letters, one for JESSICA, two for PHILIP, and departs.

PARLOURMAID: Mr. Huxtable.

PHILIP: Last post.

PARLOURMAID: Yes sir.

JESSICA: Half-past nine. I suppose your father means to come?

PHILIP: He said so.

MRS. MADRAS: Is your letter interesting, Jessica?

JESSICA: A receipt.

MRS. MADRAS: Do you run bills?

JESSICA: Lots.

MRS. MADRAS: Is that quite wise?

JESSICA: The tradesmen prefer it.

(*With that she walks to her writing table. JESSICA's manner to her mother-in-law is overcourteous, an unkind weapon against which the old lady, but half-conscious of it, is defenseless. PHILIP has opened his second letter, and whistles, at its contents, a bar of a tune that is in his head.*)

JESSICA: What's the matter, Phil?

(*To emphasise his feelings he performs that second bar with variations.*)

JESSICA: As bad as that?

(*For the final comment he brings the matter to a full close on one expressive note, and puts the letter away. JESSICA flicks at him amusedly.*)

MRS. MADRAS: How absurd! You can't tell in the least what he means.

JESSICA: No. I'm afraid we are giving you a dull evening.

MRS. MADRAS: (*With that suddenness which seems to characterise the HUXTABLE family.)* Why do you never call me Mother, Jessica?

JESSICA: Don't I?

MRS. MADRAS: *(Resenting prevarication.)* You know you don't.

JESSICA: I suppose I don't think of you just like that.

MRS. MADRAS: What has that to do with it?

JESSICA: *(More coldly courteous than ever.)* Nothing…Mother.

MRS. MADRAS: That's not a very nice manner of giving way, either, is it?

JESSICA: *(On the edge of an outburst.)* It seemed to me sufficiently childish.

MRS. MADRAS: I don't know what you mean. It's easy to be too clever for me, Jessica.

(PHILIP mercifully intervenes.)

PHILIP: Mother, what do you think parents gain by insisting on respect and affection from grown-up children?

MRS. MADRAS: Isn't it their right?

PHILIP: But I asked what they gained.

MRS. MADRAS: Isn't it natural? When an old woman has lost her husband or worse, if she's to lose her children, too, what has she left?

JESSICA: *(Recovering a little kindness.)* Her womanhood, Mother.

PHILIP: Her old-womanhood. You know, it may be a very beautiful possession.

(The PARLOURMAID announces "Mr. Constantine Madras." There stands CONSTANTINE in the bright light of the hall, more dramatically dignified than ever. As he comes in, though, it seems as if there was the slightest strain in his charming manners. He has not changed his clothes for the evening.

He goes straight to JESSICA, and it seems that he has a curious soft way of shaking hands with women.)

CONSTANTINE: How do you do, Jessica? I find you looking beautiful.

(JESSICA acknowledges the compliment with a little disdainful bend of the head and leaves him, then with a glance at PHILIP, leaves the room. CONSTANTINE comes towards his wife. She does not look up, but her face wrinkles pathetically. So he speaks at last.)

CONSTANTINE: Well, Amelia?

MRS. MADRAS: *(For MRS. MADRAS it must be resentment or tears, or both. Resentment comes first.)* Is that the way to speak to me after thirty years?

CONSTANTINE: *(Amicably.)* Perhaps it isn't. But there's not much variety of choice in greetings, is there?

(PHILIP, nodding to his father, has edged to the door and now edges out of it.)

CONSTANTINE: They leave us alone. We might be an engaged couple.

(She stays silent, distressfully avoiding his eye. He takes a chair and sits by her. He would say [as JESSICA no doubt would say of herself] that he speaks kindly to her.)

CONSTANTINE: Well, Amelia? I beg your pardon. I repeat myself, and you dislike the phrase. I hope, though, that you are quite well? Don't cry, dear Amelia…unless, of course, you want to cry. Well, then…cry. And, when you've finished crying…there's no hurry…you shall tell me why you wished to see me…and run the risk of upsetting yourself like this.

MRS. MADRAS: *(Dabbing her eyes.)* I don't often cry. I don't often get a chance.

CONSTANTINE: I fear that is only one way of saying that you miss me.

MRS. MADRAS: *(Handkerchief put away, she faces him.)* Are you really going back to that country tomorrow?

CONSTANTINE: Tomorrow morning.

MRS. MADRAS: For good?

CONSTANTINE: *(With thanksgiving.)* For ever.

MRS. MADRAS: *(Desperately resolute.)* Will you take me with you?

CONSTANTINE: *(After a moment to recover.)* No, Amelia, I will not.

MRS. MADRAS: *(Reacting a little hysterically.)* I'm sure I don't want to go, and I'm sure I never meant to ask you. But you haven't changed a bit, Constantine…in spite of your beard. I have.

CONSTANTINE: Only externally, I'm sure.

MRS. MADRAS: Why did you ever marry me? You married me for my money.

CONSTANTINE: *(Sighting boredom.)* It is so long ago.

MRS. MADRAS: It isn't…it seems like yesterday. Didn't you marry me for my money?

CONSTANTINE: Partly, Amelia, partly. Why did you marry me?

MRS. MADRAS: I wanted to. I was a fool.

CONSTANTINE: *(Evenly still.)* You were a fool, perhaps, to grumble at the consequence of getting what you wanted. It would have been kinder of me, no doubt, not to marry you. But I was more impetuous then, and I didn't realise you never could change your idea of what a good husband must be, nor how necessary it would become that you should.

MRS. MADRAS: How dare you make excuses for the way you treated me?

CONSTANTINE: There were two excuses. I was the first. I'm afraid that you ultimately became the second.

MRS. MADRAS: *(With spirit.)* I only stood up for my rights.

CONSTANTINE: You got them, too. We separated, and there was an end of it.

MRS. MADRAS: I've never been happy since.

CONSTANTINE: That is nothing to be proud of, my dear.

MRS. MADRAS: *(Feels the strangeness between them wearing off.)* What happened to that woman and her son…that Flora?

CONSTANTINE: The son is an engineer…promises very well, his employers tell me. Flora lives quite comfortably, I have reason to believe.

MRS. MADRAS: She was older than me.

CONSTANTINE: About the same age, I think.

MRS. MADRAS: You've given her money?

CONSTANTINE: *(His eyebrows up.)* Certainly…they were both provided for.

MRS. MADRAS: Don't you expect me to be jealous?

CONSTANTINE: *(With a sigh.)* Still, Amelia?

MRS. MADRAS: Do you ever see her now?

CONSTANTINE: I haven't seen her for years.

MRS. MADRAS: It seems to me she has been just as well treated as I have…if not better.

CONSTANTINE: She expected less.

MRS. MADRAS: And what about the others?

CONSTANTINE: *(His patience giving out.)* No, really, it's thirty years ago...I cannot fight my battles over again. Please tell me what I can do for you beyond taking you back with me.

MRS. MADRAS: *(Cowering to the least harshness.)* I didn't mean that. I don't know what made me say it. But it's dreadful seeing you once more and being alone with you.

CONSTANTINE: Now, Amelia, are you going to cry again?

MRS. MADRAS: *(Setting her teeth.)* No.

CONSTANTINE: That's right.

MRS. MADRAS: *(Pulls herself together and becomes intensely reasonable.)* What I really want you to do, if you please, Constantine, is not to go away. I don't expect us to live together...after the way you have behaved I could not consent to such a thing. But somebody must look after you when you are ill, and, what's more, I don't think you ought to go and die out of your own country.

CONSTANTINE: *(Meeting reason with reason.)* My dear...I have formed other ties.

MRS. MADRAS: Will you please explain exactly what you mean by that?

CONSTANTINE: I am a Mahommedan.

MRS. MADRAS: Nonsense!

CONSTANTINE: Possibly you are not acquainted with the Mahommedan marriage laws.

MRS. MADRAS: D'you mean to say you're not married to me?

CONSTANTINE: Exactly...though it was not considered necessary for me to take that into account in conforming to it...I did.

MRS. MADRAS: Well...I never thought you could behave any worse. Why weren't you satisfied in making me unhappy? If you've gone and committed blasphemy as well...I don't know what's to become of you, Constantine.

CONSTANTINE: Amelia, if I had been a Mahommedan from the beginning you might be living happily with me now.

MRS. MADRAS: How can you say such a horrible thing? Suppose it were true?

CONSTANTINE: I came from the East.

MRS. MADRAS: You didn't.

CONSTANTINE: Let us be quite accurate. My grandfather was a Smyrna Jew.

MRS. MADRAS: You never knew him. Your mother brought you up a Baptist.

CONSTANTINE: I was an unworthy Baptist. As a Baptist I owe you apologies for my conduct. What does that excellent creed owe me for the little hells of temptation and shame and remorse that I passed through because of it?

MRS. MADRAS: *(In pathetic wonder.)* Did you, Constantine?

CONSTANTINE: I did.

MRS. MADRAS: You never told me.

CONSTANTINE: *(With manly pride.)* I should think not.

MRS. MADRAS: But I was longing to have you say you were sorry, and let me forgive you. Twice and three times I'd have forgiven you...and you knew it, Constantine.

CONSTANTINE: *(Recovers his humour, his cool courtesy, and his inhumanity, which he had momentarily lost.)* Yes, it wasn't so easy to escape your forgiveness. If it weren't for Mahomet, the Prophet of

God, Amelia, I should hardly be escaping it now.

(PHILIP comes delicately in.)

PHILIP: I beg pardon…only my book. *(Which he takes from the piano.)*

CONSTANTINE: Don't go, Phil.

PHILIP: *(Joins them, and then, as silence supervenes, says with obvious cheerfulness.)* How are you getting on?

MRS. MADRAS: *(Her tongue released.)* Philip, don't be flippant. It's just as your cousin Ernest said. Your father has gone and pretended to marry a lot of wretched women out in that country you showed me on the map.

CONSTANTINE: Not a lot, Amelia.

MRS. MADRAS: My head's going round. And if anybody had told me, when I was a girl at school, and learning about such things in History and Geography, that I should ever find myself in such a situation as this, I wouldn't have believed them. Constantine, how are you going to face me Hereafter? Have you thought of that? Wasn't our marriage made in Heaven? I must know what is going to happen to us…I simply must. I have always prayed that you might come back to me, and that I might close your eyes in death. You know I have, Philip, and I've asked you to tell him so. He has no right to go and do such wicked things. You're mine in the sight of God, Constantine, and you can't deny it.

CONSTANTINE: *(Without warning, loses his temper, jumps up, and thunders at her.)* Woman…be silent. *(Then, as in shame, he turns his back on her and says in the coldest voice…)* Philip, I have several things to talk over with you. Suggest to your mother that she should leave us alone.

PHILIP: *(Protesting against both temper and dignity.)* I shall do nothing of the sort. While my father's in England, and you're in our house, he can at least treat his wife with politeness.

MRS. MADRAS: *(With meek satisfaction.)* I'd rather he didn't…it's only laughing at me. I'll go to bed. I'd much rather he lost his temper.

(She gets up to go. CONSTANTINE's bitter voice stops her.)

CONSTANTINE: Phil…when you were a boy…your mother and I once quarrelled in your presence.

PHILIP: *(In bitterness, too.)* I remember.

CONSTANTINE: I'm ashamed of it to this day.

MRS. MADRAS: *(Quite pleasantly.)* Well…I'm sure I don't remember it. What about?

CONSTANTINE: Oh…this terrible country. Every hour I stay in it seems to rob me of some atom of self-respect.

MRS. MADRAS: *(Joins battle again at this.)* Then why did you come back? And why haven't you been to see me before…or written me?

CONSTANTINE: *(In humourous despair.)* Amelia, don't aggravate me anymore. Go to bed, if you're going.

MRS. MADRAS: I wish I'd never seen you again.

PHILIP: Good night, Mother.

(PHILIP gets her to the door and kisses her kindly. Then CONSTANTINE says with all the meaning possible…)

CONSTANTINE: Goodbye, Amelia.

(She turns, the bright hall light falling on her, looks at him hatefully, makes no other

reply, goes. PHILIP comes back to the fire. All this is bitter to him, too. He eyes his father.)

CONSTANTINE: I'm sorry. I'm upset. I was upset when I came here.

PHILIP: What about? The visit to Denmark Hill?

CONSTANTINE: *(Who has apparently forgotten that.)* No…I didn't go there, after all.

PHILIP: Funked it?

CONSTANTINE: *(Accepting the gibe.)* I daresay. Once we were off the bus, Harry began to mutter about hurting their feelings. I daresay I was funking it, too. I told him to tell them how unbendingly moral he had been with me. He shed three tears as we parted.

PHILIP: Yes…you had Mother alone, at a disadvantage. But Aunt Kate…unveiled and confident, with six corseted daughters to back her!

CONSTANTINE: You think, of course, that I've always treated your mother badly?

PHILIP: Personally, I have a grudge against you both, my dear Father. As the son of a quarrelsome marriage, I have grown up inclined to dislike men and despise women. You're so full of getting the next generation born. Suppose you thought a little more of its upbringing.

CONSTANTINE: What was wrong with yours?

PHILIP: I had no home.

CONSTANTINE: You spent a Sunday with me every month. You went to the manliest school I could find.

PHILIP: Never mind how I learnt Latin and Greek. Who taught me that every pretty, helpless woman was a man's

prey…and how to order my wife out of the room?

CONSTANTINE: *(With a shrug.)* My dear boy…they like it.

PHILIP: *Do* they?

CONSTANTINE: Well…how else are you to manage them?

PHILIP: Father, don't you realise this manliness of yours is a little out of date…that you and your kind begin to look foolish?

CONSTANTINE: *(Voicing the discomfort that possesses him.)* I daresay. Thank God, I shall be quit of the country tomorrow! I got here late this evening because I travelled three stations too far in that Tube, sitting opposite such a pretty little devil. She was so alive…so crying out for conquest…she had that curve of the instep and the little trick of swinging her foot that I never could resist. How does a man resist it? Yes. That's ridiculous and degrading. I escaped from England to escape from it. Old age here…a loose lip and a furtive eye. I'd have asked you to shoot me first.

PHILIP: Was it that upset you?

CONSTANTINE: No.

(He frowns; his thoughts are much elsewhere. There is a moment's silence.)

PHILIP: Father, what do you know about this Miss Yates affair?

CONSTANTINE: *(Gives him a sharp look; then carefully casual.)* What you've told me.

PHILIP: No more?

CONSTANTINE: Is there more to know?

PHILIP: *(Fishes out and hands across the letter over which he whistled.)* This has just come from Miss Chancellor.

CONSTANTINE: Who's she?

PHILIP: The housekeeper at Uncle Harry's shop, who accused Brigstock of being the other party.

CONSTANTINE: Is he?

PHILIP: I think not. She encloses a letter from Brigstock's solicitors to the effect that both an apology and compensation is due him or the slander is to come into court. Hers faithfully, Meyrick & Hodges.

CONSTANTINE: I don't know them.

PHILIP: By their speed I should say they both are and are not a first-class firm. Suppose the whole thing is made public...then the question of the parentage must be cleared up. Miss Yates says it's nobody's business but hers. That's an odd idea, in which, if she chooses to have it, the law seems to support her.

(The steady eye and the steady voice have seemed to make the tension unbearable, and PHILIP has meant them to. But he hardly expected this.)

CONSTANTINE: *(In his own dramatically dignified way, has a fit of hysterics.)* Phil, I went back to the shop and I saw the little baggage tonight. I insisted on her meeting me. You know how I've always behaved over these matters. No one could have been kinder. But she refused money.

PHILIP: *(Calling on the gods to witness this occasion.)* Well...I might have guessed. Oh...you incorrigible old man!

CONSTANTINE: She insulted me...said she'd done with me...denied me the right to my own child. She had no intention of ever telling me about it. And you're helpless. I never felt so degraded in my life...

PHILIP: Serve you right!

CONSTANTINE: ...But the girl's mad! Think of my feelings. What does

it make of *me?* Did she know what she was doing?

PHILIP: Possibly not...but I'm thankful some woman's been found at last to put you in your place.

(These parental-filial passages have brought the two of them face to face, strung to shouting pitch. They become aware of it when JESSICA walks in very gently.)

JESSICA: Your mother gone?

PHILIP: To bed.

JESSICA: *(Conscious of thunder.)* Am I intruding? I sent Phil in for his book a while ago. He didn't return, so I judged that he was. Perhaps I'm not?

CONSTANTINE: *(Master of himself again, though the hand holding the letter which PHILIP gave him does tremble a little still.)* Well...what does Miss Chancellor want?

PHILIP: She asks my advice.

CONSTANTINE: Dismiss Baxter.

PHILIP: D'you mean Brigstock?

CONSTANTINE: Brigstock, then. Dismiss him.

PHILIP: What's he done to deserve it?

CONSTANTINE: Nonentity, without grit enough to own up to his wife and risk his place. D'you want to protect a man from the consequences of what he *is?*

PHILIP: Society conspires to.

CONSTANTINE: Then pay him fifty pounds for the damage to his little reputation. That'll be a just consequence to you of sentimentalising him.

PHILIP: And stick to Miss Chancellor?

CONSTANTINE: Certainly. Thank her from the firm for nosing out such a scandal.

PHILIP: And what about Miss Yates?

JESSICA: The girl in your office this morning?

PHILIP: Yes.

JESSICA: In the usual trouble?

PHILIP: How d'you know that?

JESSICA: I didn't.

CONSTANTINE: *(More slowly, more carefully, a little resentfully.)* Dismiss Miss Yates. Keep your eye on her…and in a year's time find her a better place…if you can…in one of these new Madras Houses of State's. He seems to pay very well. *(Then with a breath of relief he becomes his old charming self again.)* Let us change the subject. How is Mildred, Jessica?

JESSICA: Growing.

CONSTANTINE: I've an appointment with my solicitor tonight…ten o'clock. There will be five thousand pounds to come to that young lady by my will. I mean to leave it as a dowry for her marriage…its interest to be paid to her if she's a spinster at thirty…which Heaven forbid.

PHILIP: What are you doing with the rest, Father?

CONSTANTINE: There are one or two…legacies of honour, shall I call them? What remains will come to you.

PHILIP: Yes…We don't want any of it, thank you.

JESSICA: Phil?

CONSTANTINE: It isn't much.

PHILIP: Take it to your charming village on the borders of Southern Arabia. Stick it in the ground…let it breed more wheat and oil for you. We've too much of it already…it breeds idleness here.

CONSTANTINE: Dear me!

JESSICA: We have been discussing a *reduction* of our income by a few hundreds a year.

PHILIP: I'm refusing State's directorship.

JESSICA: Though I'm waiting for Phil to tell me where the saving's to come in.

PHILIP: We ought to change that school of Mildred's, for one thing.

JESSICA: Nonsense, Phil!

PHILIP: My dear Father, I spent a day there with the child, and upon my word, the only thing she's being taught which will not be a mere idle accomplishment is gardening. And even in their gardens…No vegetables allowed!

JESSICA: Phil, I don't mean to have any nonsense with Mildred about earning her living. Accomplished women have a very good time in this world… serious women don't. I want my daughter to be happy.

PHILIP: If we've only enough life left to be happy we must keep ourselves decently poor.

CONSTANTINE: *(Gets up.)* Could you get me a taxi, I wonder? It had started raining when I came.

PHILIP: There'll be one on the stand opposite.

CONSTANTINE: I mustn't be too late for Voysey. He makes a favour of coming after hours.

JESSICA: I frankly cultivate expensive tastes. I like to have things beautiful around me. I don't know what else civilisation means.

CONSTANTINE: Don't worry, Jessica, I don't think he can stop me leaving the money. I am sure that Philip will refuse you nothing. If you dismiss Miss Yates, I wonder if you could do it brutally enough to induce her to accept some compensation.

JESSICA: What for?

PHILIP: She won't take money from this gentleman...whoever he is...that is, she won't be bribed into admitting her shame.

CONSTANTINE: *(Who has stood still the while, stroking his beard.)* If your auditors won't pass a decent sum, I should be happy to send you a cheque, Phil.

PHILIP: *(With a wry smile.)* That would be very generous of you, Father.

CONSTANTINE: Goodbye, Jessica.

JESSICA: Goodbye.

CONSTANTINE: Philip is fortunate in his marriage.

JESSICA: So good of you to remind him of that.

CONSTANTINE: You have a charming home. I wonder how much of your womanly civilisation it would have needed to conquer *me*. Well...I leave you to your conversation. A pleasant life to you.

(He bends over her hand as if to kiss it. She takes it, as if fastidiously, out of his soft grasp. So he bows again and leaves her.)

CONSTANTINE: Victoria at eleven o'clock tomorrow, Philip.

PHILIP: Yes...I'll see you off.

CONSTANTINE: I have to do a little shopping quite early.

PHILIP: Shopping! What can the West send the East?

CONSTANTINE: I must take back a trinket or two.

PHILIP: To be sure! We do the same on our travels.

(PHILIP sees him through the hall to the front door, hails a stray cab, and is quit of him. JESSICA moves about as if to free the air of this visitation, and when PHILIP comes back...)

JESSICA: Does your father usually scatter cheques so generously and carelessly?

PHILIP: Jessica, while I have every respect for that young lady's independence...still two hundred pounds would be all to the good of the child's upbringing.

JESSICA: Yes, but not to Mildred's. I don't like your father. But I'm sometimes afraid that you're only an intellectual edition of him. It's very vital, of course, to go about seducing everybody to your own way of thinking. But really it's not quite civilised. You ought to learn to talk about the weather.

PHILIP: I cannot talk about what can't be helped. And I wonder more and more what the devil you all mean by civilisation. This house is civilisation. Whose civilisation? Not ours. The East End's our civilisation.

JESSICA: I've never seen it.

PHILIP: Then you don't much matter, my dear...any more than my father did with his view of life as a sort of love chase. *(He surveys the charming room that is his home.)* Persian carpets, Ghirlandajo in the drawing room...This is a museum. And down at that precious school, they are cultivating Mildred's mind into another museum...of good manners and good taste and...

(He catches JESSICA's half-scornful, half-kindly quizzical look.)

PHILIP: Are we going to have a row about this?

JESSICA: If you Idealists want Mildred to live in the East End...make it a fit place for her.

PHILIP: *(Taking the thrust and enjoyably returning it.)* When she lives in it, it will become so. Why give up running a fashion house to go on the County Council...if I can get on? Not to cut a fine figure there, but to be on committees. Not to talk finely even then...Lord keep me from that temptation...but to do dull, hard work over drains and disinfectants and...

JESSICA: Well...why, Phil? I may as well know.

PHILIP: To save my soul alive.

JESSICA: I'm sure I hope you may. But what is it we're to cultivate in poor Mildred's soul?

PHILIP: *(Stops in his walk and then...)* Have you ever really looked at a London street...walked slowly up and down it three times...carefully testing it with every cultured sense?

JESSICA: Yes...it's loathsome.

PHILIP: Then what have you done?

JESSICA: What can one do?

PHILIP: Come home to play a sonata of Beethoven! Does that drown the sights and the sounds and the smell of it?

JESSICA: Yes...it does.

PHILIP: My God...not to me!

JESSICA: *(Gently bitter.)* For so many women, Phil, art makes life possible.

PHILIP: Suppose we teach Mildred to look out of the window at life outside. You want to make that *impossible*. Neither Art nor Religion nor good manners have made the world a place I want to go on living in, if I can help it. *(He throws himself into a chair.)*

(There falls a little silence. Their voices hardly break it.)

JESSICA: Yes...a terrible world...an ugly, stupid, wasteful world. A hateful world!

PHILIP: And yet we have to teach Mildred what love of the world means, Jessica. Even if it's an uncomfortable business. Even if it means not adding her to that aristocracy of good feeling and good taste...the very latest of class distinctions. I tell you I haven't come by these doubts so easily. Beautiful sounds and sights and thoughts are all of the world's heritage I care about. Giving them up is like giving up my soul before I die.

JESSICA: *(With a sudden fling of her hands.)* To whom?

PHILIP: To everybody we are at present tempted to despise. For that's Public Life. That's Democracy. That's the Future. *(He looks across at his wife half-curiously.)* I know it's even harder for women. You put off your armour for a man you love. But otherwise you've your Honour and Dignity and Purity...

JESSICA: Do you want a world without it?

PHILIP: I rather want to know just what the world gets by it. Those six prim girls at my uncle's...what do we get from them or they from the world? We good and clever people are costing the world too much. Our brains cost too much if we don't give them freely. Your beauty costs too much if I only admire it because of all the ugliness in the world...even your virtue may cost too much, my dear. Rags pay for finery and ugliness for beauty, and sin pays for virtue. These are the riddles this Sphinx of a world presents. Your artists and scholars and preachers don't answer them...so I must turn my back for a bit on artist and scholar and preacher...all three.

JESSICA: *(Looks at him as he completes his apologia, sympathetic, if not understanding.*

Then she rallies him cheerfully.) My dear Phil, I shall not stop subscribing to the London Symphony Concerts…and I shall expect you to take me occasionally.

PHILIP: *(Jumping back from his philosophic world.)* Oh…that reminds me…I've a message for you from Tommy.

JESSICA: Have you? He was really irritating this morning.

PHILIP: Yes, we must take Tommy with a sense of humour. What it comes to is this. Will you please not flirt with him anymore because he hasn't the time, and he's too fond both of me and his wife to want to find himself seriously in love with you.

(Now PHILIP has not said this unguardedly, and JESSICA knows it. She'll walk into no little trap set for her vanity or the like. Still, it is with hardly a steady voice that she says simply…)

JESSICA: Thank you for the message.

PHILIP: *(Goes cheerfully on; he is turning the pages of his book.)* He doesn't at all suppose you are in love with him…seriously or otherwise.

JESSICA: *(Steadily.)* Do you?

PHILIP: No.

JESSICA: *(Her tone sharpening still.)* And is this the first time you've discussed me with Tommy or anyone? Please let it be the last.

PHILIP: Are you angry, Jessica?

JESSICA: I'm more than angry.

PHILIP: I'm sorry.

(Having kept her temper successfully, if not the sense of humour which PHILIP warned her he was appealing to, JESSICA now allows herself a deliberate outburst of indignation.)

JESSICA: I despise men. I despised them when I was fifteen…the first year I was

conscious of them. I've been through many opinions since…and I come back to despising them.

PHILIP: He was afraid you wouldn't be pleased with him. But he has my sympathies, Jessica.

JESSICA: *Has* he!

PHILIP: This afternoon, the entertaining Mr. State called Tommy the Mean Sensual Man.

JESSICA: *(With utter contempt.)* Yes. When we're alone, having a jolly talk about things in general, he's all the time thinking I want him to kiss me.

PHILIP: Which is what you do want, so long as he never kisses you.

JESSICA: *(In protest.)* No.

PHILIP: *(Fixing her with a finger.)* Oh yes, Jessica.

JESSICA: *(Her sense of humour returns for a moment.)* Well…I can't help it if he does.

PHILIP: You can, of course. And the Mean Sensual Man calls it being made a fool of.

(JESSICA puts a serious face on it again; not that she can keep one with PHILIP's twinkling at her.)

JESSICA: I give you my word I've never tried to flirt with Tommy…except once or twice when he was boring me. And perhaps once or twice when I was in the dumps…and there he was…and I was boring him. I know him too well to flirt with him…you can't flirt with a man you know that well. But he's been boring me a lot lately, and I suppose I've been a bit bored. Suppose I have been flirting with him…I thought he was safe enough. *(That attempt failing, there is a tack left. And on this she really manages to work herself back to indignation.)* And a caddish thing to go speaking to you about it…you should have knocked him down.

PHILIP: When he mentioned your name?

JESSICA: Yes…I wish you had.

PHILIP: Little savage.

JESSICA: I can't laugh about this. I'm hurt.

PHILIP: My dear, if you have any sense at all, you'll ask him to dinner and chaff him about it…in front of me.

JESSICA: Have you any understanding of what a woman feels when men treat her like this? Degraded and cheapened.

PHILIP: *(The high moral tone he will not stand.)* I can tell you what the man feels. He'll be either my father or me. That's your choice. Tommy's my father when you've put on your best gown to attract him, or he's me when he honestly says that he'd rather you wouldn't. Do you want him to be me or my father? That's the first question for you.

JESSICA: I want a man to treat a woman with courtesy and respect.

PHILIP: And what does that come to? My dear, don't you know that the Mean Sensual Man…not Tommy for the moment, but say Dick or Harry…looks on you all as choice morsels…with your prettiness, your dressing up, your music and art as so much sauce to his appetite. Which only a mysterious thing called your virtue prevents him from indulging…almost by force, if it weren't for the police.

JESSICA: I don't believe it.

PHILIP: Do you really believe that most men's good manners towards most pretty women are anything else but good manners?

JESSICA: I prefer good manners to yours.

PHILIP: *(With much more affection than the words convey.)* I treat you as a man would treat another man…neither better nor worse. Is the compliment wasted?

JESSICA: Is it a compliment to make me forget I'm a female? *(As amazed at this unreasonable world.)* I want to be friends with men. I'd sooner be friends with them. It's they who flirt with me. Why?

PHILIP: *(Incurably mischievous.)* Of course I've forgotten what you look like, and I never notice what you have on…but I suspect it's because you're rather pretty and attractive.

JESSICA: Do you want women not to be?

PHILIP: No.

JESSICA: It's perfectly sickening. Of course, if I had dozens of children and grew an old woman with the last one, I should be quite out of danger. But we can't all be like that…you don't want us to be.

PHILIP: *(Purely negative.)* No.

JESSICA: I do my share of things. I make a home for you. I entertain your friends. It may cost your precious world too much…my civilisation…but you want all this done. *(Then with a certain womanly reserve.)* And Phil…suppose I'm not much nicer by nature than some of you men? When I was a baby, if I'd not been fastidious I should have been a sad glutton. My culture…my civilisation…mayn't be quite up to keeping the brilliant Tommy a decent friend to me. But it has its uses.

PHILIP: Look here, if it's only your culture keeps you from kissing Tommy…kiss him.

JESSICA: *(To be so driven from pillar to post really does exasperate her.)* Phil…I sometimes think I'd sooner have been married to your father.

PHILIP: Why?

JESSICA: I should have been sorry…I should have despised him…but it would puff me up and add to my self-respect enormously! *(Then a little appealingly.)* When you're inhuman, Phil…I'm ever so little tempted…

PHILIP: *(Contrite at once.)* I know. I am. *(Then he gets up to stand looking into the fire, and what he says is heartfelt.)* But I so hate this farmyard world of sex…men and women always treating each other in an unfriendly way…I'm afraid it hardens me a bit.

JESSICA: I hate it, too…but I happen to love you, Phil.

(They smile at each other.)

PHILIP: Yes, my heart. If you'd kindly come over here…I should like to kiss you.

JESSICA: I won't. You can come over to me.

PHILIP: Will you meet me halfway?

(They meet halfway and stand together, looking into the fire.)

PHILIP: Do you know the sort of world I want to live in?

JESSICA: Aren't you going to kiss me?

(He does.)

PHILIP: Finery sits so well on the young and they strut and chase one another madly and even their quarrelling is in all good faith and innocence. But I don't see why we men and women should not find all happiness and find beauty too in soberer purposes. And with each other…why not some touch of tranquil understanding like yours and mine, dear, at the best of moments.

JESSICA: *(Happily.)* Do you mean when we sometimes suddenly want to shake hands?

PHILIP: *(Happily, too.)* That's it. And I want an art and a culture that shan't be just a veneer on savagery…but that spring from a whole people.

JESSICA: *(With one little shake of womanly common sense.)* Well, what's to be done?

PHILIP: *(Nobody more practical than he.)* I've been making suggestions. We must learn to live on less…put Mildred into a sensible school…and I must go on the County Council. That's how these great spiritual revolutions work out in practice. One begins.

JESSICA: *(As one who demands a right.)* Where's my share of the job?

PHILIP: *(Conscious of some helplessness.)* How is a man to tell you? You've the freedom to choose. And there's enough to choose from.

JESSICA: Is there? Nobody sizes you up as a good man or a bad man, pretty or plain. I know there's a trade for bad women and several professions for plain ones. But I've been taught to be charming and to like fine things. And I daresay I'd thought to continue in that vein till it bored me.

PHILIP: And doesn't it?

JESSICA: Phil, it isn't so easy for us. You don't always let us have the fairest of chances, do you?

PHILIP: No, I grant it's not easy. But unlike so many, you're free, Jessica, and it's got to be done.

JESSICA: Yes…

(She doesn't finish, for really there is no end to the subject. But for a moment or two longer, happy together, they stand looking into the fire.)

THE VOYSEY INHERITANCE

Adapted by Gus Kaikkonen

THE VALUE OF ENGLISH MONEY IN *THE VOYSEY INHERITANCE*

Amy Stoller

In 1911, the British pound sterling was made up of twenty shillings, worth twelve pence each; so that a pound equaled 240 pence. A sovereign was a gold coin worth one pound.

It isn't possible to determine the exact value of 1911 currency in 2007 (nobody bought air conditioners in 1911, and we no longer purchase buggy whips). But there are calculating formulas that allow us to estimate that £1 in 1911 had the purchasing power of £68 in 2006 (the latest year for which we have figures available).

So, the missing £300,000 in 1911 could have bought about as much as £21 million today (or 242 million in U.S. dollars)* in goods and services. Five "bob" (shillings) then would be about £15 now, or $29—enough for Beatrice's lunch (a nice one). Alice Maitland's £800 per year represents a modern annual purchasing power of £56,000, and Ethel's £1,000 dowry a contemporary $140,000. Booth and Beatrice's marriage settlement of £10,000 would buy about two-thirds of a million pounds' worth (some $1,330,000) in today's money.

By comparison with these figures for the upper middle class, the average weekly wage for a woman in 1910 was seven shillings, six pence. That's £19.5 pounds a year in 1911, or approximately $1,365 today—hardly enough to keep body and soul together! A gentleman's gentleman in service to minor aristocracy might earn £50 a year, plus a new suit of clothes and bed and board. That would have allowed for some savings with very careful management. Yet today, the equivalent amount of £3,500 ($7,000)—even with clothing, food, and shelter thrown in—might not stretch as far: expenses never dreamed of in 1911 are taken for granted now.

Amy Stoller is resident Dialect Designer/Coach and occasional Dramaturge at the Mint Theater Company, and the sole proprietor of Stoller System Dialect Coaching & Design. The Voysey Inheritance *was her second production at the Mint.*

---

*Conversion rates fluctuate; dollar amounts were calculated at 1 GBP to 2.00 USD, the rate as of April 23, 2007.

Mint Theater Company's production of *The Voysey Inheritance,* written by Harley Granville Barker, began performances on June 11, 1999, at the Mint Theater, 311 West 43rd Street, New York City, with the following cast and credits:

Mr. Voysey .... George Morfogen
Peacey.. Kurt Everhart
Edward Voysey ....Kraig Swartz
Major Booth Voysey .... Jack Koenig
Mr. George Booth .... Chet Carlin
Ethel Voysey............................ Christa Scott-Reed/Sevanne Martin
Alice Maitland... Sioux Madden
Honor Voysey.. Arleigh Richards
Beatrice Voysey.. Lisa Bostnar
Mrs. Voysey..Sally Kemp
Trenchard Voysey .... Robert Boardman/Warren Kelley

Directed by: Gus Kaikkonen
Set Design by: Vicki R. Davis
Costume Design by: Henry Shaffer
Lighting Design by: William Armstrong
Assistant Lighting Designer: Severn Clay
Original Music: Ellen Mandel
Production Stage Manager: Allison Deutsch
Assistant Stage Manager: Mazerati A. Neives/Douglas Shearer
Dialect Coach: Amy Stoller
Press Representative: David Rothenberg & Associates
Graphic Design: Aaron Lenehan/Kelrom Agency

ACT ONE

The office of Voysey and Son is in the best part of Lincoln's Inn. Its paneled rooms give out a sense of grandmotherly comfort and security, very grateful at first to the hesitating investor, the dubious litigant. MR. VOYSEY's own room, into which he walks about twenty past ten of a morning, radiates enterprise besides. There is polish on everything; on the windows, on the mahogany of the tidily packed writing table that stands between them, on the brass work of the fireplace in the other wall, on the glass of the fire screen which preserves only the pleasantness of a sparkling fire, even on MR. VOYSEY's hat as he takes it off to place it on the little red-curtained shelf behind the door. MR. VOYSEY is sixty or more and masterful; would obviously be master anywhere from his own home outwards, or wreck the situation in his attempt. Indeed there is a buccaneering air sometimes in the twist of his glance, not altogether suitable to a family solicitor. On this bright October morning, PEACEY, the head clerk, follows just too late to help him off with his coat, but in time to take it and hang it up with a quite unnecessary subservience. MR. VOYSEY is evidently not capable enough to like capable men about him. PEACEY, not quite removed from nature, has made some attempts to acquire protective colouring. A very drunken client might mistake him for his master. His voice very easily became a toneless echo of MR. VOYSEY's; later his features caught a line or two from that mirror of all the necessary virtues into which he was so constantly gazing; but how his clothes, even when new, contrive to look like the old ones of MR. VOYSEY's is a mystery, and to his tailor a most annoying one. And PEACEY is just a respectful number of years his master's junior. Relieved of his coat, MR. VOYSEY carries to his table the bunch of beautiful roses he is accustomed to bring to the office three times a week and places them for a moment only near the bowl of water there ready to receive them while he takes up his letters. These lie ready too, opened mostly, one or two private ones left closed and discreetly separate. By this time the usual salutations have passed, PEACEY's "Good morning, sir'" MR. VOYSEY's "Morning, Peacey." Then as he gets to his letters, MR. VOYSEY starts his day's work.

MR. VOYSEY: Any news for me?

PEACEY: I hear bad accounts of Alguazils Preferred, sir.

MR. VOYSEY: Oh…who from?

PEACEY: Merrit and James's head clerk in the train this morning.

MR. VOYSEY: They looked all right on…Give me the *Times*.

(PEACEY goes to the fireplace for the Times; *it is warming there.)*

MR. VOYSEY: *(Waves a letter, then places it on the table.)* Here, that's for you…Gerrard's Cross business. Anything else?

PEACEY: *(As he turns the* Times *to its Finance page.)* I've made the usual notes.

MR. VOYSEY: Thank'ee.

PEACEY: Young Benham isn't back yet.

MR. VOYSEY: Mr. Edward must do as he thinks fit about that. Alguazils, Alg—oh, yes. *(He is running his eye down the columns.)*

PEACEY: *(Leans over the letters.)* This is from Mr. Leader about the codicil…You'll answer that?

MR. VOYSEY: Mr. Leader. Yes. Alguazils. Mr. Edward's here, I suppose.

PEACEY: No, sir.

MR. VOYSEY: *(His eye twisting with some sharpness.)* What!

PEACEY: *(Almost alarmed.)* I beg pardon, sir.

MR. VOYSEY: Mr. Edward.

PEACEY: Oh, yes, sir, been in his room some time. I thought you said Headley; he's not due back till Thursday.

MR. VOYSEY: *(Discards the* Times *and sits to his desk and his letters.)* Tell Mr. Edward I've come.

PEACEY: Yes, sir. Anything else?

MR. VOYSEY: Not for the moment. Cold morning, isn't it?

PEACEY: Quite surprising, sir.

MR. VOYSEY: We had a touch of frost down at Chislehurst.

PEACEY: So early!

MR. VOYSEY: I want it for the celery. All right, I'll call through about the rest of the letters.

(PEACEY goes, having secured a letter or two, and MR. VOYSEY having sorted the rest—a proportion into the wastepaper basket—takes up the forgotten roses and starts setting them into a bowl with an artistic hand. Then his son EDWARD comes in. MR. VOYSEY gives him one glance and goes on arranging the roses, but says cheerily:)

MR. VOYSEY: Good morning, my dear boy.

*(EDWARD has little of his father in him and that little is undermost. It is a refined face, but self-consciousness takes the place in it of imagination, and in suppressing traits of brutality in his character it looks as if the young man had suppressed his sense of humour too. But whether or no, that would not be much in evidence now, for EDWARD is obviously going through some experience which is scaring him [there is no better word]. He looks not to have slept for a night or two, and his standing there, clutch-*ing and unclutching the bundle of papers he carries, his eyes on his father, half-appealingly but half-accusingly too, his whole being altogether so unstrung and desperate, makes MR. VOYSEY's uninterrupted arranging of the flowers seem very calculated indeed. At last the little tension of silence is broken.)*

EDWARD: Father...

MR. VOYSEY: Well?

EDWARD: I'm glad to see you. *(This is a statement of fact. He doesn't know that the commonplace phrase sounds ridiculous at such a moment.)*

MR. VOYSEY: I see you've the papers there.

EDWARD: Yes.

MR. VOYSEY: You've been through them?

EDWARD: As you wished me.

MR. VOYSEY: Well?

(EDWARD doesn't answer. Reference to the papers seems to overwhelm him with shame.)

MR. VOYSEY: *(Goes on with cheerful impatience.)* Now, now, my dear boy, don't take it like this. You're puzzled and worried, of course. But why didn't you come down to me on Saturday night? I expected you. I told you to come. Then your mother was wondering why you weren't with us for dinner yesterday.

EDWARD: I went through all the papers twice. I wanted to make quite sure.

MR. VOYSEY: Sure of what? I told you to come to me.

EDWARD: *(He is very near crying.)* Oh, Father!

MR. VOYSEY: Now look here, Edward, I'm going to ring and dispose of these letters. Please pull yourself together. *(He pushes the little button on his table.)*

EDWARD: I didn't leave my rooms all day yesterday.

MR. VOYSEY: A pleasant Sunday! You must learn, whatever the business may be, to leave it behind you at the Office. Why, life's not worth living else.

(PEACEY comes in to find MR. VOYSEY before the fire ostentatiously warming and rubbing his hands.)

MR. VOYSEY: Oh, there isn't much else, Peacey. Tell Simmons that if he satisfies you about the details of this lease it'll be all right. Make a note for me of Mr. Granger's address at Menton. I shall have several things to dictate to Atkinson. I'll whistle for him.

PEACEY: Mr. Burnett...Burnett and Marks...has just come in, Mr. Edward.

EDWARD: (Without turning.) It's only fresh instructions. Will you take them?

PEACEY: All right.

(PEACEY goes, lifting his eyebrows at the queerness of EDWARD's manner. This MR. VOYSEY sees, returning to his table with a little scowl.)

MR. VOYSEY: Now sit down. I've given you a bad forty-eight hours, have I? Well, I've been anxious about you. Never mind, we'll thresh the thing out now. Go through the two accounts. Mrs. Murberry's first...how do you find it stands?

EDWARD: (His feelings choking him.) I hoped you were playing some trick on me.

MR. VOYSEY: Come now.

(EDWARD separates the papers precisely and starts to detail them; his voice quite toneless. Now and then his father's sharp comments ring out in contrast.)

EDWARD: We've got the lease of her present house, several agreements...and here's her will. Here's an expired power

of attorney...over her securities and her property generally...it was made out for six months.

MR. VOYSEY: She was in South Africa.

EDWARD: Here's the Sheffield mortgage and the Henry Smith mortgage with banker's receipts...her banker's to us for the interest up to date...four and a half and five percent. Then...Fretworthy Bonds. There's a note scribbled in your writing that they are at the bank; but you don't say what bank.

MR. VOYSEY: My own.

EDWARD: (Just dwelling on the words.) Your own. I queried that. There's eight thousand five hundred in three and a half India stock. And there are her banker's receipts for cheques on account of those dividends. I presume for those dividends.

MR. VOYSEY: Why not?

EDWARD: (Gravely.) Because then, Father, there are her banker's half-yearly receipts for other sums amounting to an average of four hundred and twenty pounds a year. But I find no record of any capital to produce this.

MR. VOYSEY: Go on. What do you find?

EDWARD: Till about three years back there seems to have been eleven thousand in Queenslands which would produce...did produce exactly the same sum. But after January of that year I find no record of them.

MR. VOYSEY: In fact the Queenslands are missing, vanished?

EDWARD: (Hardly uttering the word.) Yes.

MR. VOYSEY: From which you conclude?

EDWARD: I supposed at first that you had not handed me all the papers.

MR. VOYSEY: Since Mrs. Murberry evidently still gets that four twenty a year, somehow; lucky woman.

EDWARD: *(In agony.)* Oh!

MR. VOYSEY: Well, we'll return to the good lady later. Now let's take the other.

EDWARD: The Hatherley Trust.

MR. VOYSEY: Quite so.

EDWARD: *(With one accusing glance.)* Trust.

MR. VOYSEY: Go on.

EDWARD: Father.

(His grief comes uppermost again and MR. VOYSEY meets it kindly.)

MR. VOYSEY: I know, my dear boy. I shall have lots to say to you. But let's get quietly through with these details first.

EDWARD: *(Bitterly now.)* Oh, this is simple enough. We're young Hatherley's only trustees till he comes of age in about five year's time. The property was thirty-eight thousand invested in Consols. Certain sums were to be allowed for his education; we seem to be paying them.

MR. VOYSEY: Regularly?

EDWARD: Quite. But where's the capital?

MR. VOYSEY: No record?

EDWARD: Yes…a note by you on a half-sheet…Refer Bletchley Land Scheme.

MR. VOYSEY: That must be ten years ago. Haven't I credited him with the interest on his capital?

EDWARD: You credit him with the Consol interest.

MR. VOYSEY: Quite so.

EDWARD: I've heard you say the Bletchley scheme paid seven and a half.

MR. VOYSEY: At one time. Have you taken the trouble to calculate what will be due from us to the lad?

EDWARD: Capital and compound interest…about thirty-nine thousand pounds.

MR. VOYSEY: A respectable sum. In five years' time?

EDWARD: When he comes of age.

MR. VOYSEY: That gives us, say, four years and six months in which to think about it.

(EDWARD waits, hopelessly, for his father to speak again; then says.)

EDWARD: Thank you for showing me these, sir. Shall I put them back in your safe now?

MR. VOYSEY: Yes, you'd better. There's the key.

(EDWARD reaches for the bunch, his face hidden.)

MR. VOYSEY: Put them down. Your hand shakes…why, you might have been drinking. I'll put them away later. It's no use having hysterics, Edward. Look your trouble in the face.

(EDWARD's only answer is to look at his father.)

MR. VOYSEY: I'm sorry, my dear boy. I wouldn't tell you if I could help it.

EDWARD: I can't believe it. And that you should be telling me…such a thing.

MR. VOYSEY: Let yourself go…have your cry out, as the women say. It isn't pleasant, I know. It isn't pleasant to inflict it on you.

EDWARD: How long has it been going on? Why didn't you tell me before? Oh, I know you thought you'd pull through. But I'm your partner...I'm responsible too. Oh, I don't want to shirk that...don't think I mean to shirk that, Father. Perhaps I ought to have discovered. But those affairs were always in your hands. I trusted...I beg your pardon. Oh, it's us...not you. Everyone has trusted us.

MR. VOYSEY: (*Calmly and kindly still.*) You don't seem to notice that I'm not breaking my heart like this.

EDWARD: What's the extent of the damage? When did it begin? Father, what made you begin it?

MR. VOYSEY: I didn't begin it.

EDWARD: You didn't? Who then?

MR. VOYSEY: My father before me.

(*EDWARD stares.*)

MR. VOYSEY: That calms you a little.

EDWARD: I'm so sorry! My dear Father...I'm glad. But I...it's amazing.

MR. VOYSEY: (*Shaking his head.*) My inheritance, Edward.

EDWARD: My dear Father!

MR. VOYSEY: I had hoped it wasn't to be yours.

EDWARD: D'you mean to tell me that this sort of thing has been going on here for years? For more than thirty years!

MR. VOYSEY: Yes.

EDWARD: That's a little hard to understand...just at first, sir.

MR. VOYSEY: (*Sententiously.*) We do what we must in this world, Edward. I have done what I had to do.

EDWARD: (*His emotion well cooled by now.*) Perhaps I'd better just listen quietly while you explain.

MR. VOYSEY: (*Concentrating.*) You know that I'm heavily into Northern Electrics.

EDWARD: Yes.

MR. VOYSEY: But you don't know how heavily. When I got the tip the Municipalities were organizing the purchase, I saw of course the stock must be up to a hundred and forty-five—a hundred and fifty in no time. But now that Leeds won't settle, there'll be no bill brought in for ten years. I bought at ninety-five. What are they today?

EDWARD: Seventy-two.

MR. VOYSEY: Seventy-one and a half. And in ten years I may be...! I'm getting on, Edward. That's mainly why you've had to be told.

EDWARD: With whose money are you so heavily into Northern Electrics?

MR. VOYSEY: The firm's money.

EDWARD: Clients' money?

MR. VOYSEY: Yes.

EDWARD: (*Coldly.*) Well...I'm waiting for your explanation, sir.

MR. VOYSEY: (*With a shrug.*) Children always think the worst of their parents, I suppose. I did of mine. It's a pity.

EDWARD: Go on, sir, go on. Let me know the worst.

MR. VOYSEY: There's no immediate danger. I should think anyone could see that from the figures there. There's no real risk at all.

EDWARD: Is that the worst?

MR. VOYSEY: (*His anger rising.*) Have you studied these two accounts or have you not?

EDWARD: Yes, sir.

MR. VOYSEY: Well, where's the deficiency in Mrs. Murberry's income…has she ever gone without a shilling? What has young Hatherley lost?

EDWARD: He stands to lose…

MR. VOYSEY: He stands to lose nothing if I'm spared for a little and you will only bring a little common sense to bear and try to understand the difficulties of my position.

EDWARD: Father, I'm not thinking ill of you…that is, I'm trying not to. But won't you explain how you're justified…

MR. VOYSEY: In putting our affairs in order?

EDWARD: Are you doing that?

MR. VOYSEY: What else?

EDWARD: (*Starting patiently to examine the matter.*) How bad were things when you first came to control them?

MR. VOYSEY: Oh, I forget.

EDWARD: You can't forget.

MR. VOYSEY: Well…pretty bad.

EDWARD: Do you know how it was my grandfather began…

MR. VOYSEY: Muddlement…cowardice! He invested recklessly and when the money was gone what was he to do? He'd no capital, no credit, and was in terror of his life. My dear Edward, if I hadn't found it out in time, he'd have confessed to the first man who came and asked for a balance sheet.

EDWARD: What amount was he to the bad then?

MR. VOYSEY: I forget. Several thousands.

EDWARD: But surely it hasn't taken all these years to pay off—

MR. VOYSEY: Oh, hasn't it!

EDWARD: (*Making his point.*) Then how does it happen, sir, that such a comparatively recent trust as young Hatherley's has been broken into?

MR. VOYSEY: Well, what could be safer? The investments are long term, there's no custodian, and not a sight wanted of interest or capital for five years.

EDWARD: (*Utterly beaten.*) Father, are you mad?

MR. VOYSEY: On the contrary. When my client's money is entirely under my control I sometimes reinvest it. The difference between the income it brings to them, and the profits it actually brings to me I utilize in my endeavor to fill up the deficit in the firm's accounts. Most of young Hatherley's Consol capital is now out on mortgage at four and a half and five. Safe as safe can be.

EDWARD: But he should have the full benefit.

MR. VOYSEY: We credit him his expected three percent.

EDWARD: Where are the mortgages? Are they in his name?

MR. VOYSEY: Some of them, some of them. That's a technical matter. With regard to Mrs. Murberry…those Fretworthy Bonds at my bank…I've raised five thousand on them. But I can release them tomorrow if she wants them.

EDWARD: Where's the five thousand?

MR. VOYSEY: I'm not sure. It was paid into my private account. Yes, I do remember. Some of it went to complete a purchase…that and two thousand more out of the Skipworth fund.

EDWARD: But, my dear Father…

MR. VOYSEY: Well?

EDWARD: *(Summing it all up very simply.)* It's not right.

MR. VOYSEY: *(Considers his son for a moment with a pitying shake of the head.)* Oh?…Why is it so hard for a man to see beyond the letter of the law! Will you consider, Edward, the position in which I found myself. Was I to see my father ruined and disgraced without lifting a finger to help him? Not to mention the interest of the clients. I paid back to the man who would have lost the most, by my father's mistakes, every penny of his money…and he never even knew the danger he'd been in…never passed an uneasy moment about it. It was I that lay awake. I have now somewhere a letter from that man thanking us effusively for the way in which the firm stewarded his estate. It allowed him to pursue his profession and provide for his family and leave this life in peace. Well, Edward, I stepped outside the letter of the law to do that service. For my family. For the firm. For kindness. For England. Was I right or wrong?

EDWARD: In the result, sir, right.

MR. VOYSEY: Judge me by the result. I took the risk of failure…I should have suffered. I could have kept clear of the danger if I'd liked.

EDWARD: But that's all past. The thing that concerns me is what you are doing now.

MR. VOYSEY: *(Gently reproachful now.)* My boy, can't you trust me a little? It's all very well for you to come in at the end of the day and criticize. But I who have done the day's work know how that work had to be done. And here's our firm, prosperous, respected, and without a stain on its honour. That's the main point, isn't it?

EDWARD: *(Quite irresponsive to this pathetic appeal.)* Very well, sir. Let's dismiss from our minds all prejudices about the truth, acting upon instructions, behaving as any honest firm of solicitors must behave.

MR. VOYSEY: Nonsense. I tell no unnecessary lies. If a man of any business ability gives me definite instructions about his property I follow them.

EDWARD: Father, no unnecessary lies!

MR. VOYSEY: Well, my friend go and knock it into Mrs. Murberry's head, if you can, that four hundred and twenty pounds of her income hasn't, for the last eight years, come from the place she thinks it's come from, and see how happy you'll make her.

EDWARD: But is that four hundred and twenty a year as safe to her as it was before you…

MR. VOYSEY: I see no reason why—

EDWARD: What's the security?

MR. VOYSEY: *(Putting his coping stone on the argument.)* My financial ability.

EDWARD: *(Really not knowing whether to laugh or cry.)* Why, one'd think you were satisfied with this state of things.

MR. VOYSEY: Edward, you really are most unsympathetic and unreasonable. I give all I have to the firm's work: my brain…my energies…my whole life. I can't turn my abilities into hard cash at par…I wish I could. Do you suppose if I could establish every one of these people with a separate and consistent bank balance tomorrow…I shouldn't do it?

EDWARD: *(Thankfully able to meet anger with anger.)* Do you mean to tell me that you couldn't somehow have put things right by now?

MR. VOYSEY: How?

EDWARD: If thirty years of this sort of thing hasn't brought you hopelessly to grief...there must have been opportunities.

MR. VOYSEY: Must there! Well, I hope that when I'm under ground, you may find them.

EDWARD: I?

MR. VOYSEY: Put everything right with a stroke of your pen, if it's so easy!

EDWARD: I!

MR. VOYSEY: You're my partner and my son; you inherit the business.

EDWARD: (Realizing at last that he has been led to the edge of this abyss.) Oh no, Father.

MR. VOYSEY: Why else have I had to tell you all this?

EDWARD: (Very simply.) Father, I can't. I can't possibly. I don't think you've any right to ask me.

MR. VOYSEY: Why not, pray?

EDWARD: It's perpetuating the dishonesty.

MR. VOYSEY: (Hardens at the unpleasant word.) You don't believe that I've told you the truth.

EDWARD: I want to believe it.

MR. VOYSEY: It's no proof...my earning these twenty or thirty people their rightful incomes for the last—how many years?

EDWARD: Whether what you've done has been wrong or right I can't meddle in it.

MR. VOYSEY: (For the moment MR. VOYSEY looks a little dangerous.) Very well. Forget all I've said. Go back to your room. Get back to your drudgery. My life's work—ruined! What does that matter?

EDWARD: Whatever did you expect of me?

MR. VOYSEY: (Making a feint at his papers.) Oh, nothing. (Then he slams them down with great effect.) Here's a great edifice built up by years of labour and devotion and self-sacrifice...A great arch you may call it...a bridge to carry our firm to safety with honour.

(This variation of Disraeli passes unnoticed.)

MR. VOYSEY: My work! And it still lacks the keystone. Perhaps I am to die with my work incomplete. Then is there nothing that a son might do? Do you think I shouldn't be proud of you, Edward...that I shouldn't bless you from—wherever I may be, when you completed my life's work...with perhaps just one kindly thought of your father?

EDWARD: (In spite of this oratory, the situation is gradually impressing him.) What will happen if I resign?

MR. VOYSEY: I'll protect you from the law as best I can.

EDWARD: I wasn't thinking of myself, sir.

MR. VOYSEY: (With great nonchalance.) Well, I shan't mind the exposure. It won't make me blush in my coffin...And you're not so quixotic, I hope, as to be thinking of the feelings of your brothers and sisters. Considering how simple it would have been for me to have gone to my grave and let you discover the whole thing afterwards. The fact that I didn't, that I have taken thought for the future of all of you, might perhaps have convinced you that I...! But there...consult your own safety.

EDWARD: (Has begun to pace the room; indecision growing upon him.) A queer thing to have to make up one's mind about.

MR. VOYSEY: (*Watching him closely and modulating his voice.*) My dear boy…I understand the shock this disclosure must be.

EDWARD: Yes, I came this morning thinking that next week would see us in the dock together.

MR. VOYSEY: And I suppose if I'd broken down and begged your pardon for my folly, you'd have done anything for me, gone to prison smiling, eh?

EDWARD: I suppose so.

MR. VOYSEY: Yes, it's easy enough to forgive. I'm sorry I can't go in sackcloth and ashes to oblige you. (*Now he begins to rally his son; easy in his strength.*) My dear Edward, you've lived a quiet humdrum life up to now, with your poetry and your sociology and your agnosticism and your ethics of this and your ethics of that…and you've never before been brought face to face with any really vital question. Now don't make a fool of yourself just through inexperience. I'm not angry at what you've said to me. I'm quite willing to forget it. And it's for your own sake and not for mine, Edward, that I do beg you to—to—to be a man and take a practical commonsense view of the position you find yourself in. It's not a pleasant position, I know, but it's unavoidable.

EDWARD: You should have told me before you took me into partnership.

MR. VOYSEY: (*Oddly enough, it is this last flicker of rebellion which breaks down MR. VOYSEY's caution. Now he lets fly with a vengeance.*) Should I be telling you at all if I could help it? Don't I know you're about as fit for the job as a babe unborn? Haven't I been worrying over that for these last three years? But I'm in a corner…and am I to see my firm come to smash simply because of your scruples?

If you're a son of mine you'll do as I tell you. Hadn't I the same choice to make? D'you suppose I didn't have scruples? If you run away from this, Edward, you're a coward. My father was a coward and he suffered for it to the end of his days. I was sick-nurse to him here more than partner. Good Lord!…of course it's pleasant and comfortable to keep within the law…then the law will look after you. Otherwise you have to look pretty sharp after yourself. You have to cultivate your own sense of right and wrong; deal your own justice. But that makes a bigger man of you, let me tell you. How easily…how easily could I have walked out of my father's office and left him to his fate! But I didn't. I thought it my better duty to stay and…yes, I say it with all reverence…to take up my cross. Well, I've carried that cross pretty successfully. And what's more, it's made a happy man of me. A better, stronger man. (*He changes his tone.*) I don't want what I've been saying to influence you, Edward. You are a free agent…and you must decide upon your own course of action. Now don't let's discuss the matter anymore for the moment.

EDWARD: (*Looks at his father with clear eyes.*) Don't forget to put these papers away.

(*He restores them to their bundles and hands them back. MR. VOYSEY takes them and his meaning in silence.*)

MR. VOYSEY: Are you coming down to Chislehurst soon? We've got Booth for two or three days and possibly his wife.

EDWARD: How is Emily?

MR. VOYSEY: Emily's not at all well. And Hugh and Beatrice and Alice Maitland.

EDWARD: I think I can't face them all just at present.

MR. VOYSEY: Nonsense.

EDWARD: (*A little wave of emotion going through him.*) I feel as if this thing were written on my face. How I shall get through business I don't know!

MR. VOYSEY: You're weaker than I thought, Edward.

EDWARD: (*A little ironically.*) A disappointment to you, Father?

MR. VOYSEY: No, no.

EDWARD: You should have brought one of the others into the firm... Trenchard or Booth.

MR. VOYSEY: (*Hardening.*) Trenchard! (*He dismisses that.*) Good Lord, you're a better man than Booth. Edward, you mustn't imagine that the whole world is standing on its head merely because you've had an unpleasant piece of news. Come down to Chislehurst tonight... well, say tomorrow night. It'll be good for you... stop your brooding. That's your worst vice, Edward. You'll find the household as if nothing had happened. Then you'll remember that nothing really has happened. And presently you'll come to see that nothing need happen, if you keep your head. I remember times, when things have seemed at their worst, what a relief it's been to me... my romp with you all in the nursery just before your bedtime. (*In full glow of fine feeling.*) And, my dear boy, if I knew that you were going to inform the next client you met of what I've just told you...

EDWARD: (*With a shudder.*) Father!

MR. VOYSEY: ...And that I should find myself in prison tomorrow, I wouldn't wish a single thing I've ever done undone. I have never willfully harmed man or woman. My life's been a happy one. Your dear mother has been spared to me. And

you're most of you good children, and a credit to what I've done for you.

EDWARD: (*The deadly humour of this too much for him.*) Father!

MR. VOYSEY: Run along now, run along. I must finish my letters and get into the City.

(*He might be scolding a schoolboy for some trifling fault. EDWARD turns to have a look at the keen, unembarrassed face. MR. VOYSEY smiles at him and proceeds to select from the bowl a rose for his buttonhole.*)

EDWARD: I'll think it over, sir.

MR. VOYSEY: Of course you will! And, Edward, don't brood.

(*So EDWARD leaves him; and having fixed the rose to his satisfaction he rings his table telephone and calls through to the listening clerk.*)

MR. VOYSEY: Send Atkinson to me, please. (*Then he gets up, keys in hand, to lock away Mrs. Murberry's and the Hatherley Trust papers.*)

ACT TWO

The Voysey dining room at Chislehurst, when children and grandchildren are visiting, is dining table and very little else. And at the moment in the evening when five or six men are sprawling back in their chairs, and the air is clouded with smoke, it is a very typical specimen of the middle-class English domestic temple. It has the usual red-papered walls, the usual varnished woodwork which is known as grained oak; there is the usual hot, mahogany furniture; and, commanding point of the whole room, there is the usual black marble sarcophagus of a fireplace. Above this hangs one of the two or three oil paintings, which are all that break the red pattern of the walls, the portrait, painted in 1880, of an undistinguished-looking gentleman aged sixty; he is shown sitting in a more graceful attitude than it could ever have been comfortable for him to assume. MR. VOYSEY's father it is, and the brass plate at the bottom of the frame tells us that the portrait was a presentation one. On the mantelpiece stands, of course, a clock; at either end a china vase filled with paper spills. And in front of the fire—since that is the post of vantage—stands at this moment MAJOR BOOTH VOYSEY. He is the second son, of the age that it is necessary for a Major to be, and of the appearance of many ordinary Majors in ordinary regiments. He went into the Army because he thought it would come up to a schoolboy's idea of it; and, being there, he does his little all to keep it to this. He stands astride, hands in pockets, coattails through his arms, half-smoked cigar in mouth, moustache bristling. On the side of him sits at the table an old gentleman, MR. GEORGE BOOTH, a friend of long standing and the Major's godfather. MR. GEORGE BOOTH is as gay an old gentleman as can be found in Chislehurst. An only son, his father left him at the age of twenty-five a fortune of a hundred thousand pounds. At the same time he had the good sense to dispose of his father's business, into which he had been most unwillingly introduced five years earlier, for a like sum before he was able to depreciate its value. It was MR. VOYSEY's invaluable assistance in this transaction which first bound the two together in great friendship. Since that time MR. BOOTH has been bent on nothing but enjoying himself. He has even remained a bachelor with that object. Money has given him all he wants, therefore he loves and reverences money; while his imagination may be estimated by the fact that he has now reached the age of sixty-five, still possessing more of it than he knows what to do with. At the head of the table, meditatively cracking walnuts, sits MR. VOYSEY. He has his back to the conservatory door. The MAJOR's voice is like the sound of a cannon through the tobacco smoke.

MAJOR VOYSEY: Of course…I am hot and strong for conscription…

MR. GEORGE BOOTH: My dear boy…the country won't hear of it.

MAJOR VOYSEY: I beg your pardon. If we…the Army…say to the country…upon our honour, conscription is necessary for your safety…what answer has the country? What? *(Pauses defiantly.)* There you are! None.

MR. GEORGE BOOTH: Do you imagine that because one doesn't argue with you, one has nothing to say? You ask the country.

MAJOR VOYSEY: Perhaps I will. Perhaps I'll chuck the Army and stand for Parliament. *(Then falling into the singsong of a favourite phrase.)* And I'm not a conceited man…but I believe that if I speak out on a subject I understand, and only upon that subject, the House will listen.

MR. GEORGE BOOTH: If you think the gentlemen of England will allow themselves to be herded into the army with a lot of low fellers and made to carry guns…

MAJOR VOYSEY: Just one moment. Have you thought of the physical improvement conscription would bring to the country's manhood? What England wants is chest. *(He generously inflates his own.)* Chest and discipline. Never mind how it's obtained.

MR. VOYSEY: *(With the crack of a nut.)* Your godson talks a good deal, don't he? You know, when our Major gets into a club, he gets on a committee…gets on any committee to enquire into anything…and then goes on at 'em just like this. Don't you, Booth?

MAJOR VOYSEY: *(Knuckles under easily enough to his father's sarcasm.)* Well, sir, people tell me I'm a useful man on committees.

MR VOYSEY: I don't doubt it…your voice must drown out all discussion.

MAJOR VOYSEY: You can't say I don't listen to you, sir.

MR. VOYSEY: I don't…and I'm not blaming you. But I must say I often think what a devil of a time the family will have with you when I'm gone. Fortunately for your poor mother, she's deaf.

MAJOR VOYSEY: Wouldn't you wish me, sir, as eldest son…Trenchard not counting…

MR. VOYSEY: *(With the crack of a nut.)* Trenchard not counting. By all means, bully them. Never mind whether you're right or wrong…bully them. I don't manage things that way myself, but I think it's your best chance.

MAJOR VOYSEY: *(With some discomfort.)* Ha! If I were a conceited man, sir, I could trust you to take it out of me.

MR. VOYSEY: *(As he taps MR. BOOTH with the nutcrackers.)* Help yourself, George, and drink to your godson's health. Long may he keep his chest notes! Never heard him on parade, have you?

(ETHEL appears in the open door. MR. BOOTH and the MAJOR rise from their chairs.)

ETHEL: Have you noticed how military men must display themselves. You're such a splendid fire screen, Booth.

MAJOR VOYSEY: *(Cheered to find an opponent he can tackle.)* If you want a bit of fire, say so, little sister. Because we mean to allow you to be married, you think you can be impertinent. Out!

(ETHEL exits the room.)

MR. VOYSEY: Has the Vicar left us any port?

MR. GEORGE BOOTH: The dregs.

MR. VOYSEY: By the way…you were with him at Lady Mary's yesterday? Is she giving us anything toward the new chapel window?

MR. GEORGE BOOTH: Because your son designed it: Five pounds.

MR. VOYSEY: Then how will the debt stand?

MR. GEORGE BOOTH: One hundred thirty-two pounds.

MR. VOYSEY: It's been a long time clearing it off.

MR. GEORGE BOOTH: And, now that the window is up and people can see it, they don't seem so ready to contribute as they were.

MAJOR VOYSEY: We must mention that to Hugh!

MR. GEORGE BOOTH: Not that Hugh's work is unadmired. I've heard it praised by supposedly competent judges. But it might have been wiser to have delayed the unveiling till after the money was raised.

MR. VOYSEY: Never deliver goods to a church on credit.

MAJOR VOYSEY: Well, I don't pretend to criticise art. But I think the window'd be prettier if it wasn't so broken up into bits.

(EDWARD enters the room.)

MR. VOYSEY: As it was my wish that my son should do the design, I suppose I shall have to send a cheque.

MAJOR VOYSEY: Anonymously, of course.

MR. VOYSEY: George, will you cover half of it?

MR. GEORGE BOOTH: Damned if I will! Remember that meeting of the parents and friends to decide upon the position of the names of the poor dead fellows and the regiments and coats of arms and so on…when Hugh said how violently he disapproved of the war and made all those remarks about landlords and Bibles, and threatened to put in the window a figure of Britannia blushing for shame or something…

MAJOR VOYSEY: I'm beginning to fear that may have created a bad impression.

MR. GEORGE BOOTH: These young men are so ready with their disapproval. When I was young people weren't always questioning this and questioning that.

MAJOR VOYSEY: Lack of discipline.

MR. GEORGE BOOTH: The way a man now even stops to think what he's eating and drinking.

MAJOR VOYSEY: I try to keep myself free of the disturbing influence of modern thought.

MR. GEORGE BOOTH: Edward's worse even than Hugh is.

EDWARD: What have I done?

MR. GEORGE BOOTH: Well, aren't you another of those young men who go about making difficulties?

EDWARD: What sort?

MR. GEORGE BOOTH: *(Triumphantly.)* Just so…I never can make out. I look back over a fairly long life and…perhaps I should say by Heaven's help…I find nothing that I can honestly reproach myself with. And yet I don't think I ever took more than five minutes to come to a decision upon any important point. I'm not speaking of private life. That is, I think, one's own affair…I should allow no one to pry into that. But as to worldly things…well, I have come into several sums of money and my capital is still intact…ask your father.

(MR. VOYSEY nods gravely.)

MR. GEORGE BOOTH: I've never robbed any man. I've never lied over anything that mattered. As a citizen I pay my taxes without grumbling very much. Yes, and I consider that any man who takes the trouble can live the life of a gentleman.

MAJOR VOYSEY: *(Not to be outdone by this show of virtue.)* Well, I'm not a conceited man, but—

(ETHEL reenters.)

ETHEL: Are you sure of that, Booth?

(MR. BOOTH and the MAJOR rise, but before the MAJOR can send ETHEL from the room again, EDWARD reaches for her hand.)

MAJOR VOYSEY: Shut up. I was going to say when my young cub of a bride-to-be sister interrupted me, that Training, for which we all have to be thankful to you, sir, has much to do with it. *(Suddenly pulls his trousers against his legs.)* I say, I'm scorching. Want one of those new cigars, Mr. Booth?

MR. GEORGE BOOTH: No, thank you.

MAJOR VOYSEY: I do. *(He glances round.)*

(ETHEL sees a box on the table and reaches it.)

MR. GEORGE BOOTH: I must be taking my departure.

MR. VOYSEY: Already!

MAJOR VOYSEY: *(Frowning upon the cigar box.)* No, not those. Where are the

Ramon Allones. What on earth has Honor done with them?

MR. VOYSEY: Spare time for a chat with my wife before you go. She's talking with the Vicar about a children's tea-fight.

MR. GEORGE BOOTH: Certainly I will.

MAJOR VOYSEY: *(Scowling helplessly around.)* My goodness!…one can never find anything in this house.

(MR. GEORGE BOOTH is sliding through the half-opened door.)

MR. VOYSEY: I say! It's cold again to-night! Ass of an architect who built this place…such a draught!

(ALICE enters.)

ETHEL: I think we've stayed in here quite long enough.

MR. VOYSEY: That's to say, Ethel thinks her Denis has been kept out of her pocket too long.

ETHEL: Ethel wants billiards, not proper billiards, snooker, or something…Oh Papa, what a dessert you've eaten. Greedy pig!

ALICE: Crack me a filbert, please, Edward…I had none.

EDWARD: *(Jumping up, rather formally well-mannered.)* I beg your pardon, Alice. Won't you sit down?

ALICE: No.

(MR. VOYSEY takes ETHEL on his knee.)

MR. VOYSEY: Come here, puss. Have you made up your mind yet what you want for a wedding present?

ETHEL: *(Rectifying a stray hair on his forehead.)* After mature consideration, I decide on a cheque.

MR. VOYSEY: Do you!

ETHEL: Yes. I think that a cheque will give most scope to your generosity. If you desire to add any trimmings in the shape of a piano or a Turkish carpet you may…and Denis and I will be grateful. But I think I'd let yourself go over a cheque.

MR. VOYSEY: You're a minx.

ETHEL: What's the use of having money if you don't spend it on me?

MAJOR VOYSEY: *(Giving up the cigar search.)* Here, who's going to play?

MR. VOYSEY: Well, if my wrist will hold out…

MAJOR VOYSEY: *(Strides from the room, his voice echoing through the hall.)* Honor, where are those Ramon Allones?

ALICE: *(Calling after.)* She's in the drawing room with Auntie and the Vicar.

MR. VOYSEY: Now I suggest you go find Denis and take off the billiard table cover. You'll find folding it up a very excellent amusement. *(He illustrates his meaning with his table napkin and by putting together the tips of his forefingers, roguishly.)*

ETHEL: I am not going to blush. I do kiss Denis…occasionally…when he asks me. And if you think we're ashamed of being in love, we're not, we're very proud of it. *(Goes to the door and calls.)* Denis, my dear, come along solemnly and show them how much you love me. And if you flinch I'll never forgive you.

OFFSTAGE VOICE: *(Calls back.)* Ethel, I can't after dinner.

ETHEL: Denis! *(She goes off.)*

MR. VOYSEY: Women play that game better than men.

(The MAJOR comes stalking back followed in a flurry by his elder sister, HONOR.)

MAJOR VOYSEY: Honor, they are not in the dining room.

HONOR: But they must be!—Where else can they be? (She has the habit of accentuating one word in each sentence and often the wrong one.)

MAJOR VOYSEY: That's what you ought to know.

MR. VOYSEY: (As he moves toward the door.) Well, will you have a game?

MAJOR VOYSEY: I'll play you fifty up.

HONOR: Here you are, Booth.

(She triumphantly discovers the discarded box, at which the MAJOR becomes pathetic with indignation.)

MAJOR VOYSEY: Oh, Honor, don't be such a fool. I want the Ramon Allones.

HONOR: I don't know the difference.

MAJOR VOYSEY: No, you don't but you might learn.

MR. VOYSEY: (In a voice like the crack of a very fine whip.) Booth!

MAJOR VOYSEY: (Subduedly.) What is it, sir?

MR. VOYSEY: Look for your cigars yourself. Honor, go back to your reading or your sewing or whatever you were fiddling at, and fiddle in peace.

(VOYSEY departs, leaving the room rather hushed. Then ALICE insinuates a remark very softly.)

ALICE: Have you looked in the library?

MAJOR VOYSEY: (Relapsing to an injured manner.) Where's my wife?

HONOR: Emily's lying down upstairs.

MAJOR VOYSEY: Honor. Why don't you stop looking for those cigars?

HONOR: If you don't mind I want my reading glasses while I am here.

MAJOR VOYSEY: I daresay they're in the library. What a house! (He departs.)

HONOR: Booth is so trying.

ALICE: Honor, why do you put up with it?

HONOR: Someone has to.

ALICE: (Discreetly nibbling a nut, which EDWARD has cracked for her.) I'm afraid I think Master Major Booth ought to have been taken in hand early…with a cane.

HONOR: (As she vaguely burrows into corners.) Papa did. But it never did any good. He's been booming at us ever since he was a baby. Now he's flustered me so I simply can't remember where they are.

ALICE: The Pettifers desired to be remembered to you, Edward.

HONOR: (But she goes on looking.) I sometimes think, Alice, that we're a very difficult family…except perhaps Edward.

EDWARD: Why except me?

HONOR: And you were always difficult…to yourself. (Then she starts to go, threading her way through the disarranged chairs.) The Vicar will shout so at Mother, and she hates people to think she's so very deaf…I thought Mary Pettifer looking old. (She talks herself out of the room.)

ALICE: (After her.) She's getting old. I was glad not to spend August abroad for once. We drove into Cheltenham to a dance. I golfed a lot.

EDWARD: How long were you with them?

ALICE: A fortnight. It doesn't seem three months since I was here.

EDWARD: I'm down so very little.

ALICE: I'm here a disgraceful deal.

EDWARD: You know they're always pleased.

ALICE: Well, being a homeless person! But what a cartload to descend…yesterday and today. The Major and Emily…Emily's not at all well. Hugh and Mrs. Hugh. And me. Are you staying?

EDWARD: No. I must get a word with my father.

ALICE: Edward…you look more like half-baked pie crust than usual.

EDWARD: *(A little enviously.)* You're very well.

ALICE: I'm always well and nearly always happy.

(MAJOR BOOTH returns. He has the right sort of cigar in his mouth and is considerably mollified.)

ALICE: You found them?

MAJOR VOYSEY: Of course they were there. Thank you very much, Alice. Now I want a knife.

ALICE: I must get you a cigar cutter for Christmas, Booth.

MAJOR VOYSEY: Beastly things, I hate 'em. *(He eyes the dessert disparagingly.)* Nothing but silver ones.

(EDWARD hands him a carefully opened pocketknife.)

MAJOR VOYSEY: Thank you, Edward. And I must take one of the candles. Something's gone wrong with the library ventilator and you never can see a thing in that room.

ALICE: Is Mrs. Hugh there?

MAJOR VOYSEY: Writing letters. Things are neglected, Edward, unless one is constantly on the lookout. The Pater only cares for his garden. I must speak seriously to Honor. *(He has returned the knife, still open, and having now lit his cigar at the candle he carries this off.)*

EDWARD: *(Giving her a nut, about the fifteenth.)* Here. 'Scuse fingers.

ALICE: Thank you. *(Looking at him, with her head on one side and her face more humorous than ever.)* Edward, why have you given up proposing to me?

EDWARD: *(He starts, flushes; then won't be outdone in humour.)* One can't go on proposing forever.

ALICE: Have you seen anyone you like better?

EDWARD: No.

ALICE: Well…I miss it.

EDWARD: What satisfaction did you find in refusing me?

ALICE: *(As she weighs the matter.)* I find satisfaction in feeling that I'm wanted.

EDWARD: Without any intention of giving…of throwing yourself away.

ALICE: *(Teasing his sudden earnestness.)* Ah, now we come from mere vanity to serious questions.

EDWARD: Mine was a very serious question.

ALICE: But, Edward, all questions are serious to you. I call you a perfect little pocket guide to life…all questions answered; what to eat, drink, and avoid, what to believe and what to say.

EDWARD: One must lay down principles.

ALICE: I prefer my plan. I always do what I know I want to do. Crack me another nut.

EDWARD: Haven't you had enough?

ALICE: I *know* I want one more.

(*He cracks another with a sigh which sounds ridiculous in that connection.*)

ALICE: I know it just as I knew I didn't want to marry you. Each time.

EDWARD: Oh, you hadn't made a rule of saying no?

ALICE: On principle? No I always gave you a fair chance. I'll give you one now if you like. Courage, I might say yes…all in a flash.

EDWARD: I think we won't run the risk.

ALICE: Edward! There's nothing wrong, is there?

EDWARD: Nothing at all.

(*They are interrupted by the sudden appearance of MRS. HUGH VOYSEY, a brisk, bright little woman, in an evening gown which she has bullied a cheap dressmaker into making look exceedingly smart. BEATRICE is hard as nails and clever as paint. But if she keeps her feelings buried pretty deep it is because they are precious to her; and if she is impatient with fools it is because her own brains have had to win her everything in the world, so perhaps she does overvalue them a little. She speaks always with great decision and little effort.*)

BEATRICE: I believe I could write business letters upon an island in the middle of Fleet Street. But while Booth is poking at a ventilator with a billiard cue…no, I can't.

(*She goes to the fireplace, waving her half-finished letter. MAJOR VOYSEY appears at the door, billiard cue in hand, and says solemnly…*)

MAJOR VOYSEY: Edward, I wish you'd come and have a look at this ventilator, like a good fellow.

(*Then he turns and goes again, obviously with the weight of an important matter on his shoulders. With the ghost of a smile EDWARD gets up and follows him.*)

ALICE: If I belonged to this family I should hate Booth. (*With which comment she joins BEATRICE at the fireplace.*)

BEATRICE: A good day's shopping?

ALICE: The baby bride and I bought clothes all the morning. Then we had lunch with Denis and bought furniture.

BEATRICE: Nice furniture?

ALICE: Very good and very new. They neither of them know what they want. (*Then suddenly throwing up her chin and exclaiming.*) Beatrice…when it's a question of money I can understand it…but if a woman can provide for herself or is independent why get married? Of course with Ethel and Denis it's different. They've both been caught young. They're two little birds building their nest and it's all ideal. They'll soon forget they've ever been apart.

(*Now HONOR flutters into the room, patient but wild-eyed.*)

HONOR: Mother wants last week's *Notes and Queries*. Have you seen it?

BEATRICE: (*Exasperated at the interruption.*) No.

HONOR: It ought not to be here. (*So she proceeds to look for it.*) She's having a long argument with the Vicar over Oliver Cromwell's relations.

ALICE: I thought Auntie didn't approve of Oliver Cromwell.

HONOR: She doesn't and she's trying to prove that he was a brewer or something. I suppose someone has taken it away. (*So she gives up the search and flutters out again.*)

ALICE: This is a most unrestful house.

BEATRICE: I once thought of putting the Voyseys into a book of mine. Then I concluded they'd be as dull there as they are anywhere else.

ALICE: They're not duller than most people.

BEATRICE: But how very dull that is!

ALICE: They're a little noisier and perhaps not quite so well-mannered. But I love them.

BEATRICE: I don't. I should have thought love was just what they couldn't inspire.

ALICE: Your husband excepted I suppose.

BEATRICE: Hugh has most of their bad points. But then I don't love Hugh.

ALICE: *(Her eyebrows up, though she smiles.)* Beatrice, you shouldn't say so.

BEATRICE: Sounds affected, doesn't it?

ALICE: *(Her face growing a little thoughtful.)* Beatrice…weren't you in love with Hugh when you married him?

BEATRICE: I married him for his money.

ALICE: He hadn't much.

BEATRICE: I had none…and I wanted to write books. Yes, I loved him.

ALICE: And you thought you'd be happy?

BEATRICE: *(Considering carefully.)* No, I didn't. I hoped he'd be happy. My dear Alice, how are you to comprehend this? You've nine hundred pounds a year.

ALICE: What has that to do with it?

BEATRICE: *(Putting her case very precisely.)* Fine feelings, my dear, are as much a luxury as clean gloves. For ten years I had to earn my own living; consequently there isn't one thing in my life that I have ever done quite genuinely for its own sake…but always with an eye towards bread-and-butter…pandering to the people who were to give me that. I warned Hugh…he took the risk.

ALICE: What risk?

BEATRICE: That one day I'd be able get on better without him.

ALICE: And Hugh?

BEATRICE: My dear Alice, it's degrading to let one's happiness depend upon someone else.

(The conservatory door opens and through it come MR. VOYSEY and MR. GEORGE BOOTH in the midst of a discussion.)

MR. VOYSEY: My dear man, stick to the shares and risk it.

MR. GEORGE BOOTH: No, of course if you seriously advise me.

MR. VOYSEY: I never advise greedy children; I let 'em overeat 'emselves and take the consequences.

ALICE: *(Shaking a finger.)* Uncle Trench, you've been in the garden without a hat after playing billiards in that hot room.

MR. VOYSEY: We had to give up…my wrist was bad. They've started pool.

BEATRICE: Is Booth going to play?

MR. VOYSEY: We left him instructing Ethel how to hold a cue.

BEATRICE: Ah! I can finish my letter.

(Off she goes. ALICE is idly following with a little journal her hand has fallen on behind the clock.)

MR. VOYSEY: Don't run away, my dear.

ALICE: I'm taking this to Auntie…*Notes and Queries*, she wants it.

MR. VOYSEY: This room's cold. Why don't they keep the fire up? (*He proceeds to put coals on it.*)

MR. GEORGE BOOTH: You were too hot in the billiard room. You know, Voysey…about those Alguazils?

MR. VOYSEY: (*Through the rattling of the coals.*) What?

MR. GEORGE BOOTH: (*Trying to pierce the din.*) Those Alguazils.

MR. VOYSEY: (*With surprising inconsequence, points a finger at the silk handkerchief across MR. BOOTH's shirt front.*) What have you got your handkerchief there for?

MR. GEORGE BOOTH: Measure of precau— (*At that moment he sneezes.*) Damn it…if you've given me a chill dragging me through your infernal garden.

MR. VOYSEY: (*Slapping him on the back.*) You're an old crock.

MR. GEORGE BOOTH: Well, I'll be glad of this winter in Egypt. (*He returns to his subject.*) And if you think seriously that I ought to sell out of the Alguazils before I go…? Well, I'll give you power of attorney or whatever it is, and you can sell out if things look bad.

(*At this moment HONOR comes in, looking disconsolately at the table. Like an expert fisherman VOYSEY lets loose the thread of the conversation.*)

MR. VOYSEY: Do you want to clear, Honor? Leave that for the servants.

HONOR: It doesn't matter, Papa.

MR. VOYSEY: All right, Honor. Go on…go on.

(*So HONOR starts to clear the table, which fidgets poor MR. BOOTH considerably. He sits shrivelled up in the armchair by the fire; and now MR. VOYSEY attends to him.*)

MR. VOYSEY: What d'you want with high interest at all…you never spend half your income?

MR. GEORGE BOOTH: I like to feel that my money's doing useful things, and forty-two percent is pleasing.

MR. VOYSEY: You're an old gambler.

MR. GEORGE BOOTH: (*Propitiatingly.*) Ah, but then I've you to advise me. I always do what you tell me in the end…you can't deny that.

MR. VOYSEY: The man who don't know must trust in the man who do.

MR. GEORGE BOOTH: (*Modestly insisting.*) There's nine thousand in Alguazils. What else could we put it into?

MR. VOYSEY: I can get you something at four and a half.

MR. GEORGE BOOTH: Oh, Lord… that's nothing!

MR. VOYSEY: (*With a sudden serious friendliness.*) I wish, my dear George, you'd mind your own accounts a bit better. You know—what with one thing and the other—I've got control of practically all you have in the world. I might be playing Old Harry with it for all you know.

MR. GEORGE BOOTH: My dear feller…If I'm satisfied, well then…! But, my friend, what'll happen to your firm when you depart this life!…not before my time, I hope.

MR. VOYSEY: (*With a little frown.*) What d'ye mean?

MR. GEORGE BOOTH: Edward's no use.

MR. VOYSEY: I beg your pardon…very sound in business.

MR. GEORGE BOOTH: Maybe…but I tell you he's no use. Men have confidence in a personality, not in principles.

MR. VOYSEY: I fear you dislike Edward.

MR. GEORGE BOOTH: (With pleasant frankness.) Yes, I do.

MR. VOYSEY: That's a pity. That's a great pity.

MR. GEORGE BOOTH: (With a flattering smile.) He's not his father and never will be. What's the time?

MR. VOYSEY: Twenty to ten.

MR. GEORGE BOOTH: I must be trotting.

(As he goes to the door he meets EDWARD, who comes in apparently looking for his father; at any rate he catches his eye immediately, while MR. BOOTH obliviously continues.)

MR. GEORGE BOOTH: And I've not said a word to Mrs. Voysey. Stroll home with me?

MR. VOYSEY: I can't.

MR. GEORGE BOOTH: (Mildly surprised at the short reply.) Well, good night. Good night, Edward. (He trots away.)

MR. VOYSEY: Leave the table, Honor.

HONOR: But, Papa…

MR. VOYSEY: You can come back in ten minutes.

(HONOR departs and the door is closed. Alone with his son MR. VOYSEY does not move. His face grows a little keener, that's all.)

MR. VOYSEY: Well, Edward?

(EDWARD starts to move restlessly about, like a cowed animal in a cage; silently for a moment or two. Then when he speaks his voice is toneless, and he does not look at his father.)

EDWARD: Would you mind, sir, dropping with me for the future all these protestations about putting the firm's affairs straight…about all your anxieties and sacrifices. I see now, of course…a cleverer man than I could have seen it yesterday…that for some time, ever since, I suppose, you recovered from the first shock and got used to the double dealing, this hasn't been your object at all. You've used your clients' capital to produce your own income…to bring us up and endow us with. Booth's ten-thousand-pound legacy; what you're giving Ethel on her marriage…! It's odd it never struck me yesterday that my own pocket money as a boy must have been drawn from some client's account. I suppose about half the sum you've spent on us first and last would have put things right?

MR. VOYSEY: No, it would not.

EDWARD: (Appealing for the truth.) Oh…at some time or other!

MR. VOYSEY: Well, if there have been good times there have been bad. At present the three hundred a year I'm to allow your sister is going to be rather a pull.

EDWARD: Three hundred a year…and no attempt to put a single account straight. Since it isn't lunacy, sir, I can only conclude that you enjoy being in this position.

MR. VOYSEY: Three trusts…two of them big ones…have been wound up within this last year and the accounts have been above suspicion. What's the object of this rodomontade, Edward?

EDWARD: If I'm to remain in the firm it had better be with a very clear understanding of things as they are.

MR. VOYSEY: (Firmly, not too anxiously.) Then you do remain?

EDWARD: (In a very low voice.) I must remain.

MR. VOYSEY: *(Quite gravely.)* That's wise of you…I'm very glad.

EDWARD: But I make one condition. And I want some information.

MR. VOYSEY: Well?

EDWARD: Of course no one has ever discovered…and no one suspects this state of things?

MR. VOYSEY: Peacey knows.

EDWARD: Peacey!

MR. VOYSEY: His father found out.

EDWARD: Oh. Does he draw hush money?

MR. VOYSEY: *(Curling a little at the word.)* It is my custom to make him a little present every Christmas. *(He becomes benevolent.)* I don't grudge the money…Peacey's a devoted fellow.

EDWARD: Yes, it's a heavily taxed industry. *(With entire comprehension.)* The condition I wish to make is a very simple one. That we should really try…as unobtrusively as you like and put things straight.

MR. VOYSEY: *(With a little polite shrug.)* I've no doubt you'll prove an abler man of business than I.

EDWARD: We can begin by halving the salary I draw from the firm.

MR. VOYSEY: I see.

EDWARD: And it seems to me that you can't give Ethel this five-thousand-pounds dowry.

MR. VOYSEY: *(Shortly, with one of the quick twists of his eye.)* I have given my word to Denis.

EDWARD: Because the money isn't yours to give.

MR. VOYSEY: *(In an indignant crescendo.)* I should not dream of depriving Ethel of what, as my daughter, she has every right to expect. I am surprised at your suggesting such a thing.

EDWARD: *(Pale and firm.)* I am set on this, Father.

MR. VOYSEY: Don't be such a fool, Edward. What would it look like…suddenly refusing without rhyme or reason? What would old Tregoning think?

EDWARD: Oh, can't you see it's my duty to prevent this?

MR. VOYSEY: You can prevent it by telling the nearest policeman. It is my duty to pay no more attention to these scruples of yours than a nurse pays to her child's tantrums. Understand, Edward, I don't want to force you to continue. Come with me gladly, or don't come at all.

EDWARD: *(Dully.)* It is my duty to be of what use I can to you, sir. Father, I want to save you if I can.

(He flashes into this exclamation of almost broken-hearted affection. MR. VOYSEY looks at his son for a moment and his lip quivers. Then he steels himself.)

MR. VOYSEY: Thank you! I have been saving myself quite satisfactorily for the last thirty years, and you must please believe that by this time I know my own business best.

EDWARD: *(Hopelessly.)* Can't we find the money some other way? How do you manage about your own income?

MR. VOYSEY: I have a bank balance and a cheque book, haven't I? I spend what I think well to spend. What's the use of earmarking this or that as my own? You say none of it is my own. I might say it's all my own. I think I've earned it.

EDWARD: *(Anger coming on him.)* That's what I can't forgive. If you'd lived poor...if you'd really done all you could for your clients and not thought of your own wealth...then, even though things were no better than they are now why, somehow I could have been proud of you. But, Father, own the truth, at least...I deserve that much from you. Didn't you simply seize this opportunity as a means to enrich yourself?

MR. VOYSEY: *(With a sledge-hammer irony.)* Certainly. I sat that morning in my father's office, studying the helmet of the policeman in the street below, and thinking what a glorious path I had happened on to wealth and honour and renown. *(Then he begins to bully EDWARD in the kindliest way.)* My dear boy, you haven't begun to grasp the A.B.C. of my position. What has carried me to victory? The confidence of my clients. What has earned me that confidence? A decent life, my integrity, my brains? No, my reputation for wealth...that, and nothing else. Business nowadays is run on the lines of the confidence trick. What makes old George Booth so glad to trust me with every penny he possesses? Not affection...he's never cared for anything in his life but his collection of prints.

EDWARD: *(Stupefied, helpless.)* Is he involved?

MR. VOYSEY: Of course he's involved, and he's always after high interest, too... it's little one makes out of him. But there's a further question here, Edward. Should I have had confidence in myself, if I'd remained a poor man? No, I should not. You must either be the master of money or its servant. And if one is not opulent in one's daily life one loses that wonderful...financier's touch. One must be confident oneself...and I saw from the first that I must at any cost inspire confidence. My whole public and

private life has tended to that. All my surroundings...you and your brothers and sisters that I have brought into, and up, and put out in the world so worthily...you in your turn inspire confidence.

EDWARD: I sat down yesterday to make a list of the people who are good enough to trust their money to us. From George Booth with his enormous wealth growing—at least that's what he thinks—to old Nursie with her savings, which she brought you so proudly to invest. But you've let those be, at least.

MR. VOYSEY: Five hundred pounds. I never troubled to invest it.

EDWARD: But that's damnable.

MR. VOYSEY: Indeed? I give her seventy-five pounds a year for it. Would you like to take charge of that account, Edward? I'll give you five hundred to invest tomorrow.

EDWARD: *(Hopelessly beaten, falls into an almost comic state of despair.)* My dear Father, putting every moral question aside... it's all very well your playing Robin Hood in this magnificent manner; but have you given a moment's thought to the sort of inheritance you'll be leaving me?

MR. VOYSEY: *(Pleased for the first time.)* Ah! that's a question you have every right to ask.

EDWARD: If you died tomorrow could we pay eight shillings in the pound...or seventeen...or five? Do you know?

MR. VOYSEY: And the answer is, that by your help I have every intention, when I die, of leaving you all an inheritance running into six figures. D'you think I've given my life and my talents for a less result than that? I'm fond of you all...and I want you to be proud of me...and I mean that the name of Voysey shall be carried high in the world by my children and grandchildren. Don't you be afraid, Edward. Ah, you lack experience, my boy… you're not full grown yet…your impulses are a bit chaotic. You emotionalise over your work, and you reason about your emotions. You must sort yourself. You must realise that moneymaking is one thing, and religion another, and family life a third…and that if we apply our energies wholeheartedly to each of these in turn, and realise that different laws govern each, that there is a different end to be served, a different ideal to be striven for in each. *(His coherence is saved by the sudden appearance of his wife, who comes round the door smiling benignly. Not in the least put out, in fact a little relieved, he greets her with an affectionate shout, for she is very deaf.)*

MR. VOYSEY: Hullo, Mother!

MRS. VOYSEY: Oh, there you are, Trench. I've been deserted.

MR. VOYSEY: George Booth gone?

MRS. VOYSEY: Are you talking business? Perhaps you don't want me.

MR. VOYSEY: No, no…no business.

MRS. VOYSEY: *(Who has not looked for his answer.)* I suppose the others are in the billiard room.

MR. VOYSEY: *(Vociferously.)* We're not talking business, old lady.

EDWARD: I'll be off, sir.

MR. VOYSEY: *(Genial as usual.)* Why don't you stay? I'll come up with you in the morning.

EDWARD: No, thank you, sir.

MR. VOYSEY: Then I shall be up about noon.

EDWARD: Good night, Mother.

MRS. VOYSEY: *(Places a plump, kindly hand on his arm and looks up affectionately.)* You look tired.

EDWARD: No, I'm not.

MRS. VOYSEY: What did you say?

EDWARD: *(Too weary to repeat himself.)* Nothing, Mother dear.

(He kisses her cheek, while she kisses the air.)

MR. VOYSEY: Good night, my boy.

(Then he goes. MRS. VOYSEY is carrying her Notes and Queries. *This is a dear old lady, looking older too than probably she is. Placid describes her. She has had a life of little joys and cares, has never measured herself against the world, never even questioned the shape and size of the little corner of it in which she lives. She has loved an indulgent husband and borne eight children, six of them surviving, healthy. That is her history.)*

MRS. VOYSEY: George Booth went some time ago. He said he thought you'd taken a chill walking round the garden.

MR. VOYSEY: I'm all right.

MRS. VOYSEY: D'you think you have?

MR. VOYSEY: *(In her ear.)* No.

MRS. VOYSEY: You should be careful, Trench. What did you put on?

MR. VOYSEY: Nothing.

MRS. VOYSEY: How very foolish! Let me feel your hand. You are quite feverish.

MR. VOYSEY: *(Affectionately.)* You're a fuss-box, old lady.

MRS. VOYSEY: *(Coquetting with him.)* Don't be rude, Trench.

(HONOR descends upon them. She is well into that nightly turmoil of putting everything and everybody to rights which always precedes her bedtime. She carries a shawl which she clasps round her mother's shoulders, her mind and gaze already on the next thing to be done.)

HONOR: Mother, you left your shawl in the drawing room.

MR. VOYSEY: Now who's careless!

MRS. VOYSEY: Thank you, Honor. You'd better look after your father; he's been walking round the garden without his cape.

HONOR: Papa.

MR. VOYSEY: Honor, you get that little kettle and boil it, and brew me some whiskey and water. I shall be all right.

HONOR: (Fluttering more than ever.) I'll get it. Where's the whiskey? Here it is! And Hugh coming back at ten o'clock with no dinner. No wonder his work goes wrong. Papa, you do deserve to be ill.

(Clasping the whiskey decanter, she is off again. MRS. VOYSEY sits at the dinner table and adjusts her spectacles. She returns to Notes and Queries, one elbow firmly planted and her plump hand against her plump cheek. This is her favourite attitude; and she is apt, when reading, to soliloquise in her deaf woman's voice. At least, whether she considers it soliloquy or conversation is not easy to discover. MR. VOYSEY stands with his back to the fire, grumbling and pulling faces.)

MRS. VOYSEY: This is a very perplexing correspondence about the Cromwell family. One can't deny the man had good blood in him...his grandfather Sir Henry, his uncle Sir Oliver...

MR. VOYSEY: There's a pain in my back.

MRS. VOYSEY: ...And it's difficult to discover where the taint crept in.

MR. VOYSEY: I believe I strained myself putting in those strawberry plants.

MRS. VOYSEY: Yes, but then how was it he came to disgrace himself so? I believe the family disappeared. Regicide is a root and branch curse. You must read the letter signed C.W.A....it's quite interesting. There's a misprint in mine about the first umbrella-maker...now where was it... (And so the dear lady will ramble on indefinitely.)

ACT THREE

The dining room looks very different in the white light of a July noon. Moreover, on this particular day, it isn't even its normal self. There is a peculiar luncheon spread on the table. The embroidered cloth is placed cornerwise and on it are decanters of port and sherry; sandwiches, biscuits, and an uncut cake; two little piles of plates and one little pile of napkins. There are no table decorations, and indeed the whole room has been made as bare and as tidy as possible. The first to enter are MRS. VOYSEY and MR. BOOTH, she on his arm; and the fact that she is in widow's weeds makes the occasion clear. The little old man leads his old friend very tenderly.

MR. GEORGE BOOTH: Will you come in here?

MRS. VOYSEY: Thank you.

(With great solicitude he puts her in a chair; then takes her hand.)

MR. GEORGE BOOTH: Now I'll intrude no longer.

MRS. VOYSEY: You'll take some lunch?

MR. GEORGE BOOTH: No.

MRS. VOYSEY: Not a glass of wine?

MR. GEORGE BOOTH: If there's anything I can do just send round.

MRS. VOYSEY: Thank you.

(MR. GEORGE BOOTH reaches the door only to be met by the MAJOR and

BEATRICE. He shakes hands with them both.)

MR. GEORGE BOOTH: My dear Beatrice! My dear Booth!

(The MAJOR, though his grief is most sincere, has an irresistible air of being responsible for, and indeed rather proud of, the whole affair.)

MAJOR VOYSEY: I think it all went off as he would have wished.

MR. GEORGE BOOTH: *(Feeling that he is called on for praise.)* Great credit...great credit. It must be particularly hard for you. Another funeral, so soon after your dear wife's.

MAJOR VOYSEY: Poor little Emily.

BEATRICE: Poor Emily.

(MR. GEORGE BOOTH makes another attempt to escape, and is stopped this time by TRENCHARD VOYSEY, to whom he was extending a hand and beginning his formula. But TRENCHARD speaks first.)

TRENCHARD: Have you the right time?

MR. GEORGE BOOTH: *(Taken aback and fumbling for his watch.)* I think so...I make it fourteen minutes to one. *(He seizes the occasion.)* Trenchard, as a very old and dear friend of your father's you won't mind me saying how glad I was that you were present today. Death closes all. Indeed...it must be a great regret to you that you did not see him before...before...

TRENCHARD: *(His cold eye freezing this little gush.)* I don't think he asked for me.

MR. GEORGE BOOTH: *(Stoppered.)* No? No! Well...well...

(At this third attempt to depart he actually collides with someone in the doorway. It is ETHEL, several months pregnant.)

MR. GEORGE BOOTH: My dear Ethel...I won't intrude. *(Determined to escape, he grasps her hand, gasps out his formula, and is off.)*

(TRENCHARD has the cocksure manner of the successful barrister. The self-respect of his appearance is immense, and he cultivates that air of concentration on any trivial matter, or even upon nothing at all, which will someday make him an impressive figure of the Bench; he conscientiously preserves an air of the indifference which he feels. MAJOR VOYSEY stands statuesque at the mantelpiece; while BEATRICE is by MRS. VOYSEY, whose face in its quiet grief is nevertheless a mirror of many happy memories of her husband.)

MAJOR VOYSEY: I wouldn't hang over her, Beatrice.

BEATRICE: No, of course not.

TRENCHARD: I hope your husband is well, Ethel.

ETHEL: Thank you, Trench: I think so. Denis is in America...

BEATRICE: With Hugh.

ETHEL: ...Giving some lectures there.

TRENCHARD: Really! Oh, Booth, did you bring Honor back?

MAJOR VOYSEY: Yes. A glass of wine, Mother?

MRS. VOYSEY: What?

(MAJOR VOYSEY hardly knows how to turn his whisper decorously into enough of a shout for his mother to hear. But he manages it.)

MAJOR VOYSEY: Have a glass of wine?

MRS. VOYSEY: Sherry, please.

(While he pours it out with an air of its being medicine on this occasion and not wine at all, EDWARD comes quickly into the

room, his face very set, his mind obviously on other matters than the funeral. No one speaks to him for the moment and he has time to observe them all.)

MAJOR VOYSEY: Lunch, Beatrice?

BEATRICE: I suppose so, Booth, thank you.

EDWARD: How are you, Ethel?

ETHEL: A little smashed, but no harm done.

(ALICE comes in brisk and businesslike; a little impatient of this universal cloud of mourning.)

ALICE: Edward, Honor has gone to her room; I must take her some food and make her eat it. She's very upset.

EDWARD: Make her drink a glass of wine, and say it is necessary she should come down here. And d'you mind not coming back yourself, Alice?

ALICE: *(Her eyebrows up.)* Certainly, if you wish.

MAJOR VOYSEY: What's this? What's this?

(ALICE gets her glass of wine and goes. The MAJOR is suddenly full of importance.)

MAJOR VOYSEY: What is this, Edward?

EDWARD: I have something to say to you all.

MAJOR VOYSEY: What?

EDWARD: Well, Booth, you'll hear when I say it.

MAJOR VOYSEY: Is it business?...because I think this is scarcely the time for business.

EDWARD: Why?

MAJOR VOYSEY: Do you find it easy to descend from your natural grief to the

consideration of money?...I do not. *(He finds TRENCHARD at his elbow.)* I hope you are getting some lunch, Trenchard.

EDWARD: This is business and rather more than business, Booth. I choose now, because it is something I wish to say to the family, not to write each individually...and it will be difficult to get us all together again.

MAJOR VOYSEY: *(Determined at any rate to give his sanction.)* Well, Trenchard, as Edward is in the position of trustee...executor...I don't know your terms...I suppose...

TRENCHARD: I don't see what your objection is.

MAJOR VOYSEY: *(With some superiority.)* Don't you? I should not call myself a sentimental man, but...

EDWARD: You had better stay, Beatrice; you represent Hugh.

(HONOR has obediently come down from her room. She is pale and thin, shaken with grief and worn out besides; for needless to say the brunt of her father's illness, the brunt of everything, has been on her. Six weeks' nursing, part of it hopeless, will exhaust anyone. Her handkerchief is to her eyes, and every minute or two they flood over with tears. EDWARD goes and affectionately puts his arms round her.)

EDWARD: My dear Honor, I am so sorry to be so...so merciless. There!...there!

(He hands her into the room; then turns and once more surveys the family, who this time mostly return the compliment. Then he says shortly:)

EDWARD: I think you might all sit down.

(And then since the MAJOR happens to be conveniently near...)

EDWARD: Shut the door, Booth.

MAJOR VOYSEY: Shut the door!

(But he does so, with as much dignity as possible. EDWARD goes close to his mother and speaks very distinctly, very kindly.)

EDWARD: Mother, we're all going to have a little necessary talk over matters... now, because it's most convenient. I hope it won't...I hope you won't mind. Will you come to the table?

MRS. VOYSEY: (Looks up as if understanding more than he says.) Edward...

EDWARD: Yes, Mother dear?

MAJOR VOYSEY: (Commandingly.) You'll sit here, Mother, of course.

(He places her in her accustomed chair at the foot of the table. One by one the others sit down, EDWARD apparently last. But then he discovers that ETHEL has lost herself in a corner of the room and is gazing into vacancy.)

EDWARD: (With a touch of kindly exasperation.) Ethel, would you mind attending?

ETHEL: What is it?

EDWARD: There's a chair.

(ETHEL takes it. Then for a moment— while EDWARD is trying to frame in coherent sentences what he must say to them—for a minute there is silence, broken only by HONOR's sniffs, which culminate at last in a noisy little cascade of tears.)

MAJOR VOYSEY: Honor, control yourself. (And to emphasize his own perfect control he helps himself majestically to a glass of sherry. Then says...) Well, Edward?

EDWARD: I'll come straight to the point that concerns you. Our father's will gives certain sums to you all...the gross amount would be something over a hundred thousand pounds. There will be no money.

(He can get no further than the bare statement, which is received only with varying looks of bewilderment; until MRS. VOYSEY, discovering nothing from their faces, breaks this second silence.)

MRS. VOYSEY: I didn't hear.

BEATRICE: (In her mother-in-law's ear.) Edward says there's no money.

TRENCHARD: (Precisely.) I think you said..."will be."

MAJOR VOYSEY: (In a tone of mitigated thunder.) Why will there be no money?

EDWARD: (Letting himself go.) Because every penny by right belongs to the clients Father spent his life defrauding. I mean that in the worst sense...swindling... thieving. And now I must collect every penny, any money that you can give me; put the firm into bankruptcy; pay back all we can. I'll stand trial...it'll come to that with me...and as soon as possible. (He pauses partly for breath, and glares at them all.) Are none of you going to speak? Quite right, what is there to be said? (Then with a gentle afterthought.) I'm sorry to hurt you, Mother.

(The VOYSEY FAMILY is simply buried deep beneath this avalanche of horror. MRS. VOYSEY, though, who has been watching EDWARD closely, says very calmly...)

MRS. VOYSEY: I can't hear quite all you say, but I guess what it is. You don't hurt me, Edward...I have known of this for a long time.

EDWARD: (With a muted cry.) Oh Mother, did he know you knew?

MRS. VOYSEY: What do you say?

TRENCHARD: (Collected and dry.) I may as well tell you, Edward; I suspected everything wasn't right about the time of my last quarrel with my father. As there was nothing I could do I did not pursue my suspicions. Was Father aware that you knew, Mother?

MRS. VOYSEY: We never discussed it. There was once a great danger, I believe... when you were all younger...of his being found out. But we never discussed it.

EDWARD: *(Swallowing a fresh bitterness.)* I'm glad it isn't such a shock to you.

ETHEL: *(Alive to the dramatic aspect of the matter.)* My God...before the earth has settled on his grave!

EDWARD: I thought it wrong to put off telling you.

HONOR: *(The word swindling having spelt itself out in her mind, at last gives way to a burst of piteous grief.)* Oh, poor Papa!...poor Papa!

EDWARD: *(Comforting her kindly.)* Honor, we shall want your help and advice.

MAJOR VOYSEY: *(The MAJOR has recovered from the shock, to swell with importance. It being necessary to make an impression, he instinctively turns first to his sister-in-law.)* I think, Beatrice, there is no further need for you to be present at this exposure, and that you had better retire.

BEATRICE: No, Booth.

MAJOR VOYSEY: *(An awful thought strikes him.)* Good heavens...I hope the servants haven't been listening! See where they are, Honor...open the door suddenly.

(She does so more or less and there is no one behind it.)

MAJOR VOYSEY: That's all right. *(He turns with gravity to his brother.)* I have said nothing as yet, Edward. I am thinking.

TRENCHARD: *(A little impatient at this exhibition.)* That's the worst of these family practices...a lot of money knocking around and no audit ever required.

The wonder to me is to find an honest solicitor at all.

MAJOR VOYSEY: Really, Trenchard!

TRENCHARD: Well, think of the temptation.

EDWARD: And how naïve most clients are...

TRENCHARD: The world's getting more and more into the hands of its experts...

EDWARD: Here were all these funds... simply a lucky bag into which he dipped.

TRENCHARD: Did he keep accounts of any sort?

EDWARD: Scraps of paper. Most of the original investments I can't even trace. The money doesn't exist.

MAJOR VOYSEY: Where's it gone?

EDWARD: *(Very directly.)* You've been living on it.

MAJOR VOYSEY: Good God!

TRENCHARD: What can you pay in the pound?

EDWARD: As we stand?...six or seven shillings, I daresay. But we must do better than that.

(To which there is no response.)

MAJOR VOYSEY: All this is very dreadful. Does it mean beggary for the whole family?

EDWARD: Yes, it should.

TRENCHARD: *(Sharply.)* Nonsense.

EDWARD: *(Joining issue at once.)* What right have we to a thing we possess?

TRENCHARD: He didn't make you an allowance, Booth? Your capital's your own, isn't it?

MAJOR VOYSEY: *(Awkwardly placed between the two of them.)* Really…I…I suppose so. The Pater gave it me when I received my commission.

TRENCHARD: Beatrice?

BEATRICE: Oh…he was very generous when Hugh and I married…

MAJOR VOYSEY: Then that's all right.

EDWARD: *(Vehemently.)* It was stolen money.

TRENCHARD: Most likely, but maybe not. And they took it in good faith.

MAJOR VOYSEY: I should hope so!

EDWARD: *(Dwelling on the words.)* It's stolen money.

MAJOR VOYSEY: *(Bubbling with distress.)* I say, what ought I to do?

TRENCHARD: Do…my dear Booth? Nothing.

EDWARD: *(With great indignation.)* Trenchard, we owe reparation.

BEATRICE: Quite so. But to whom? From which client's account was the money taken? You say yourself you don't know.

EDWARD: Trenchard!

TRENCHARD: My dear Edward, the law will take anything it has a right to and all it can get; you needn't be afraid. But what about your own position…can we get you clear?

EDWARD: Oh, I'll get what's coming to me.

(MAJOR VOYSEY's head has been turning incessantly from one to the other and by this he is just a bristle of alarm.)

MAJOR VOYSEY: But I say, you know, this is awful! Will this have to made public?

TRENCHARD: No help for it.

(The MAJOR's jaw drops; he is speechless. MRS. VOYSEY's dead voice steals in.)

MRS. VOYSEY: What is all this?

TRENCHARD: Edward suggests that the family beggar itself in order to pay back to every client to whom Father owed a pound perhaps seven shillings instead of six.

MRS. VOYSEY: He will find that my estate has been kept quite separate.

(EDWARD hides his face in his hands.)

TRENCHARD: I'm very glad to hear it, Mother.

MRS. VOYSEY: When Mr. Barnes died, your father agreed to appointing another trustee.

ETHEL: *(Diffidently.)* I suppose, Edward, Denis and I are involved?

EDWARD: *(Lifting his head quickly.)* Denis, I hope not. I didn't know that anything of his…

ETHEL: Yes…all he got under his aunt's will.

EDWARD: See how things are…I've not found a trace of that, yet. We'll hope for the best.

ETHEL: *(Setting her teeth.)* It can't be helped.

MAJOR VOYSEY: *(In the loudest of whispers.)* Let me advise you not to worry about this too much Ethel, at such a critical time.

ETHEL: I thank you, Booth.

(HONOR, by a series of contortions, has lately been giving evidence of a desire or intention to say something.)

EDWARD: Well, what is it, Honor?

HONOR: I have been wondering... if he can hear this conversation. *(Her remark brings on a fresh bout of tears.)* Oh, poor Papa... poor Papa!

MRS. VOYSEY: I think I'll go to my room. I can't hear what any of you are saying. Edward can tell me afterwards.

EDWARD: Would you like to go too, Honor?

HONOR: *(Through her sobs.)* Yes, please, I would.

ETHEL: I'll get out, Edward. Whatever you think fit to do...! I wish... for our child's sake... That's all.

(By this time MRS. VOYSEY and HONOR have been got out of the room. ETHEL follows them. EDWARD does not speak. MAJOR VOYSEY looks at BEATRICE, who settles herself at the table.)

TRENCHARD: How long have things been wrong?

EDWARD: He told me the trouble began in his father's time and he'd been battling it ever since.

TRENCHARD: *(Smiling.)* Oh, come now... that's impossible.

EDWARD: I believed him. But looking through all the papers, such as they are, there's not record enough to trace any irregularities further than ten years back, except those that have to do with old George Booth's business.

MAJOR VOYSEY: But the Pater never touched his money... why, he was a personal friend.

TRENCHARD: When did you find out?

EDWARD: October.

TRENCHARD: What did you do?

EDWARD: I urged him at least to put some of the smaller people right. He said

that would be penny wise and pound foolish. So I've done what I could myself... since he's been ill... Nothing to count.

TRENCHARD: What was his object in telling you? He didn't think you'd take a hand?

EDWARD: He always protested that things would come right... that he'd clear the firm and have two hundred thousand to the good. Perhaps he only told me so he'd have someone to boast to of his financial exploits.

TRENCHARD: *(Appreciatively.)* I daresay.

MAJOR VOYSEY: Scarcely a thing to boast of!

TRENCHARD: Depends on your point of view.

EDWARD: You know what the Pater was. Last winter he drew up an extremely generous will. Though he hadn't a penny really. But he left thousands to his family, his staff, charities. And I'm the sole executor... and there's an added five hundred for my time!

TRENCHARD: What on earth made you stay with him once you knew?

EDWARD: *(Does not answer for a moment.)* I thought I might prevent things getting worse.

TRENCHARD: You knew the personal risk you were running?

EDWARD: *(Bowing his head.)* Yes.

TRENCHARD: *(The only one of the four who fully comprehends, he looks at EDWARD for a moment with something that might almost be admiration. Then he stirs himself.)* I must be off to court. Work waiting... end of term.

MAJOR VOYSEY: Shall I walk to the station with you?

TRENCHARD: I'll spend a few minutes with Mother. *(He says at the door, very respectfully.)* You'll count on me for any legal help I can give, please, Edward.

EDWARD: *(Simply.)* Thank you, Trenchard.

(So TRENCHARD goes. The MAJOR who has been endeavoring to fathom his final attitude, then comments—)

MAJOR VOYSEY: No heart, y'know! Great brain! If it hadn't been for that distressing quarrel, he might have saved our poor father. Don't you think so, Edward?

EDWARD: Perhaps.

BEATRICE: *(Giving vent to her thoughts at last with something of a relish.)* The more I think this out, the more devilishly humorous it gets. Old Booth breaking down by the grave. The Vicar reading the service...

EDWARD: Yes, the Vicar's badly hit. The Pater managed his business for years.

MAJOR VOYSEY: Good God...how shall we ever look old Booth in the face again?

EDWARD: I don't worry about him; he can die quite comfortably enough on our six shillings in the pound. It's one or two of the smaller fry who will suffer.

MAJOR VOYSEY: Now, just explain to me...I didn't interrupt while Trenchard was speaking...of what exactly did this defrauding consist?

EDWARD: Speculating with a client's capital. You pocket the gains...and keep paying the client his ordinary income.

MAJOR VOYSEY: So that he doesn't find out?

EDWARD: Quite so.

MAJOR VOYSEY: In point of fact, he doesn't suffer?

EDWARD: He doesn't suffer till he finds it out.

MAJOR VOYSEY: And all that's wrong now is that some of their capital is missing.

EDWARD: *(Half-amused, half-amazed at this process of reasoning.)* Yes, that's all that's wrong.

MAJOR VOYSEY: What is the—ah—deficit? *(The word rolls from his tongue.)*

EDWARD: Anything between two and three hundred thousand pounds.

MAJOR VOYSEY: *(Impressed, and not unfavourably.)* Dear me...this is a big affair!

BEATRICE: *(Following her own line of thought.)* Quite apart from the rights and wrongs of this, only a very able man could have kept a straight face to the world all these years, as your father did.

MAJOR VOYSEY: I suppose he sometimes made money by these speculations?

EDWARD: Very often. His own expenditure was heavy...as you know.

MAJOR VOYSEY: *(With gratitude for favours received.)* He was a very generous man.

BEATRICE: Did nobody ever suspect?

EDWARD: You see, Beatrice, when there was any pressing danger...if a big trust had to be wound up...he'd make a great effort and put the accounts straight.

MAJOR VOYSEY: Then he did put some accounts straight?

EDWARD: Yes, when he couldn't help himself.

(MAJOR VOYSEY looks very enquiring, and then squares himself up to the subject.)

MAJOR VOYSEY: Now look here, Edward. You told us that he told you that it was the object of his life to put these accounts straight. Then you laughed at that. Now you tell me that he did put some accounts straight.

EDWARD: *(Wearily.)* My dear Booth, you don't understand.

MAJOR VOYSEY: Well, let me understand…I am anxious to understand.

EDWARD: We can't pay ten shillings in the pound.

MAJOR VOYSEY: That's very dreadful. But do you know that there wasn't a time when we couldn't have paid five?

EDWARD: *(Acquiescent.)* Perhaps.

MAJOR VOYSEY: Very well, then! If it was true about his father and all that…and why shouldn't we believe him if we can?…and he did effect an improvement, that's to his credit, isn't it? Let us at least be just, Edward.

EDWARD: *(Patiently polite.)* I am sorry if I seem unjust. But he has left me in a rather unfortunate position.

MAJOR VOYSEY: Yes, his death was a tragedy. It seems to me that if he had been spared he might have succeeded at length in this tremendous task and restored to us our family honour.

EDWARD: Yes, Booth, he spoke very feelingly of that.

MAJOR VOYSEY: *(Irony lost upon him.)* I can well believe it. And I can tell you that now…I may be right or I may be wrong…I am feeling far less concerned about the clients' money than I am at the terrible blow to the family which this exposure will strike. Money, after all, can to a certain extent be done without…but honour—

(This is too much for EDWARD.)

EDWARD: Our honour! Do either of you mean to give me a single penny towards undoing all the wrong that has been done?

MAJOR VOYSEY: I take Trenchard's word for it that…there's no need.

EDWARD: Then don't talk to me of honour.

MAJOR VOYSEY: *(Somewhat nettled at this outburst.)* I am speaking of the public exposure. Edward, can't that be prevented?

EDWARD: *(With quick suspicion.)* How?

MAJOR VOYSEY: Well, how was it being prevented before he died…before we knew anything about it?

EDWARD: *(Appealing to the spirits that watch over him.)* Oh, listen to this! First Trenchard…and now you! You've the poison in your blood, every one of you. Who am I to talk! I daresay I so have I.

MAJOR VOYSEY: *(Reprovingly.)* I am beginning to think that you have worked yourself into rather an hysterical state over this unhappy business.

EDWARD: *(Rating him.)* Perhaps you'd have been glad…glad if I'd gone on lying and cheating…and married and begotten a son to go on lying and cheating after me. And to pay you your interest in the lie and the cheat.

MAJOR VOYSEY: *(With statesmanlike calm.)* Look here, Edward, this rhetoric is exceedingly out of place. The simple question before us is…what is the best course to pursue?

EDWARD: There is no question before us. There's only one course to pursue.

MAJOR VOYSEY: *(Crushingly.)* You will let me speak, please. Insofar as our poor father was dishonest to his clients, I pray that he may be forgiven. Insofar as he spent his life honestly endeavouring to right a wrong which he had found already committed...I forgive him...I admire him, Edward...and I feel it my duty to—er—reprobate most strongly the—er—gusto with which you have been holding him up in memory to us... ten minutes after we'd been standing round his grave...as a monster of wickedness. I think I knew him as well as you—better. And...thank God!...there was not between him and me this...this unhappy business to warp my judgment of him. *(He warms to his subject.)* Did you ever know a more charitable man...a larger-hearted? He was a faithful husband...and what a father to all of us!...putting us out into the world and fully intending to leave us comfortably settled there. Further as I see this matter, Edward...when as a young man he was told this terrible secret and entrusted with such a frightful task...did he turn his back on it like a coward? No. He went through it heroically to the end of his life. And, as he died, I imagine there was no more torturing thought than that he had left his work unfinished. *(He is pleased with this peroration.)* And now...if all these clients can be kept receiving their natural incomes...and if Father's plan could be carried out, of gradually replacing the capital...

EDWARD: *(At this, raises his head and stares with horror.)* You're asking me to carry on this...? Oh, you don't know what you're talking about.

MAJOR VOYSEY: *(The MAJOR, having talked himself back to a proper eminence, remains good-tempered.)* Well, I'm not a conceited man...but I do think that I can understand a simple financial problem when it has been explained to me.

EDWARD: You don't know the nerve... the unscrupulous daring it requires to...

MAJOR VOYSEY: Of course, if you're going to argue round your own incompetence.

EDWARD: *(Very straight.)* D'you want your legacy?

MAJOR VOYSEY: *(With dignity.)* In one moment I shall get very angry. Here am I doing my best to help you and your clients...and there you sit imputing to me the most sordid motives. Do you suppose I should touch, or allow to be touched, the money which Father has left us till every client's claim was satisfied?

EDWARD: My dear Booth, I know you mean well...

MAJOR VOYSEY: I'll come down to your office and work with you.

EDWARD: *(At this cheerful prospect even poor EDWARD can't help smiling.)* I'm sure you would.

MAJOR VOYSEY: *(Feeling that it is a chance lost.)* If the Pater had ever consulted me...

(At this point TRENCHARD looks round the door to say:)

TRENCHARD: Are you coming, Booth?

MAJOR VOYSEY: Yes, certainly. I'll talk this over with Trenchard. *(As he gets up and automatically stiffens, he is reminded of the occasion and his voice drops.)* I say...we've been speaking very loud. You must do nothing rash. I've no doubt he and I can devise something which will obviate...and then I'm sure I shall convince you.

(Catches his eldest brother's impatient eye, for he departs abruptly, saying:)

MAJOR VOYSEY: ...All right, Trenchard, you've eight minutes.

(The MAJOR and TRENCHARD exit.)

BEATRICE: *(At ease.)* This is an experience for you, Edward!

EDWARD: *(Bitterly.)* And I feared what the shock might be to you all! Booth has made a good recovery.

BEATRICE: You wouldn't have him miss such a chance of booming at us.

EDWARD: It's strange that people will believe you can do right by means they know to be wrong.

BEATRICE: *(Taking great interest in this.)* Come, what do we know about right and wrong? Let's say legal and illegal. You're so down on the Governor because he has trespassed against the etiquette of your own profession. But now he's dead...and if there weren't any scandal to think of...it's no use the rest of us pretending to feel him a criminal, because we don't. Which just shows that money...and property...

(At this point she becomes conscious that ALICE MAITLAND is standing behind her, her eyes fixed on EDWARD. So she interrupts herself to ask...)

BEATRICE: D'you want to speak to Edward?

ALICE: Please, Beatrice.

BEATRICE: I'll go. *(She looks a little martyr-like, not to conclude the evolution of her theory, but she goes.)*

(ALICE still looks at EDWARD, and he at her rather appealingly.)

ALICE: Auntie has told me.

EDWARD: He was fond of you. Don't think worse of him than you can help.

ALICE: I'm thinking of you.

EDWARD: I may just escape.

ALICE: So Trenchard says.

EDWARD: My hands are clean, Alice.

ALICE: I know that.

EDWARD: Mother's not very upset.

ALICE: She'd expected a smash in his lifetime.

EDWARD: I'm glad that didn't happen.

ALICE: Yes. I've put Honor to bed. It was a mercy to tell her just at this moment. She can grieve for his death and his disgrace at the same time...and the one grief will soften the other perhaps.

EDWARD: Oh, they're all shocked enough at his disgrace but will they open their purses to lessen the disgrace?

ALICE: Will it seem less disgraceful to have stolen ten thousand pounds than twenty?

EDWARD: I should think so.

ALICE: I should think so; but I wonder if that's the Law. If it isn't, Trenchard as a barrister wouldn't consider the point. I'm sure Public Opinion doesn't say so...and that's what Booth is considering.

EDWARD: *(With contempt.)* Yes.

ALICE: *(Ever so gently ironical.)* Well, he's in the Army. He's almost in Society...and he has got to get on in both; one mustn't blame him.

EDWARD: *(Very serious.)* But when one thinks how the money was obtained!

ALICE: When one thinks how most money is obtained!

EDWARD: They've not earned it.

ALICE: *(Her eyes humorous.)* If they had they might have given it you and earned more. Did I ever tell you what my guardian said to me when I came of age?

EDWARD: I'm thankful you're out of the mess.

ALICE: I wouldn't have been, but I was made to look after my money myself...much against my will. My guardian was a person of great character and no principles, the best and most lovable man I've ever met...I'm sorry you never knew him, Edward...and he said once to me: You've no particular right to your money...you've not earned it or deserved it in any way. Therefore don't be either surprised or annoyed when any enterprising person tries to get it from you. He has at least as much ethical right to it as you...if he can use it better perhaps he has more. Shocking sentiments, aren't they? But perhaps that's why I've less sympathy with some of these clients than you have, Edward.

EDWARD: *(Shakes his head, treating these paradoxes as they deserve.)* Alice...one or two of them will be beggared.

ALICE: *(Sincerely.)* Yes, that is bad. What's to be done?

EDWARD: There's old Nurse...with her poor little savings gone!

ALICE: Surely, she can be helped.

EDWARD: The Law's no respecter of persons...that's its boast. Old Booth with more than he wants will keep enough and to spare. My old nurse, with just enough, may starve. But it'll be a relief to clear out this nest of lies, even though one suffers one's self. I've been ashamed to walk into that office. I'll hold my head high in prison though. *(He shakes himself stiffly erect, his chin high.)*

ALICE: *(Quizzes him.)* Edward, I'm afraid you're feeling heroic.

EDWARD: I!

ALICE: You looked quite like Booth for the moment.

(This effectually removes the starch.)

ALICE: Please don't glory in your martyrdom. It will be very stupid to send you to prison, and you must do your very best to keep out. *(Her tone is most practical.)* We were discussing what could be done for these people who'll be beggared.

EDWARD: I suppose I was feeling heroic. I didn't mean to.

ALICE: It's the worst of acting on principle...one thinks more of one's attitude than of the use of what one is doing.

EDWARD: But what can I do? The fraud must be exposed.

ALICE: And people must be ruined? Well...

EDWARD: There's nothing else to be done.

ALICE: I'm afraid I've no use for that principle.

(He looks at her; she is smiling, it is true, but smiling quite gravely. EDWARD is puzzled. Then the yeast of her suggestion begins to work in his mind slowly, perversely at first.)

EDWARD: Unless you expect me to take Booth's advice. Go on with the game...as an honest cheat...plunge, just as wildly as my father did, on the chance that things might come out right. Oh, I might as well give the money to Booth and send him to Monte Carlo. For don't think I've any talents that way, principles or no. What have I done so far? Sat in shame of it for a year. I did take a hand...if you want to know...and managed to prevent one affair from going from bad to worse.

ALICE: Was that worth doing?

EDWARD: It's illegal. It will cost me now when they find out...at best I'll be struck off as a solicitor...my livelihood gone.

ALICE: The cost is your own affair.

EDWARD: There is something else I could do.

ALICE: What?

EDWARD: It's just as irregular. I could take the firm's money that's in my father's name and use it to right the smaller accounts. There are four or five I might get square. Mrs. Travers...well, I could fix it so she'd never starve, and I'd like to see those two Lyndhursts safe. It'd take a year or so to get it right and cover the tracks. Cover the tracks...sounds well doesn't it? But I would like to do it. Shall I?

ALICE: My dear, don't ask me.

EDWARD: You've taken my principles from me, give me some advice in exchange.

ALICE: I'm a woman. I'm lawless by birthright.

EDWARD: Good Lord.

ALICE: After a year you'd give yourself up as you'd meant to do now?

EDWARD: Yes...I'd have to call the police and tell them to come collect me.

ALICE: Would it be worse for you at the trial?

EDWARD: You said that would be my affair.

ALICE: Oh, Edward!

EDWARD: Shall I do it? It means lying and shuffling.

ALICE: In a good cause.

EDWARD: And it wouldn't be easy. For I'm no good at that sort of thing. The deficit's so large I could never put it right. But the smaller fry...Alice, I'd most likely muddle it.

ALICE: I wouldn't think so. In fact I'd be so proud.

EDWARD: You want me to try?

(She dares only to put out her hand, and he takes it.)

ALICE: Oh, my dear!

EDWARD: *(Excitedly.)* Everyone must hold their tongues. I needn't have told them. But honestly, I rather enjoyed it.

ALICE: Oh, Edward! I'm thrilled! I hardly recognize you.

EDWARD: You have a right to be. If I bring any of this off, it will be because of you.

ALICE: Thank you. I've always wanted something useful to my credit. I'd almost given up hope.

EDWARD: *(Then suddenly his face changes, his voice changes.)* Alice, what if my father's story is true? He must have begun like this. Trying to do the right thing in the wrong way...then doing the wrong thing...then bringing himself to what he was...and so me to this. My dear, if I take this first step down, there's a worse risk than any failure...I might succeed. What you said is true. I don't recognize myself.

ALICE: *(Stands very still, looking at him.)* Yes, my dear, you might. That's quite a risk. Well, I'll take it.

EDWARD: *(Turns to her in wonder.)* You?

ALICE: I'll risk your becoming a criminal. And that's a big risk for me now.

EDWARD: *(He is calmed by this and made happy.)* Then there's no more to be said, is there?

ALICE: Not now.

(He does not ask what she means by this.)

ALICE: I must go back to Honor. Poor girl, I wonder she has a single tear left. *(As she opens the door:)*

MAJOR VOYSEY: *(Off.)* Honor!

ALICE: And here's Booth back again. What will you tell him?

EDWARD: He'll be so glad he's convinced me.

ACT FOUR

MR. VOYSEY's room at the office is EDWARD's room now. It has somehow lost that brilliancy which the old man's occupation seemed to give it. Perhaps it is only because this December morning is dull and depressing; but the fire isn't bright and the panels and windows don't shine as they did. There are no roses on the table either. EDWARD, walking in as his father did, hanging his hat and coat where his father's used to hang, is certainly the palest shadow of that other masterful presence. A depressed, drooping shadow, too. This may be what PEACEY feels; for he looks very surly as he obeys the old routine of following his chief to this room on his arrival. Nor has EDWARD so much as a glance for his clerk. They exchange the formalest of greetings. EDWARD sits joylessly at his desk, on which the morning's pile of letters lays, unopened now.

PEACEY: Good morning, sir.

EDWARD: Good morning, Peacey. Any notes for me?

PEACEY: Well, I've hardly been through the letters yet sir.

EDWARD: *(His eyebrows meeting.)* Oh… and I'm late myself this morning.

PEACEY: I'm very sorry, sir.

EDWARD: If Mr. Bullen calls, you had better show him those papers I gave you. Write to Metcalfe; say I've seen Mr. Vickery myself this morning and he does not wish to proceed. Better show me the letter.

PEACEY: Very good, sir.

EDWARD: That's all, thank you.

PEACEY: *(Gets to the door, where he stops, looking not only surly but nervous now.)* May I speak to you a moment, sir?

EDWARD: Certainly

PEACEY: *(After a moment, makes an effort, purses his mouth, and begins.)* Bills are beginning to come in upon me as is usual at this season, sir. My son's allowance at Cambridge is now rather a heavy item of my expenditure. I hope that the custom of the firm isn't to be neglected now that you are the head of it, Mr. Edward. Two hundred your father always made it at Christmas…in notes if you please.

EDWARD: *(Towards the end of this, EDWARD begins to pay attention. When he answers his voice is harsh.)* Oh to be sure…your hush money.

PEACEY: *(Bridling.)* That's not a very pleasant word.

EDWARD: This is an unpleasant subject.

PEACEY: Well, it's not one I wish to discuss. Your father always gave me the notes in an envelope when he shook hands with me at Christmas.

EDWARD: Why notes now? Why not a rise in salary?

PEACEY: Mr. Voysey's custom, sir, from before my time. My father…

EDWARD: Yes. It's an hereditary pull you have over the firm, isn't it?

PEACEY: I remember my father saying when he retired…been dead twenty-six years, Mr. Edward…I have told the governor you know what I know. Then Mr. Voysey saying…I treat you as I did your father, Peacey. I'd never another word with him on the subject.

EDWARD: A decent arrangement…and the cheapest no doubt. Of the raising of salaries there might have been no end.

PEACEY: Mr. Edward, that's uncalled for. We have served you and yours most faithfully. I know my father would sooner have cut off his hand than do anything to embarrass the firm.

EDWARD: But business is business, Peacey. Surely he could have had a partnership for the asking.

PEACEY: That's another matter, sir.

EDWARD: Is it?

PEACEY: A matter of principle, if you'll excuse me. I must not be taken to approve of the firm's conduct. Nor did my dear father approve. And at anything like partnership he surely would have drawn the line.

EDWARD: I beg your pardon.

PEACEY: Well, that's all right, sir. Always a bit of friction in coming to an understanding about anything, isn't there, sir? *(He is going when EDWARD's question stops him.)*

EDWARD: Why didn't you speak about this last Christmas?

PEACEY: You were so upset at your father's death.

EDWARD: My father died the August before that.

PEACEY: Well…truthfully, Mr. Edward?

EDWARD: As truthfully as you think suitable.

PEACEY: *(The irony of this is wasted on PEACEY, who becomes pleasantly candid.)* Well, I'd always thought there must be a smash when your father died…but it didn't come. I couldn't make you out. So I thought I'd better keep quiet and say nothing.

EDWARD: I see. Your son's at Cambridge?

PEACEY: Yes.

EDWARD: I wonder you didn't bring him into the firm.

PEACEY: *(Taking this very kind.)* Thank you. But I hope James may go to the bar. Our only son…I didn't grudge him my small savings to help him wait for his chance. Ten years if need be.

EDWARD: I hope he'll make his mark before then. I'm glad to have had this talk with you, Peacey. I'm sorry you can't have the money. *(He returns to his letters, a little steely-eyed.)*

PEACEY: *(Quite at his ease, makes for the door yet again, saying:)* Oh, any time will do, sir.

EDWARD: You can't have it at all.

PEACEY: *(Brought up short.)* Can't I?

EDWARD: No. I made up my mind about this eighteen months ago. The business of the firm is not conducted as it used to be. Since we no longer make illicit profits out of our clients, there are none for you to share.

(EDWARD goes on with his work. PEACEY has flushed up.)

PEACEY: Mr. Edward…I'm sorry we began this discussion. You'll give me my two hundred as usual, please, and we'll drop the subject.

EDWARD: By all means drop the subject.

PEACEY: I want the money. And it's not gentlemanly in you, Mr. Edward, to try and get out of paying it me. Your father would never have made such an excuse.

EDWARD: Do you think I'm lying to you?

PEACEY: That's no concern of mine, sir.

EDWARD: So long as you get your money.

PEACEY: You can drop the sarcasm, sir.

EDWARD: Then I should have to tell you plainly what I think of you.

PEACEY: That I'm a thief because I've taken money from a thief?

EDWARD: Worse! You're content that others should steal for you.

PEACEY: And who isn't?

EDWARD: *(Really pleased with the retort. He relaxes and changes his tone, which had indeed become a little bullying.)* Ah, my dear Peacey…I see you study politics. What I'm telling you is that I have for the moment at some inconvenience to myself, ceased to receive stolen goods, so I am in a position to throw a stone at you. I have thrown it.

PEACEY: *(Who would far sooner be bullied than talked to like this, turns very sulky.)* Then I resign my position here.

EDWARD: Very well.

PEACEY: And I happen to think the secret's worth its price.

EDWARD: Perhaps someone will pay it you.

PEACEY: *(Feebly threatening.)* Don't presume upon it's not being worth my while to make use of what I know.

EDWARD: *(Not unkindly.)* My good Peacey, it happens to be the truth I told you, just now. How on earth do you suppose you can successfully blackmail a man who has so much to gain by exposure and so little to lose?

PEACEY: *(Peeving.)* I don't want to ruin you, sir, and I have a great regard for the firm. But you must see that I can't have my income reduced in this way without a struggle.

EDWARD: *(With great cheerfulness.)* Very well…struggle away.

PEACEY: *(His voice rising high and thin.)* Well, is it fair dealing on your part to dock the money suddenly like this? I have been counting on it most of the year, and I have been led into heavy expenses. Why couldn't you have warned me?

EDWARD: Yes, that's true, Peacey…it was stupid of me. I'm sorry.

PEACEY: *(A little comforted by this quite candid acknowledgment.)* Things may get easier for you by and by.

EDWARD: I hope so.

PEACEY: Will you reconsider the matter then?

EDWARD: *(At this gentle insinuation EDWARD looks up exasperated.)* Then you don't believe what I told you?

PEACEY: Yes, I do.

EDWARD: But you think that the fascination of swindling one's clients will ultimately prove irresistible?

PEACEY: That's what your father found, I suppose you know.

EDWARD: *(This gives EDWARD such pause that he drops his masterful tone.)* I didn't.

PEACEY: He got things as right as rain once.

EDWARD: Did he?

PEACEY: So my father told me. But he started again.

EDWARD: Are you sure of this?

PEACEY: *(Expanding pleasantly.)* Well, sir, I knew your father pretty well. When I first came into the firm I simply hated him. He was that sour...so snappy with everyone as if he had a grievance against the whole world.

EDWARD: *(Pensively.)* It seems he had in those days!

PEACEY: His dealings with his clients were no business of mine. I speak as I find. After a bit he was very kind to me...thoughtful and considerate. Pleasant and generous to everyone.

EDWARD: You have hopes of me yet?

PEACEY: *(Who has a simple mind.)* No, Mr. Edward, no. You're different from your father...one must make up one's mind to that. And you may believe me or not, but I should be very glad to know that the firm was going straight. I'm getting on in years myself, now. I'm not much longer for the business, and there have been times when I have sincerely regretted my connection with it. If you'll let me say so, I think it's very noble of you to have undertaken the work you have. *(Then, as everything seems smooth again.)* And if you'll give me enough to cover this year's extra expense, I think I may promise you that I shan't expect money again.

EDWARD: *(Good-tempered, as he would speak to an importunate child.)* No, Peacey, no.

PEACEY: *(Fretful again.)* Well, sir, you make things very difficult for me.

EDWARD: Here's a letter from Mr. Cartwright which you might attend to. If he wants an appointment with me, don't make one till the New Year. His case can't come on before February.

PEACEY: *(Taking the letter.)* I show myself anxious to meet you in every way...

(He is handed another.)

EDWARD: "Percival Building Estate"... that's yours too.

PEACEY: *(Putting them both down, resolutely.)* But I refuse to be ignored. I must consider my whole position. I hope I may not be tempted to make use of the power I possess. But if I am driven to proceed to extremities...

EDWARD: *(Breaking in upon this bunch of tags.)* My dear Peacey, don't talk nonsense...you couldn't proceed to an extremity to save your life. You've taken this money without thinking for all these years. You'll find you're no longer capable even of such a thoughtless act as tripping up your neighbour.

PEACEY: *(This does completely upset the gentle blackmailer. He loses one grievance in another.)* Really, Mr. Edward, I am a considerably older man than you and I think that whatever our positions...!

EDWARD: I apologise. Don't forget the letters.

PEACEY: I will not, sir. *(He takes them with great dignity and is leaving the room.)* There's Miss Beatrice waiting.

EDWARD: To see me? Ask her in.

PEACEY: Come in, Mrs. Voysey, please.

(BEATRICE comes in, PEACEY holding the door for her with a frigid politeness of which she is quite oblivious. At this final slight PEACEY goes out in dudgeon.)

EDWARD: How are you?

BEATRICE: Good Lord. *(She sits in the chair by the fire, distracted as if she were quite capable of sitting by the fire for the entire morning.)*

EDWARD: How's Hugh?

BEATRICE: He's very busy.

(EDWARD asks her at last:)

EDWARD: Do you want anything?

BEATRICE: Yes…tube fare home, Edward. I went out without my purse.

EDWARD: How did you get here?

BEATRICE: On foot.

EDWARD: From Hampstead?

BEATRICE: Yes, I walked here this morning from Hampstead. The streets are so dirty I wanted to curse. You'd think that an Empire could keep its streets clean! But then I saw that the children were dirty, too.

EDWARD: That's because of the streets.

BEATRICE: Any child old enough to cross the road by herself selling holiday trimmings, earning a bit of money, and covered in mud. London at Christmas. I want it destroyed, please.

EDWARD: What d'you want?

BEATRICE: I want a machine gun planted in Regent Street…and one in the Haymarket…and one in Leicester Square and one in the Strand…and a dozen in the City. An earthquake would be simpler. Or why not a nice clean tidal wave? Don't you feel, even in your calmer moments, that this whole country is simply hideous? I want it destroyed.

EDWARD: It has been promised.

BEATRICE: Well, I'm sick of waiting for other nations to do it. I'm patriotic. Why not do it ourselves? If it weren't for the Voyseys, I would.

EDWARD: I suppose we would be put out. You might make a book of it.

BEATRICE: It wouldn't sell.

EDWARD: Or Hugh might paint it.

BEATRICE: Oh, he doesn't care. Nor could he capture it. Oh, he paints, in a sort of way, Edward. But the only thing he can do or be—the only thing his canvasses reflect is the drawing room at Chislehurst. His tragedy is that he's sharp enough to know he's mediocre. And no sharper.

EDWARD: Well, Beatrice…much as I love your society…this morning I'm rather busy…

BEATRICE: You too? *(She's surprised to say what must have brought her here.)* Edward, take that money your father settled on us for your miserable clients…what's left of it. You ought to have had it when you asked for it.

EDWARD: But, Beatrice, you can't afford…

BEATRICE: No we can't. *(Taking the coins from EDWARD's desk.)* And remind me that I owe you tube fare, as well.

EDWARD: And what does Hugh say?

BEATRICE: Now that we're separating…

EDWARD: *(Taken aback.)* What?

BEATRICE: We mean to separate.

EDWARD: The first I've heard of it.

BEATRICE: Ethel knows.

EDWARD: Have you told anyone else?

BEATRICE: We must now, I suppose.

EDWARD: Don't say anything to Mother till after Christmas.

BEATRICE: Hugh will be in Italy, and I don't believe I'll be down for Christmas.

EDWARD: Nonsense! You can't upset the family…

BEATRICE: Edward, has one member of your family taken a scrap of interest in what you're doing here? I know I haven't! Because I'm afraid to know. When will you be quit of the beastly business?

EDWARD: Some day.

BEATRICE: What do you gain by hanging on now?

EDWARD: I'm not in gaol.

BEATRICE: *(Really startled by this.)* Edward, don't be dramatic…

EDWARD: Beatrice, at any moment a policeman may knock on the door. Any moment. I take no precautions. I made up my mind that at least I wouldn't lower myself to that. And perhaps that's why it doesn't happen. At first I listened for him, day by day. Then I said to myself…next week. But a year has gone by and more. I've ceased expecting to hear the knock at all. I sit here now drudging honestly. I've done some good—robbing Peter to pay Paul, I'll suffer for it eventually, but no one will be quite beggared now. The deficit is still hundreds of thousands. And I declare I do begin to understand my father better.

BEATRICE: Yes, he was a lesson in values wasn't he? If I can't destroy England myself, perhaps a few more like him might do the job for me.

(The door is opened and MR. GEORGE BOOTH comes in. He looks older than he did and besides is evidently not in a happy frame of mind.)

MR. GEORGE BOOTH: Hullo, Beatrice. How are you, Edward?

EDWARD: Good morning, Mr. Booth.

BEATRICE: Well, I'm going.

EDWARD: About the other matter, Beatrice, I should wait till summer and see how you feel.

BEATRICE: I don't think so. By the way Edward, did you know that your old Nursie is furious with you about something?

EDWARD: *(Shortly.)* Yes, I know.

BEATRICE: Good Lord…what a business! Goodbye. *(BEATRICE departs.)*

EDWARD: Will you come here…or will you sit by the fire?

MR. GEORGE BOOTH: This'll do. I shan't detain you long.

EDWARD: Are you feeling all right again?

MR. GEORGE BOOTH: A bit dyspeptic. How are you?

EDWARD: Quite well thanks.

MR. GEORGE BOOTH: I'm glad…I'm glad.

EDWARD: I have the Wyndham papers for you to sign…

MR. GEORGE BOOTH: Yes, I'm afraid it isn't very pleasant business I've come upon.

EDWARD: D'you want to go to court with anyone?

MR. GEORGE BOOTH: No…oh, no. I'm getting too old to quarrel. No. I've decided to withdraw my securities from the custody of your firm. *(And he adds apologetically.)* With the usual notice, of course.

EDWARD: *(Feels at this moment perhaps something of the shock that the relief of death may be as an end to pain so long endured that it has been half-forgotten. He answers very quietly, without a sign of emotion.)* Thank you…May one ask why?

MR. GEORGE BOOTH: *(Relieved that the worst is over.)* Oh…certainly…certainly! I think you must know, Edward,

I have never been able to feel that implicit confidence in your ability which I had in your father's. Well it is hardly to be expected, is it?

EDWARD: *(With a grim smile.)* No.

MR. GEORGE BOOTH: Men like your father are few and far between. No doubt things go on here as they have always done, but…since his death. I have not been happy about my affairs. For the first time in my long life I have been worried about my money. I don't like the feeling. The possession of money has always been something of a pleasure to me. For what are perhaps my last years I don't wish it to be otherwise. Remember, you have practically my entire property unreservedly in your control.

EDWARD: Perhaps we can arrange to hand you over the reins to an extent which will ease your mind, and at the same time not…

MR. GEORGE BOOTH: I thought of that. I had not moved in the matter for eighteen months. But I saw my doctor yesterday, Edward, and he told me…well, it was a warning. And so I felt it my duty…especially as I made up my mind to it some time ago…in point of fact more than a year before your father died I had quite decided that I could never trust my affairs to you as I had to him.

EDWARD: *(Starts; his face pale, his eyes black.)* Did he know that?

MR. GEORGE BOOTH: *(Resenting this new attitude.)* I may not have said it in so many words. But I fancy he guessed.

EDWARD: Don't say so…I prefer to believe that he never guessed. *(A fresh impulse.)* Let me persuade you not to do this, Mr. Booth.

MR. GEORGE BOOTH: No. I have quite made up my mind. I shall make a point of telling the family that you are in no way to blame.

EDWARD: *(Still quite unstrung really.)* For I believe my father would have wanted me to if I can.

MR. GEORGE BOOTH: My idea is for the future to employ merely a financial agent…

EDWARD: Of course. *(Speaking half to himself.)* Well…here's the way out. And it isn't my fault. *(EDWARD laughs.)*

MR. GEORGE BOOTH: You're making a fearful fuss about a simple matter, Edward. The loss of one client, however important he may be…Why this is one of the best family practices in London. I am surprised at your lack of dignity, but then that's your personality.

EDWARD: *(Yields, smilingly, to this assertiveness.)* Yes. Will you walk off with your papers now?

MR. GEORGE BOOTH: What notice is usual?

EDWARD: To a good solicitor, five minutes. Ten to a poor one. *(EDWARD settles at his desk again, with a certain grim enjoyment.)*

MR. GEORGE BOOTH: You'll have to explain matters a bit to me.

EDWARD: I will. Mr. Booth, how much do you think you're worth?

MR. GEORGE BOOTH: *(Easily.)* Do you know, I actually couldn't say offhand. But I have a rough idea, to be sure.

EDWARD: To be sure. You'll get not quite half of that out of us.

MR. GEORGE BOOTH: *(Precisely.)* I think I said I had made up my mind to withdraw the whole amount.

EDWARD: You should have made it up sooner.

MR. GEORGE BOOTH: I don't understand you, Edward.

EDWARD: The greater part of your capital doesn't exist.

MR. GEORGE BOOTH: *(With some irritation.)* Nonsense. It must exist. I needn't cash them in. You can hand me over the securities. I don't want to reinvest simply because…

EDWARD: I can't hand you over what I haven't got.

MR. GEORGE BOOTH: Is anything… wrong?

EDWARD: How many more times am I to say that we have robbed you of half your property?

MR. GEORGE BOOTH: *(His senses failing him.)* Say that again.

EDWARD: It's quite true.

MR. GEORGE BOOTH: My money… gone?

EDWARD: Yes.

MR. GEORGE BOOTH: *(Clutching at a straw of anger.)* And you've been the thief?…you…you…

EDWARD: I wouldn't tell you if I could help it…my father.

(That actually calls the old man back to something like dignity and self-possession. He thumps on EDWARD's table furiously.)

MR. GEORGE BOOTH: I'll make you prove that.

EDWARD: Oh, you've fired a mine. *(EDWARD goes off into hysterics.)*

MR. GEORGE BOOTH: *(Scolding him well.)* Slandering your dead father, and lying to me…revenging yourself by frightening me…because I detest you!

EDWARD: Why…haven't I thanked you for putting an end to my troubles? I do…I promise you I do.

MR. GEORGE BOOTH: *(Shouting; and his sudden courage failing as he shouts.)* Prove it…prove it to me. You don't frighten me so easily. One can't lose half of all one has and then be told of it in two minutes…sitting at a table. *(His voice tails off to a piteous whimper.)*

EDWARD: *(Quietly now and kindly.)* If my father had told you this in plain words, you'd have believed him.

MR. GEORGE BOOTH: *(Bowing his head.)* Yes.

EDWARD: *(Looks at the poor old thing with great pity.)* What on earth did you want to do this for? You need never have known…you could have died happy. Settling with all those charities in your will would certainly have smashed us up. But proving your will is many years off yet, we'll hope.

MR. GEORGE BOOTH: *(Pathetic and bewildered.)* I don't understand. No, I don't understand…because your father…! But I must understand, Edward.

EDWARD: Don't try to understand my father, for you never will. Pull yourself together, Mr. Booth. After all, this isn't a vital matter to you. It's not even as if you had a family to consider…like some of the others.

MR. GEORGE BOOTH: *(Vaguely.)* What others?

EDWARD: Don't imagine your money has been specially selected for pilfering.

MR. GEORGE BOOTH: *(With solemn incredulity.)* One has read of this sort of thing. But I thought people always got found out.

EDWARD: *(Brutally humorous.)* Well… you've found us out.

MR. GEORGE BOOTH: *(Rising to the full appreciation of his wrongs.)* Oh…I've been foully cheated!

EDWARD: *(Patiently.)* You have, I've told you so.

MR. GEORGE BOOTH: *(His voice breaks, he appeals pitifully.)* But by you, Edward…say it's by you.

EDWARD: *(Unable to resist his quiet revenge.)* I've not the ability or the personality for such work, Mr. Booth…nothing but the remains of a few principles, which forbid me even to lie to you.

MR. GEORGE BOOTH: *(The old gentleman draws a long breath and then speaks with great awe, blending into grief.)* I think your father is in Hell. I'd have gone there myself for him, Edward. I loved him. Very truly. How he could have had the heart! We were friends for forty years. Am I to think he only cared for me to cheat me?

EDWARD: *(Venturing the comfort of an explanation.)* No…he didn't value money quite as you do.

MR. GEORGE BOOTH: *(With sudden shrill logic.)* But he took it. What d'you mean by that?

EDWARD: *(Leans back in his chair and changes the tenor of their talk.)* Well, you are master of the situation now. What are you going to do?

MR. GEORGE BOOTH: To get the money back?

EDWARD: No, that's gone.

MR. GEORGE BOOTH: Then give me what's left and—

EDWARD: Are you going to prosecute?

MR. GEORGE BOOTH: *(Shifting uneasily in his chair.)* Oh, dear is that necessary? Can't somebody else do that? I thought the law…! What'll happen if I don't?

EDWARD: What do you suppose I'm doing here still?

MR. GEORGE BOOTH: *(As if he were being asked a riddle.)* I don't know.

EDWARD: *(Earnestly.)* As soon as my father died, I began to try and put things straight. Doing as I thought best that is, as best I could. Then I made up my accounts…showing who has lost and who hasn't…they can review those as they please and do what they will about it. And now I've set myself to a duller sort of work. I throw penny after penny hardly earned into the half-filled pit of our deficit. I've been doing that…for what it's worth…till this should happen. If you choose to let things alone…and hold your tongue…I can go on with the job till the next smash comes…and I'll beg that off too if I can. This is my duty…and it's my duty to ask you to let me go on with it.

(He searches Mr. Booth's face and finds there only disbelief and fear. He bursts out.)

EDWARD: Oh, you might at least believe me. It can't hurt you to believe me.

MR. GEORGE BOOTH: You must admit, Edward, it isn't easy to believe anything in this office…just for the moment.

EDWARD: *(Bowing to the extreme reasonableness of this.)* I suppose not. I can prove it to you. I'll take you through the books…you won't understand them…but I can do that much.

MR. GEORGE BOOTH: I think I'd rather not. Do you think I ought to hold any further communication with you at all? *(And at this he takes his hat.)*

EDWARD: *(With a little explosion of contemptuous anger.)* Certainly not. Prosecute…prosecute!

MR. GEORGE BOOTH: *(With dignity.)* Don't lose your temper. It's my place to be angry with you.

EDWARD: But I shall be grateful if you'll prosecute.

MR. GEORGE BOOTH: *(Hesitating, fidgeting.)* Surely I oughtn't have to make up my mind! There must be a right or a wrong thing to do. Edward, can't *you* tell me?

EDWARD: I'm prejudiced, you see.

MR. GEORGE BOOTH: I believe you're simply trying to practice on my goodness of heart. Certainly I ought to prosecute. Oughtn't I? *(At the nadir of helplessness.)* I'll have to consult another solicitor.

EDWARD: *(His chin in the air.)* You may as well write to the *Times* about it!

MR. GEORGE BOOTH: *(Shocked and grieved at his attitude.)* Edward, how can you be so cool and heartless?

EDWARD: *(Changing his tone.)* D'you think I shan't be glad to sleep at night?

MR. GEORGE BOOTH: Perhaps you'll be put in prison.

EDWARD: I am in prison…a less pleasant one than Wormwood Scrubs. But we're all prisoners, Mr. Booth.

MR. GEORGE BOOTH: *(Wagging his head.)* Yes. This is what comes of your philosophy. Why aren't you on your knees?

EDWARD: To you?

MR. GEORGE BOOTH: *(This was not what MR. BOOTH meant, but as he gets up from his chair he feels all but mighty.)*

And why should you expect me to shrink from vindicating the Law?

EDWARD: *(Shortly.)* I don't. I've explained you'll be doing me a kindness. When I'm wanted you'll find me here at my desk. *(Then as an afterthought.)* If you take long to decide don't alter your behaviour to my family in the meantime. They know the main points of the business, and…

MR. GEORGE BOOTH: *(Knocked right off his balance.)* Do they? Good God! I'm invited there to dinner the day after tomorrow, that's Christmas Eve. The hypocrites!

EDWARD: *(Unmoved.)* I shall be there… that will have given you two days. Will you tell me then?

MR. GEORGE BOOTH: *(Protesting violently.)* I can't go…I can't have dinner with them. I must be ill.

EDWARD: *(With a half-smile.)* I remember I went to dine at Chislehurst to tell my father of my decision.

MR. GEORGE BOOTH: *(Testily.)* What decision?

EDWARD: To remain in the firm when I first knew what was happening.

MR. GEORGE BOOTH: *(Interested.)* Was I there?

EDWARD: I daresay.

(MR. BOOTH stands there, hat, stick, gloves in hand, shaken by this experience, helpless, at his wits' end. He falls into a sort of fretful reverie, speaking half to himself, but yet as if he hoped that EDWARD, who is wrapped in his own thoughts, would have the decency to answer, or at least listen to what he is saying.)

MR. GEORGE BOOTH: Yes, how often I dined with him! Oh, it's monstrous! *(His eyes fall on the clock.)* It's nearly lunchtime now. Do you know I can still hardly believe it all. I wish I hadn't found it out. If he hadn't died, I should never have found it out. I hate to have to be vindictive…it's not my nature. I'm sure I'm more grieved than angry. But it isn't as if it were a small sum. And I don't see that one is called upon to forgive crimes…or why does the Law exist? I feel this will go near to killing me. I'm too old to have such troubles. It isn't right. And if I have to prosecute…

EDWARD: *(At last throwing in a word.)* Well…you need not.

MR. GEORGE BOOTH: *(Thankful for the provocation.)* Don't you attempt to influence me, sir. *(He turns to go.)*

EDWARD: And what's more…with the money you have left…

(EDWARD follows him politely. MR. BOOTH flings the door open.)

MR. GEORGE BOOTH: You'll make out a cheque for that at once, sir, and send it me.

EDWARD: You might…

MR. GEORGE BOOTH: *(Clapping his hat on, stamping his stick.)* I shall do the right thing, sir…never fear.

(So he marches off in fine style, he thinks, having had the last word and all. But EDWARD, closing the door after him, mutters…)

EDWARD: Save your soul…I'm afraid I was going to say.

ACT FIVE

Naturally it is the dining room consecrated as it is to the distinguishing orgy of the season—which bears the brunt of what an English household knows as Christmas decorations. They consist chiefly of the branches of holly, stuck cockeyed behind the top edges

of the pictures. The one picture conspicuously not decorated is that which hangs over the fireplace, a portrait of MR. VOYSEY, with its new gilt frame and its brass plate marking it also as a presentation. Otherwise the only difference between the dining room's appearance at half-past nine on Christmas Eve and on any other evening in the year is that little piles of queer-shaped envelopes seem to be lying about, and quite a lot of tissue paper and string is to be seen peeping from odd corners.

MR. GEORGE BOOTH: Thank you, but this room is empty and will do. Go tell Mr. Edward I'm here.

OFFSTAGE VOICE: Very well, sir.

(In a very short time EDWARD comes in, shutting the door and taking stock of the visitor before he speaks.)

EDWARD: Well?

MR. GEORGE BOOTH: *(Feebly.)* I hope my excuse for not coming to dinner was acceptable. I did have…I have a very bad headache.

EDWARD: I daresay they believed it.

MR. GEORGE BOOTH: I have come immediately to tell you my decision.

EDWARD: What is it?

MR. GEORGE BOOTH: I couldn't think the matter out alone. I went this afternoon to talk it over with the Vicar.

(At this EDWARD's eyebrows contract and then rise.)

MR. GEORGE BOOTH: What a terrible shock to him!

EDWARD: Oh, three of his four thousand pounds are quite safe.

MR. GEORGE BOOTH: That you and your father…you, whom he baptized… should have robbed him! I never saw a man so utterly prostrate with grief. That it should have been your father! And his poor wife...though she never got on with your father.

EDWARD: *(With cheerful irony.)* Oh, Mrs. Colpus knows too, does she?

MR. GEORGE BOOTH: Of course he told Mrs. Colpus. This is an unfortunate time for the storm to break on him. What with Christmas Day and Sunday following so close they're as busy as can be. He has resolved that during this season of peace and goodwill he must put the matter from him if he can. But once Christmas is over...! *(He envisages the old Vicar giving EDWARD a hell of a time then.)*

EDWARD: *(Coolly.)* So you mean to prosecute. If you don't, you've inflicted on the Colpuses a lot of unnecessary pain and a certain amount of loss by telling them.

MR. GEORGE BOOTH: *(Naïvely.)* I never thought of that. No, Edward, I have decided not to prosecute.

EDWARD: *(Hides his face for a moment.)* And I've been hoping to escape! Well, it can't be helped. *(And he sets his teeth.)*

MR. GEORGE BOOTH: *(With touching solemnity.)* I think I could not bear to see the family I have loved brought to such disgrace. And I want to ask your pardon, Edward, for some of the hard thoughts I have had of you. I consider this effort of yours a very striking one. You sacrifice your profits, I understand, to replacing the capital that has been misappropriated. Very proper.

EDWARD: No. No. To pay interest on the money that doesn't exist but ought to...for the profits don't really cover that or anything like it...Mr. Booth, you see the help you could give us, don't you?

MR. GEORGE BOOTH: By not prosecuting?

EDWARD: *(Earnestly.)* Beyond that. If you'd cut your losses...for now, and take only the return on that portion of your estate that still exists...why that would relieve me of four thousand three hundred a year...and I could do so much with it. There are one or two bad cases still. One woman—I believe you know her—it's not that she's so poor...and perhaps I'm not justified now in doing anything special...but she's got children...and if you'd help...

MR. GEORGE BOOTH: Stop, Edward...stop at once. If you attempt to confuse me I must seek professional advice. The Vicar and I have discussed this and quite made up our minds. And I've made a note or two.

(He produces a bit of paper and a pencil. EDWARD stiffens.)

MR. GEORGE BOOTH: May we understand that in straightening affairs you can show a proper preference for one client over another?

EDWARD: *(Pulled up, draws back in his chair.)* No...you had better not understand that.

MR. GEORGE BOOTH: Edward, do please be straightforward. Why can't you?

EDWARD: Why should I?

MR. GEORGE BOOTH: You certainly should. Do you mean to compare your father's ordinary business transactions— the hundreds of them—with his black treachery to the Vicar or to me?

EDWARD: Besides that, holding your tongue should be worth something extra now, shouldn't it?

MR. GEORGE BOOTH: I don't want to argue. My own position morally—and otherwise—is a strong one...so the Vicar impresses on me…and he has some head for business.

EDWARD: Well, what are your terms?

MR. GEORGE BOOTH: This is my note of them. (He takes refuge in his slip of paper.) I make these conditions, if you please, Edward, on the Vicar's behalf and my own. First, that you return to us any of our investments which have not been tampered with…then, that you continue, of course, to pay us the usual interest upon the rest of the capital, which ought to exist and does not. And finally, that you should, year by year, as a first priority, pay us back our capital…We will agree upon the sum…say a thousand a year. I doubt if you can ever restore to us all we have lost, but do your best to pay us back first, and we shan't complain, nor prosecute. There, and we both think that is extremely fair dealing!

(EDWARD does not take his eyes off MR. BOOTH until the whole meaning of the proposition has settled in his brain. Then without warning, he goes off into peals of laughter, much to the alarm of MR. BOOTH, who has never thought him over-sane.)

EDWARD: How funny! How very funny!

MR. GEORGE BOOTH: Edward…don't laugh!

EDWARD: I never heard anything quite so funny!

MR. GEORGE BOOTH: Edward, stop laughing.

EDWARD: Oh, you Christian gentlemen!

MR. GEORGE BOOTH: Don't be hysterical. The money's ours.

EDWARD: (EDWARD's laughter gives way to the deepest anger of which he is capable.) I'm giving my soul and body to restoring you and the rest to your precious moneybags. And you'll wring me dry… won't you? Won't you?

MR. GEORGE BOOTH: Now be reasonable.

EDWARD: Go to the devil, sir.

(He turns away from the flabbergasted old gentleman.)

MR. GEORGE BOOTH: Don't be rude.

EDWARD: I beg your pardon.

(There is a knock at the door.)

EDWARD: Come in.

(HONOR intrudes an apologetic head.)

HONOR: Am I interrupting business?

EDWARD: (Mirthlessly joking.) No. Business is over…quite over. Come in, Honor.

(HONOR puts on the table a market basket bulging with little paper parcels, and, oblivious of MR. BOOTH's distracted face, tries to fix his attention.)

HONOR: I thought, dear Mr. Booth, perhaps you wouldn't mind carrying round this basket of things yourself. It's so very damp underfoot that I don't want to send one of the maids out tonight if I can possibly avoid it…and if one doesn't get Christmas presents the very first thing on Christmas morning quite half the pleasure in them is lost, don't you think?

MR. GEORGE BOOTH: Yes…yes.

HONOR: (Fishing out the parcels one by one.) This is a bell for Mrs. Williams… something she said she wanted so that you can ring for her, which saves the maids; cap and apron for Mary; cap and apron for Ellen; shawl for Davis when she goes out to the larder—all useful presents—and that's something for you, but you're not to look at it till the morning.

(Having shaken each of them at the old gentleman, she proceeds to repack them. He is now trembling with anxiety to escape before any more of the family find him there.)

MR. GEORGE BOOTH: Thank you… thank you! I hope my lot has arrived. I left instructions…

HONOR: Quite safely…and I have hidden them. Presents are put on the breakfast table tomorrow.

(EDWARD speaks with an inconsequence that still further alarms MR. BOOTH.)

EDWARD: When we were children our Christmas breakfast was mostly made of chocolates.

(Before the basket is packed, MRS. VOYSEY sails slowly into the room, as smiling and as deaf as ever. MR. BOOTH does his best not to scowl at her.)

HONOR: Mother, have you left Booth all alone in the billiard room?

MRS. VOYSEY: Yes, dear.

(HONOR exits.)

MRS. VOYSEY: Are you feeling better, George?

MR. GEORGE BOOTH: No. *(Then he elevates his voice with a show of politeness.)* No thank you…I can't say I am.

MRS. VOYSEY: You don't look better.

MR. GEORGE BOOTH: I still have my headache. *(With a distracted shout.)* Headache!

MRS. VOYSEY: Bilious, perhaps! I quite understood you didn't care to dine. But why not have taken your coat off? How foolish in this warm room!

MR. GEORGE BOOTH: Thank you. I'm—er—just off.

(He seizes the market basket. At that moment BEATRICE appears.)

BEATRICE: Your shawl, Mother. *(And she clasps it round MRS. VOYSEY's shoulders.)*

MRS. VOYSEY: Thank you Beatrice, I thought I had it on. *(Then to MR. BOOTH who is now entangled in his comforter.)* A merry Christmas to you.

BEATRICE: Good evening, Mr. Booth.

MR. GEORGE BOOTH: I beg your pardon. Good evening, Beatrice.

(ETHEL enters, once again pregnant and carrying a sleeping infant.)

ETHEL: Why shouldn't we sit in here, now the table's cleared.

MR. GEORGE BOOTH: *(Sternly, now he is safe by the door.)* Will you see me out, Edward?

EDWARD: Yes.

(He follows the old man and his basket, leaving the others to distribute themselves about the room. It is the custom of the female members of the Voysey family, especially about Christmas time, to return to the dining room, when the table has been cleared, and occupy themselves in various ways which involve space and untidiness. BEATRICE has a little workbasket containing a buttonless glove and such things which she is rectifying. MRS. VOYSEY settles to the fire, opens the Nineteenth Century, *and is instantly absorbed in it.)*

BEATRICE: Does anyone want cocoa? Where's Honor?

ETHEL: Well…I'm afraid she's talking to Booth.

BEATRICE: Talking to Booth; good Heavens! I suspect she has taken my scissors.

ETHEL: And I think she's telling him about you.

BEATRICE: What about me?

ETHEL: About you and Hugh.

BEATRICE: Who set her on? It was carefully arranged no one was to be told till after Christmas.

ETHEL: But you told me…and Edward knows…and Mother knows…

BEATRICE: I warned Mother a year ago.

ETHEL: And I told Honor. And everyone seems to know except Booth.

(At this moment HONOR comes in, looking rather trodden upon. ETHEL concludes in the most audible of whispers.)

BEATRICE: Honor…

ETHEL: Don't say anything…it's my fault.

BEATRICE: *(Fixing her with a sever forefinger.)* …Have you taken my best scissors?

HONOR: *(Timidly.)* No, Beatrice.

BOOTH: *(From offstage.)* Beatrice!

ETHEL: *(Who is diving into the recesses of her sewing basket.)* Oh, here they are! I must have taken them. I do apologize!

HONOR: *(More timidly still.)* I'm afraid Booth's rather cross.

BEATRICE: *(With a shake of her head.)* Ethel…I've a good mind to make you do this sewing for me.

(In comes the MAJOR, strepitant. He takes, so to speak, just enough time to train himself on BEATRICE and then fires.)

MAJOR VOYSEY: Beatrice, what on earth is this Honor been telling me?

BEATRICE: *(With elaborate calm.)* Honor, what have you been telling Booth?

MAJOR VOYSEY: Please…please do not prevaricate.

MRS. VOYSEY: *(Looking over her spectacles.)* What did you say, Booth?

MAJOR VOYSEY: Do not prevaricate!

MRS. VOYSEY: I thought you were playing billiards together.

(EDWARD strolls back from dispatching MR. BOOTH, his face thoughtful.)

BEATRICE: I know quite well what you want to talk about, Booth. Discuss the matter by all means if it amuses you…but don't shout.

MAJOR VOYSEY: I use the voice nature has gifted me with, Beatrice.

BEATRICE: *(As she searches for a glove button.)* Nature did let herself go over your lungs.

HONOR: This is a family matter. Any member of the family has a right to express an opinion. I want Mother's. Mother, what do you think?

MRS. VOYSEY: *(Amicably.)* What about?

HONOR: Hugh and Beatrice separating.

MRS. VOYSEY: They haven't separated.

HONOR: But she means to.

MRS. VOYSEY: Fiddle-de-dee!

MAJOR VOYSEY: I quite agree with you.

BEATRICE: *(With a charming smile.)* Such reasoning would convert a stone.

MAJOR VOYSEY: Why have I not been told?

BEATRICE: You have just been told.

MAJOR VOYSEY: *(Thunderously.)* Before.

(ETHEL exits with the baby.)

BEATRICE: The truth is, dear Booth, we're all so afraid of you.

MAJOR VOYSEY: *(A little mollified.)* Ha...I should be glad to think that.

BEATRICE: *(Sweetly.)* Don't you?

MAJOR VOYSEY: *(Intensely serious.)* Beatrice, your callousness shocks me! That you can dream of deserting Hugh...a man who of all others, requires constant care and attention.

BEATRICE: Why do you suppose he spends most of his time abroad? The separation is as much Hugh's wish as mine.

MAJOR VOYSEY: I don't believe that.

BEATRICE: *(Her eyebrows up.)* Really!

MAJOR VOYSEY: All my life I've had to stand up for him...and by Jove, I'll continue to do so.

EDWARD: Booth...it's Christmas Eve.

BEATRICE: Is one never to be free of your bullying?

HONOR: You ought to be grateful.

BEATRICE: Well, I'm not.

HONOR: This is a family affair.

BEATRICE: It is not!

MAJOR VOYSEY: *(At the top of his voice.)* If all any of you can do is contradict...you'd better listen to what I've got to say...quietly.

(A hushed pause.)

MRS. VOYSEY: Would you like me to go, Booth?

MAJOR VOYSEY: *(Severely.)* No, Mother. Unless anything has been going on which cannot be discussed before you. *(To BEATRICE, more severely still.)* And I hope that is not so.

BEATRICE: Booth, you have a cheap mind.

MAJOR VOYSEY: Why do you wish to separate?

BEATRICE: *(Who sews on undisturbed.)* What's the use of telling you? You won't understand. We don't get on well together.

MAJOR VOYSEY: *(Amazedly.)* Is that all?

BEATRICE: *(Snapping at him.)* Yes, that's all. Can you find a better reason?

MAJOR VOYSEY: I've given up expecting common sense from you, Beatrice.

BEATRICE: It doesn't seem to me to make any sense that people should live together for purposes of mutual irritation.

MAJOR VOYSEY: *(Protesting.)* My dear girl, that sounds like a quotation from your last book.

BEATRICE: It isn't. I do think that you might read that book...for the honour of the family.

MAJOR VOYSEY: I bought several copies at once, Beatrice, and...

BEATRICE: That's the principal thing, of course.

MAJOR VOYSEY: *(...And discovering it.)* But do let us keep to the subject.

BEATRICE: *(With flattering sincerity.)* Certainly Booth. Hugh and I will be happier apart.

MAJOR VOYSEY: *(Obstinately.)* Why?

BEATRICE: *(With resolute patience, having vented a little sigh.)* He finds that my opinions distress him. And I have lost patience.

MRS. VOYSEY: *(Who has been trying to follow this through her spectacles.)* What does Beatrice say?

HONOR: *(Translating into a loud sing-song.)* That she wishes to leave her husband because she has lost patience.

MRS. VOYSEY: *(With considerable acrimony.)* Then you must be a very ill-tempered woman. All of my children are sweet natured.

MAJOR VOYSEY: *(Shouting self-consciously.)* Nonsense, Mother!

BEATRICE: *(Shouting good-humouredly.)* I quite agree with Booth. Still it has taken seven years working up to it to get angry with Hugh, and now that I am angry I shall never get pleased again.

MAJOR VOYSEY: *(The MAJOR returns to his subject refreshed by a moment's repose.)* How has he failed in his duty to you? Tell us.

BEATRICE: If I tell you, you won't understand. You understand nothing.

MRS. VOYSEY: *(MRS. VOYSEY leaves her armchair for her favourite station at the dining table.)* Booth is the only one of you I can hear at all distinctly. But if you foolish young people think you want to separate...try it. You'll soon come back to each other and be glad to. People can't fight against Nature for long. And marriage is a natural state...once you're married.

MAJOR VOYSEY: *(With intense approval.)* Quite right, Mother.

MRS. VOYSEY: I know.

(She resumes reading the Nineteenth Century. *And the MAJOR, to the despair of everybody, makes yet another start; trying oratory this time. ETHEL returns to the room.)*

MAJOR VOYSEY: My own opinion is, Beatrice, that you don't realize the meaning of the word marriage. I don't call myself a religious man...but, dash it all,

you were married in a Church. And you then entered upon an awful compact...! Surely, as a woman, Beatrice, the religious point of it ought to appeal to you. Good Lord...suppose everybody were to carry on like this! And have you considered that...whether you are right or whether you are wrong...if you desert Hugh you cut yourself off from the Family.

BEATRICE: *(With the sweetest of smiles.)* That will distress me terribly.

MAJOR VOYSEY: *(Not doubting her for a moment.)* Of course.

ETHEL: I wish to God I'd been able to cut myself off from the family! Look at Trenchard!

MAJOR VOYSEY: *(Gobbling a little at this unexpected attack.)* I do not forgive Trenchard for quarrelling with and deserting our father.

ETHEL: He quarrelled because that was his only way of escape.

MAJOR VOYSEY: Escape from what?

ETHEL: From tyranny...from hypocrisy...from boredom! From his happy English home...

BEATRICE: Now, my dear Ethel...it's no use...

MAJOR VOYSEY: *(Attempting sarcasm.)* Speak so that Mother can hear you!

ETHEL: Why are we all dull, cubbish, uneducated?...hopelessly middle class!

MAJOR VOYSEY: *(Taking this as very personal.)* Cubbish!

BEATRICE: Middle class! Ethel!

ETHEL: Yes...and pretentious as well! That's what happens when you're born to comfort. You only learn too late what the world wants of you and what it doesn't.

MAJOR VOYSEY: Who ever heard such nonsense?

BEATRICE: She's right, Booth. You escaped to the Army so of course you've never discovered what a Neanderthal you are. But think for a moment how easily the world could do without you! Strip yourself of your bourgeois income, and walk outside.

MAJOR VOYSEY: What would be the point of that? One must live.

BEATRICE: And if Booth can be said to think, he honestly thinks he's living.

MAJOR VOYSEY: (*Dignified and judicious.*) We will return, if you please, to the original subject of discussion. The question of separation...

BEATRICE: I mean to separate. And nothing you may say will prevent it. The only question is money. Can we come up with enough to live apart comfortably.

ETHEL: Comfortably!

HONOR: Well?

BEATRICE: Well, at the moment we can't.

MAJOR VOYSEY: Well?

BEATRICE: So we can't separate.

MAJOR VOYSEY: (*Speaking with bewilderment.*) Then what in heaven's name have we been discussing it for?

BEATRICE: I haven't discussed it. I don't want to discuss it. Can't you mind your own business?

MAJOR VOYSEY: I'm not an impatient man...but really...!

HONOR: You have never made the best of Hugh.

BEATRICE: I have spared him that indignity.

HONOR: But I am very glad that you can't separate.

BEATRICE: As soon as I am sure of earning enough I shall walk off from him.

MAJOR VOYSEY: (*His manly spirit stirs.*) You will do nothing of the sort, Beatrice.

BEATRICE: (*Unruffled.*) How will you stop me, Booth?

MAJOR VOYSEY: I shall tell Hugh he must command you to stay.

BEATRICE: It was one of the illusions of my girlhood that I'd love a man who would master me.

MAJOR VOYSEY: Hugh must assert himself.

BEATRICE: Ah...if only I'd married you, Booth!

MAJOR VOYSEY: (*The MAJOR's face grows beatific.*) Well, I must own to thinking that I am a masterful man...that it's the duty of every man to be so. (*He adds forgivingly.*) Poor old Hugh!

BEATRICE: If I tried to leave you, Booth, you'd have me whipped...wouldn't you?

MAJOR VOYSEY: (*Ecstatically complacent.*) Ha...well...!

BEATRICE: Do say yes. Think how it will frighten Honor.

(*HONOR leaves. The MAJOR strokes his mustache and is most friendly.*)

MAJOR VOYSEY: I quite see your point of view, Beatrice. (*The MAJOR leaves them.*)

BEATRICE: Do you find men difficult, Ethel?

ETHEL: (*Putting her knitting down to consider the matter.*) No. It's best to let them talk themselves out. When Denis has done that he'll often come to me for advice. Though I like him to get his own way as much as possible…or think he's getting it. Otherwise he becomes so depressed.

BEATRICE: (Quietly amused.) Edward shouldn't hear this. (Then to him.) These are women's secrets.

EDWARD: I won't tell…and I'm a bachelor.

ETHEL: (Solemnly as she takes up her knitting again.) Do you really mean to leave Hugh?

BEATRICE: (Slightly impatient.) Ethel, I've said so.

(ALICE MAITLAND comes in gaily.)

ALICE: What's Booth shouting about in the billiard room?

ETHEL: (Pained.) Oh, on Christmas Eve, too!

BEATRICE: Don't you take any interest in my matrimonial affairs?

MRS. VOYSEY: (Shuts up the Nineteenth Century and removes her spectacles.) That's a very interesting article. The Chinese Empire must be in a shocking state. Is it ten o'clock yet?

EDWARD: Past.

MRS. VOYSEY: (As EDWARD is behind her.) Can anyone see the clock?

ALICE: It's past ten, Auntie.

MRS. VOYSEY: Then I think I'll go to my room.

ETHEL: Shall I come and look after you, Mother?

MRS. VOYSEY: If you'll find Honor for me, Ethel.

(ETHEL goes in search and MRS. VOYSEY begins her nightly chant of departure.)

MRS. VOYSEY: Good night, Alice. Good night, Edward.

EDWARD: Good night, Mother.

MRS. VOYSEY: (With sudden severity.) I'm not pleased with you, Beatrice.

BEATRICE: I'm sorry, Mother.

(But without waiting to be answered, the old lady has sailed out of the room. BEATRICE, EDWARD, and ALICE, now left together, are attuned to each other enough to be able to talk with ease.)

BEATRICE: They, none of them, speak of your fate, Edward. That's too shameful.

EDWARD: Yes. I sit at my desk daily as the poor servant of men whose ultimate ideal is three thousand pounds a year.

BEATRICE: Edward…however scandalous your father was, he left you a man's work to do.

EDWARD: An outlaw's.

BEATRICE: Well, that's what I mean.

EDWARD: Do you know what I discovered the other day about him? He actually saved the firm once. It's true. A pretty capable piece of heroism! Then, eight years afterwards…he started thieving again.

BEATRICE: (Greatly interested.) Did he now?

EDWARD: He must have found himself in trouble…

BEATRICE: Never! He knew what he was doing. He had imagination, didn't he? A great financier must find scope for his abilities or die. I'm sure he despised your fat little clients, living snugly in their three-thousand-pound-a-year world…and so one day he woke up and thought, why not put them and their money to the best use he could. Do you see?

EDWARD: Fine phrases for a robber, Beatrice.

BEATRICE: Quite so. But he was a bit of a genius too. You can't admit it, Edward. Splendid criminals like your father leave honest men too much mess to tidy up. But he *had* genius, Edward, hadn't he?

EDWARD: Yes.

BEATRICE: And he must have made a great deal of honest money, in his time.

EDWARD: A great deal.

BEATRICE: Perhaps, as much as he stole?

EDWARD: Well, perhaps half as much. Almost. Who knows?

BEATRICE: Well. And everyone loved him.

ALICE: I did.

EDWARD: My father was a swindler and a cheat.

BEATRICE: But my dear, Edward... hasn't your own golden deed been robbing your rich clients to benefit the poor?

EDWARD: *(Gently.)* But Beatrice, we're all a bit in debt to the poor, aren't we?

BEATRICE: If you think about it, Edward, your father's lack of conscience sprang from a taste for power and display. Yours comes from charity. That's all the difference between you. But even a brittle little cynic like myself, who spends her life scribbling cynical disapproving phrases, can, when no one's looking, appreciate how sacred that difference may be. Robbery! In your hands, Edward. Can it be a beautiful word?

EDWARD: I think he might have told me the truth sooner.

BEATRICE: Perhaps he didn't know it! Or perhaps he thought you'd go to the police. Why didn't you?

EDWARD: I thought I could do some good. And after he died I thought if I put some of the mischief he'd done right, it might make a difference for him, wherever he is. For Beatrice, you know, I loved him, too.

BEATRICE: Through it all?

EDWARD: Yes, and not just from habit.

BEATRICE: Well... *(With reverence in her voice now.)* That might silence a bench of judges. *(Another moment, and she collects her sewing, gets up and goes.)*

(ALICE has had all the while a keen eye on EDWARD.)

ALICE: Something has happened...since dinner.

EDWARD: Can you see that?

ALICE: What is it?

EDWARD: *(With sudden exultation.)* The smash has come and not by my fault. Old George Booth...

ALICE: I saw him leaving.

EDWARD: Can you imagine? That old man forced me to tell him the truth. I told him to take his money...what there was of it...and prosecute. Well, he won't prosecute. Instead he bargains to take whatever's left, and then bleed us, sovereign by sovereign, as I earn sovereign by sovereign with the sweat of my soul till he has everything. And the vicar has been told...who has told his wife, who has telegraphed to Canterbury by now. So it's all over at last, and I'm glad.

ALICE: And now?

EDWARD: Who knows? The half-dozen poor souls I've pulled from the fire are safe. The police won't easily discover how I managed it. And I shan't confess. But the firm's done, and so am I. So it's prison I suppose. And Peace on Earth, goodwill toward men. Good night, now, Alice.

ALICE: And bankruptcy?

EDWARD: No doubt.

ALICE: How will you live?

EDWARD: Well, if I'm not a long-term guest of His Majesty, I'll live poorly at best, Alice.

ALICE: How lucky for me.

EDWARD: How's that?

ALICE: It gives me a bargaining chip.

EDWARD: For what?

ALICE: Edward, why have you become such a sloven? You've let yourself go.

EDWARD: I'm sorry.

ALICE: And you don't eat properly. You're deliberately unhappy.

EDWARD: Is happiness under one's control?

ALICE: My dear, you shouldn't neglect your happiness any more than you neglect to wash your face.

EDWARD: Alice, I apologize, but I've been forced to put every effort into work…Don't scold me.

ALICE: What shall we do about it, Edward? Is there nothing you still want from life…want for its own sake? *(She looks at him for a moment.)* That's a test.

EDWARD: Nothing.

ALICE: Of course there is! Dare. Go ahead. You needn't be afraid. It's so long past—that awful time when I thought you were a prig.

EDWARD: Did you?

ALICE: I'm afraid so. But I think he's mostly gone.

EDWARD: I'm glad.

ALICE: Go on. What are you afraid of?

EDWARD: Alice, they may put me in prison.

ALICE: Yes?

EDWARD: And who'll be the man who comes out?

ALICE: I shall be most interested to see.

EDWARD: No, no! You're out of this, thank God. It's the one thing I have to be grateful for. I stand alone. And when the disgrace comes it may leave me homeless, but it won't touch you.

(There he sits shaken. ALICE waits a moment, not taking her eyes off him; then speaks.)

ALICE: Edward, there's something else. You've still given up proposing to me. Certainly that shows a lack of character…and of perseverance.

EDWARD: No, no, no we mustn't be stupid.

ALICE: *(With serene strength.)* I know you want me. And while I live…where I am will be your home.

EDWARD: No, it's too late. And be glad it's too late. If you'd said yes to me before…

ALICE: Marry you when you were only a well-principled prig…Thanks! I didn't want you…But now I do and one must always take what one wants.

EDWARD: My dear, what would we have to build a marriage on? Poverty and prison.

ALICE: You seem to think that all the money in the world was invested in your precious firm. I have nine hundred a year of my own. At least let me tempt you with that.

EDWARD: You can't.

ALICE: Oh, my dear, don't be afraid if you love me.

EDWARD: *(Sets his teeth against temptation.)* I don't.

ALICE: *(She smiles.)* I don't believe you.

EDWARD: No, Alice…let it end here. It's absurd.

ALICE: Am I unworthy? All right, if you don't think me your equal as woman to man we'll drop it and never speak of it again. But if you do, know I love you with all my heart. If I didn't should I embarrass myself like this? Now look at me and make your choice.

EDWARD: If they don't put me in prison…

ALICE: No, Edward, now or never. I won't take you later. Refuse me my life and happiness, and yours, at this moment…or take my hand.

(She puts out her hand frankly, as a friend should. With only a second's thought he takes it as frankly.)

EDWARD: Alice, we can't be married now.

ALICE: *(With firmness enough for two.)* Yes, it will surprise the vicar when we call. *(She sits beside him and quite cheerfully changes the subject.)* Now, about old George Booth. What will he do?

EDWARD: Nothing, I'll turn myself in before he has a chance.

ALICE: Can't we bargain with him and the others to keep the firm going somehow? Throw ourselves on their mercy? For if we can I'm afraid we must.

EDWARD: *(Makes a last attempt to abandon himself to his troubles.)* No, Alice, let it end. It's useless. They'll all be round in a day or two after their capital like wasps after honey. And when they find how little is left, what sort of mercy will they have?

ALICE: Suppose we have them meet. Gather them all together and tell them what's happened. And that you're willing to continue as you have been. I don't think they'd put you in prison, then, for it wouldn't pay them.

EDWARD: Good Lord, I don't want to continue. I want to be free. To rest, or turn round and say I've either succeeded or failed.

ALICE: That's asking too much.

EDWARD: You don't know what it's like…

ALICE: No, you've kept it to yourself. But it will be better now, for the fear of discovery will be gone. You'll be able to sleep. And you won't be alone. For there's to be our life now. And that will matter.

EDWARD: I suppose they might agree to syndicate themselves, and keep me at it for life.

ALICE: You'll convince them. They aren't all so stupid.

EDWARD: They believed in my father.

ALICE: And he swindled them. Now they'll have you. What more could they ask?

EDWARD: It's good to be praised sometimes…by you.

ALICE: *(Close to him.)* Yes. Well, I'm foolish proud.

EDWARD: So, I'll make a stab at it.

ALICE: I thought you might. So then, I suppose it's late.

EDWARD: Yes, good night. Merry Christmas, Alice.

ALICE: Good night. You know, Edward, you still haven't…

EDWARD: *Will* you marry me?

ALICE: I will. I will. I will.

(They look at each other.)

ALICE: Well?

EDWARD: Yes, all right.

(He kisses her for the first time.)

ALICE: *(Steps back from him, adding happily, with perhaps just a touch of shyness.)* My heart. Till tomorrow.

(She walks to the doorway, turns around, and they both laugh.)

EDWARD: *(Echoing in gratitude the hope and promise in her voice.)* Till tomorrow.

FAREWELL TO THE THEATRE

Mint Theater Company's production of *A Farewell to the Theater*, written by Harley Granville Barker, began performances on November 10, 2000, at the Mint Theater, 311 West 43rd Street, New York City, with the following cast and credits:

Edward...George Morfogen
Dorothy...Sally Kemp

Directed by: Gus Kaikkonen
Set Design by: Sarah Lambert
Costume Design by: Henry Shaffer
Lighting Design by: William Armstrong
Original Music: Ellen Mandel
Production Stage Manager: Rachel R. Bush
Assistant Stage Manager: Erin Riggs
Press Representative: David Gersten & Associates
Graphic Design: Jude Dvorak

This talk took place in EDWARD's office. He is a London solicitor and his office reflects his standing. It is, that is to say, a musty dusty room in a house two hundred years old or so, now mercilessly chopped into offices. The woodwork is so old and cracked that new paint looks old on it and fresh paper on the walls looks dingy in a day. You may clean the windows (and it is sometimes done) but nothing will make them shine. The floor has been polished and stained and painted and scraped and painted again till it hardly looks like wood at all. And the furniture is old, not old enough to be interesting, old enough to be very respectable. There are some pictures on the wall. One is a good print of Lord Mansfield, one represents a naval battle, the third a nondescript piece of mountain scenery. How the battle and the nondescript came there nobody knows. One pictures some distracted client arriving with them under his arm. They were left to lean against the wall ten years or so; then a clerk hung them up. The newest thing in the room and quite the strangest seeming there is a photograph on the mantelpiece of EDWARD's daughter, and that has been here nine years or so, ever since she died. A pretty child.

Well, the papers renew themselves and the room is full of them, bundles and bundles and bundles. They spread about poor ED-WARD like the leaves of a forest; they lie packed close like last year's leaves and in time are buried deep like leaves of the year before last. His clerk knows what they all are and where everything is. He flicks a feather duster over them occasionally and has been observed to put some—very reluctantly—away. Very reluctantly. For, after all, these are the fabric of a first-class practice and it is his instinct to have them in evidence. EDWARD has never thought about it. Thus was the room when his uncle walked out of it and he walked in and thus he will leave it in a few years for some junior partner.

Note the signs then by which a lawyer marks himself above reproach. Beware the businesslike well-polished office, clicking with machinery. There works a man who does not practice law so much as make a practice of it. Beware!

EDWARD is at his desk. Wherever else is he, unless he rises wearily to stretch his long limbs before the fire? Thin, humourous, and rather more than middle-aged, a sensitive, distinguished face. One likes EDWARD.

His clerk shows in DOROTHY TAVERN-ER. Everybody knows MISS DOROTHY TAVERNER. The clerk beams at her with forgetful joy—shamelessly at her while he tries to say to EDWARD, "Miss Taverner, sir." Then he departs.

EDWARD: How punctual!

DOROTHY: Twelve ten by the clock out there. Your note said eleven thirty.

EDWARD: And I said "How punctual!"

(They shake hands like the oldest friends. He bends a little over her pretty hand.)

DOROTHY: You have no right to send for me at all when I'm rehearsing...and you know it.

EDWARD: It was urgent. Sit down.

DOROTHY: My dear Edward, nothing is more urgent than that my rehearsals should go right...and if I leave the company to the mercy of my understudy and this author-boy...though he's a nice author-boy...they don't.

EDWARD: I'm sure they don't.

DOROTHY: His beating heart tells him that we must all be bad actors because we don't live and move just like the creatures as he began thinking them into being. He almost weeps. Then I tell him God called him into collaboration fifty-three flying years too late as far as I'm concerned.

EDWARD: Oh…Oh!

DOROTHY: Fifty-four will have flown on November the next eighteenth. And that cheers us all up and we start again. Well, dear friend, you are fifty-seven and you…look it. *(Having made her point, she pauses for effect.)*

EDWARD: *(Carefully places legal documents on one side.)* My dear Dorothy…

DOROTHY: That tone means that a little business talk has now begun. Where's the rickety paper-knife that I play with? Thank you.

EDWARD: Vernon Dix and…Boothby, is that the name of your treasurer?…paid me a formal visit yesterday afternoon.

DOROTHY: Behind my back! What about?

EDWARD: They complain you won't look at your balance sheets…

DOROTHY: *(With cheerful charm.)* But they're liars. I look at them every week.

EDWARD: …That you won't study them.

DOROTHY: I'm studying a new part.

EDWARD: They brought me a pretty full statement. I spent some hours over it.

DOROTHY: More money wanted?

EDWARD: They also brought me the estimate for this new play.

DOROTHY: It'll be exceeded.

EDWARD: Can more money be found?

DOROTHY: We can search.

EDWARD: You remember the last search.

DOROTHY: The rent's paid till Christmas.

EDWARD: Trust your landlord!

DOROTHY: This play may do well.

EDWARD: It may not.

DOROTHY: *(Gives a sigh. With an impatient gesture or two she takes off her hat and puts it obliviously on EDWARD's inkstand. She runs her fingers through her front hair, takes out a hairpin, and viciously replaces it. Signs, these are, that she is worried.)* Yes, I remember the last search. Nearly kissed by old James Levison for Dear Art's sake. At my age! I wonder did he guess what an even choice it was between five thousand pounds and boxing his flat white ears.

EDWARD: There was Shelburne's five thousand and Mrs. Minto's…

DOROTHY: Well, I did kiss Lord Shelburne…he's a dear. Blue-eyed and over seventy or under twenty…then I always want to kiss them. Why?

EDWARD: My eyes…alas…were never blue and never will be now.

DOROTHY: Because I suppose then they don't care whether I do or not. All that money gone? I'm sorry. Mrs. Minto can't afford it.

EDWARD: No, it's not all gone. And another five thousand will make you safe through this season. Another ten thousand unless you've very bad luck should carry you to Christmas…otherwise, if this new play isn't an instant success, you must close.

DOROTHY: *(Sits upright in her chair.)* I have been in management for sixteen years. I have paid some dividends. "Dividends" is correct, I think.

EDWARD: I keep a sort of abstract which reminds me of the fearful and wonderful way you have been financed.

DOROTHY: Dear Edward, I should have cheated everybody but for you.

EDWARD: I have also managed mostly to stop you from cheating yourself. Dorothy, it is odd that the people who put money in only to make some did often manage to make it out of you, while the people who stumped up for art's sake and yours never got anything at all.

DOROTHY: I don't see anything odd in that. They got what they wanted. People always do. Some of them got the art...and one of them nearly got me.

EDWARD: Why didn't you marry him, Dorothy? A good fellow...a good match.

DOROTHY: Oh, my dear! Marry him? Marry! Confound him...why did he ask me? Now I can't ever ask *him* for a penny again. Yes...on that bright Sunday morning the manageress was tempted, I won't deny.

EDWARD: But the record of the past five years does not warrant your promising more dividends...and that's the truth.

DOROTHY: Well...shall we hide the balance sheets away and shall I gird myself with boastfulness once more...once weary more? What is our record for Dear Art's Sake? Shakespeare...without scenery...Molière, Holberg, Ibsen, Strindberg, Maeterlinck, Shaw, Hauptmann, d'Annunzio, Benevente, Giacosa, Parraval, Ostrowsky, Lavalliere, Chekhov, Galsworthy, Masefield, Henniker and Borghese, Brieux, Yeats, van Arpent, and Claudel. Some of it sounds quite old-fashioned already...and some has begun to pay. When a Knight of the Garter dies, you know, they proclaim his title over his tomb. You'll have to come to my burning, Edward, and through a trumpet of rolled-up balance sheets proclaim my titles to fame. "She, here deceased, did her duty by them, Shakespeare, Ibsen"...How I hate boasting! And boasting to millionaires to get money out of them. I'm as vain as a peacock still...but boasting I hate.

EDWARD: Then consider. You can see through the production of this...what's it called?

DOROTHY: "The Salamander." Good title!

EDWARD: If it fails...shut up...finally.

DOROTHY: Yes...I've been thinking of doing that, Edward. "The Salamander" won't succeed in the fine full business sense...though now I've whispered that for the first time it most perversely may.

EDWARD: Then what on earth are you putting it up for?

DOROTHY: Because it's good enough ...and then the next can be better. It won't succeed because I've only a small part in it. Say Egoist...say Actress.

EDWARD: Wiser to keep out altogether.

DOROTHY: And then it wouldn't succeed because the dear Public would think I didn't believe in it enough. Queer silly children the dear Public are, aren't they? For ten years now my acting is held to have grown steadily worse, so quite rightly they won't rush to plays with me in them. But then they won't have my plays with me out of them either. So what's a poor body to do?

EDWARD: I don't hold that your acting has grown steadily worse.

DOROTHY: Well...not steadily perhaps. But I never was steady, was I? And you don't like the parts I choose?

EDWARD: Not when you hide yourself behind them.

DOROTHY: I never do.

EDWARD: Your old self! But I want you to finish with it all anyway.

DOROTHY: Why?

EDWARD: Because I fear I see heartbreak ahead.

DOROTHY: That you need never look to see...

EDWARD: You still do care...far too much.

DOROTHY: Do I hanker for the old thrill...like wine bubbling in one's heart...and then the stir in the audience when...on I came. Dear friend, you now prefer my acting...off the stage. My well-known enthusiasm. It seems to me it rings more tinny every day. I'm glad it takes you in. Still, even that's only an echo...growing fainter since I died.

EDWARD: My dear Dorothy.

DOROTHY: Oh...but you knew I was dead. You own now to mourning me. You know the day and hour I died. Hypocrite...I remember how you congratulated me on the tragic occasion...kissing my hand...you're the only man that does it naturally. Doesn't that abstract remind you when we produced "The Flight of the Duchess"?

EDWARD: Many of us thought you very good.

DOROTHY: Because I was far, far better than many a bad actress would have been. It is the queerest sensation, Edward, to be dead...though after a while you get quite used to it. Are you still alive, by the way?

EDWARD: There is the same feeble flicker that there has ever been.

DOROTHY: Burn on, dear Edward, burn on...that I may warm my poor hands sometimes at the flames you are.

EDWARD: It can serve no better purpose.

DOROTHY: No...so I'm sure I think.

(There falls a little silence. Then EDWARD speaks, the more bitterly that it is without anger.)

EDWARD: Damn them! I'd damn their souls, if they had any. They've helped themselves to you at so much a time for... how many years? Dorothy...what have they ever given you in return?

DOROTHY: Oh, if that were all my grievance I'd be a happy ghost this day. If I'd a thousand souls and they wanted them...the dear Public...as they need them...God knows they do...they should have every one, for me. What does the law say, Edward? Is a soul private property?

EDWARD: There are decisions against it.

DOROTHY: Then I prefer your law to your religion. It's more public-spirited.

EDWARD: My ancestral brand of religion, my dear, taught me to disapprove very strongly of the theatre.

DOROTHY: And after watching my career you've found out why. How long have you been in this office, Edward?

EDWARD: Thirty years, nearly.

DOROTHY: The weight of them! Do you remember having tea at Richmond...at the Roebuck at Richmond...when they'd offered you this billet and we talked wisely of the future?

EDWARD: I do.

DOROTHY: And I made you take it, didn't I?

EDWARD: You did.

DOROTHY: And I wouldn't marry you.

(EDWARD looks at her. One side of his mouth twitches a little. You might charitably call it a smile. But his eyes are smiling.)

DOROTHY: Don't say you didn't ask me to marry you.

EDWARD: On that occasion?

DOROTHY: Yes...on that occasion, too. That's what one calls the Past, isn't it? How right I was...and what successes we've both been.

EDWARD: My son Charles tells me that I have done very well. Do you know, I was moved to ask him the other night as we sat in the box whether he wasn't in love with you?

DOROTHY: Do you think it's hereditary?

EDWARD: He said he had been as a boy.

DOROTHY: How old is he?

EDWARD: Twenty-three.

DOROTHY: Bless him! I do regret sometimes.

EDWARD: What did happen...so suddenly?

DOROTHY: To us? What happens to the summer? You go walking one day and you feel that it has gone.

EDWARD: You've been that to the Theatre.

DOROTHY: A summer day...a long, long summer day. Thank you. I prefer the sonnet which calls me a breath of spring. But truly he died, my famous poet...oh, that lion's head of his!...before I was full blown.

EDWARD: I know it by heart.

DOROTHY: It's a good sonnet.

EDWARD: It makes history of you.

DOROTHY: And it never made me vain a bit because indeed I knew it was true. Yes, I like to be standard literature.

EDWARD: Easy enough for a poet to be public-spirited over you.

DOROTHY: But from the time I was born, Edward, I believe I knew my destiny. And I've never quarrelled with it...never. I can't imagine how people get along if they don't know by sheer instinct what they're meant to be and do. What muddles they must make of life!

EDWARD: They do...and then come to me for advice. It's how you told me to earn my living.

DOROTHY: You only tell them what the law says and what two and two make. That's all you ever tell me. But what I was alive for I have always known. So of course I knew when I died.

EDWARD: Dorothy, my dear, it hurts me to hear you say it.

DOROTHY: Why? We must all die and be born again...how many times in our lives? I went home that night and sent poor old Sarah to bed. And I didn't curse and break things...I'd always let myself do that a little on occasion...it seemed so much more human...when I was alone...oh, only when I was quite alone. But that night it had all been different...and I sat still in the dark...and wondered...wondered what was to happen now. It's a frightening thing at best to lose your old and well-trained trusted self...and not know what the new one's going to be. I was angry. I had rehearsed the wretched play so well too. Why do people think I've no brains, Edward?

EDWARD: I suppose because you're so pretty.

DOROTHY: Or perhaps because I don't use them for the things they were never meant to be used for. I've sometimes thought, since I can't act any longer, I might show the dear Public my rehearsing.

That'd teach them! But there...I've come down to wanting to teach them. Time to retire. For, you see, after that night I wasn't born again. Something...didn't happen. And a weary business it has been finding out what. With the dear Public helping me to discover...hard on them, they've thought it. And you so patient with my passion to keep on failing...hard on you. For you've not understood. I've disappointed you these later years. Own up.

EDWARD: If it's admitted that all my heart is your most humble servant I'll own up again to disapproving of the Theatre...to disapproving most thoroughly of acting and of actors too...and to doubly disapproving when any new nonsense about them is added to life's difficulties.

DOROTHY: Yes...if life's so important! Well...I have four hundred a year, *safe*, to retire on, haven't I, Edward?

EDWARD: As safe as money can be.

DOROTHY: I do think that money ought to learn to be safe. It has no other virtues. And I've got my Abbey.

EDWARD: Milford Abbey is safe for you from everything but earthquake.

DOROTHY: How utterly right that I should end my days in a shanty built out of the stones of that great Abbey and buttressed up in its shell.

EDWARD: Is it?

DOROTHY: Oh. Edward, if you had but the artist's sense of the eternal fitness of things, you'd find it such a help...

EDWARD: ...To imagining Miss Dorothy leading the Milford monks a dance.

DOROTHY: Well...their religion was not of this world, nor is mine. But yours is, dear Edward. Therefore the follies of art

and saintliness must seem to you two sorts of folly and not one. St. Francis would have understood me. I should have been his dear sister Happiness. But you and the railway trains running on time would have puzzled him no end.

EDWARD: What foolishness makes you say you're dead, my dear?

DOROTHY: While...if I'd lived the cautious life, I shouldn't be. If I'd sold my fancies for a little learning, virginity for a gold ring, likings for good manners, hate for silence...if I ever could have learnt the world's way...to measure out gifts for money and thanks...well, I'd have been married to you perhaps, Edward. And then you never could have enjoyed my Imogen as you used to enjoy it. You used to say it was a perfect tonic.

EDWARD: So it was!

DOROTHY: Yes, dear, you never had a gift for subtle expression, had you?

EDWARD: From the beginning I suppose you expected more of life than ever I could find in it.

DOROTHY: Whatever I expected, my friend, I bargained for nothing at all.

EDWARD: I'd like you to know this, Dorothy, that...for all my rectangular soul, as you used to call it...when I asked you to marry me...

DOROTHY: On which of those great occasions?

EDWARD: On the various occasions I did ask you before I did...otherwise... marry.

DOROTHY: I think there were five...or six. I recall them with pride.

EDWARD: But not with enough of it to ensure accuracy.

DOROTHY: And was it never just for the sake of repeating yourself?

EDWARD: No. When I was most ridiculously in love I used to think three times before I faced a life with you in that...

DOROTHY: Well?

EDWARD: That flowery wilderness which was your life. I knew there were no safe roads for me there. And yet I asked you...knowing that very well.

DOROTHY: I'm glad...for your sake...that you risked it.

EDWARD: Glad, for your own, *you* didn't?

DOROTHY: Did you really only marry her because I told you to?

EDWARD: I fear so.

DOROTHY: That was a wrong reason for doing the right thing. But I could not have one of the ablest men of his set in everything else said at his club to be sentimentalizing his life away about me...I really couldn't. They told me she was desperately in love with you. And I never would have spoken to you again if you hadn't married her. Edward, it was never hard on her, was it?

EDWARD: No, Dorothy, I hope and think it never was. I made her happy in every ordinary sense...at least I felt she felt so.

DOROTHY: And you did love her, didn't you, Edward?

EDWARD: I shouldn't put this into words perhaps. I thought through those twenty-five years I gave her all the love that her love asked for. But the world of...folly, one calls it...into which your laugh had once lifted me...

DOROTHY: Or was it wisdom?

EDWARD: That, my dear Dorothy, was the problem you would never consent to try and solve.

DOROTHY: She never could have liked me, Edward.

EDWARD: She thought you a great artist. She had judgment and taste, you know.

DOROTHY: Yes...she thought me an attack of scarlet fever, let us say...and that it was a very beautiful scarlet.

EDWARD: Dorothy, somehow that hurts.

DOROTHY: I'm sorry.

EDWARD: Some years before she died, her nature seemed to take a fresh start, as it were. It shot out in the oddest ways...over a home for horses and cooking reforms...and a most romantic scheme for sending strayed servant girls to Australia to get married. If there had been any genius in my love for her...would she have had to wait till forty-five and then find only those crabbed half-futile shoots of inner life begin to show? While her children were amused...and I was tolerant! For quite incurably middle-aged she was by then...

DOROTHY: Had she dreaded that?

EDWARD: Not a bit. Not even in fun...as we made such a fuss of doing.

DOROTHY: Admirable Ethel! Clear-eyed and so firm-footed on this spinning earth. And Life her duty...to be punctually and cheerfully done. But overtrained a little, don't you think...just for her happiness sake.

EDWARD: She didn't count *her* happiness.

DOROTHY: She should have.

EDWARD: She shouldn't have died when she did.

DOROTHY: The doctors were fools.

EDWARD: Well, it was a while after...remembering my love for you...I suddenly saw how perhaps, after all, I had wronged her.

DOROTHY: It was just three years after that you asked me to marry you again.

EDWARD: You forgave me. Let's forget it. It was good to feel I was still a bit of a fool.

DOROTHY: Folly for certain, it was then?

EDWARD: And not so old at heart as you thought.

DOROTHY: I like your declarations, Edward. They're different. But never from the beginning have you been like the others.

EDWARD: And I was never jealous of any of the three.

DOROTHY: Four.

EDWARD: Four?

DOROTHY: One that you never knew about. I told you though I should never marry...and I never have. Perhaps I'm as frightened at the meaning I might find in it...as you ought to have been.

EDWARD: They made you just as miserable at times, Dorothy, as if you had married them.

DOROTHY: Poor dears.

EDWARD: And two out of the three were really perfect fools.

DOROTHY: Three out of the four, my friend, were perfect fools...helpless fools.

EDWARD: Then which wasn't?

DOROTHY: The one you never guessed about. Don't try to, even now. He never really cared for me, you see...and I knew he didn't...and so I was ashamed to tell you.

EDWARD: Now when was that?

DOROTHY: You're trying to guess.

EDWARD: No, honestly...

DOROTHY: Do you remember a time when I was very cross with life and wouldn't act for a whole year...in the days when I still could? I went down to Grayshott and started a garden...a failure of a garden. And you came down to see me...and we talked into the dark. And I said I ought to have married Father's scrubby-headed assistant and had ten children...

EDWARD: I vaguely remember.

DOROTHY: Well, it wasn't then...but shortly after.

EDWARD: You wanted that experience...

DOROTHY: No, no! How dare you? Am I that sort of a creature...collecting sensations? Sometimes, Edward, I find you the biggest fool of the lot...a fool at heart, which is worse than a fool at head... and wickeder.

EDWARD: I'm sorry!

DOROTHY: Never mind, it's not your fault now if fresh air disagrees with you. And you can't open the window here, for only dust comes in.

EDWARD: Is the room stuffy?

DOROTHY: Yes...but so's London... and so's life.

EDWARD: I do remember there was a time when I thought you were hardening a little.

DOROTHY: Well, it wasn't from that bruising. No man or woman in this world shall make me hard.

EDWARD: Dorothy, will you marry me?

DOROTHY: *(Her voice pealing out.)* Oh, my dear!

EDWARD: That's what you said to Blackthorpe when he offered you his millions on a bright Sunday morning. Don't say it to me.

DOROTHY: I never called him My Dear...I was much too proper...and so is he! But you are the Dear of one corner of my heart...it is the same old corner always kept for you. No, no...that sort of love doesn't live in it. So for the...seventh?...Let's make it the seventh time...oh, yes, I wear them on my memory's breast like medals...no, I won't.

EDWARD: Very well. If you don't want to raise five thousand pounds you'd better close the theatre after this next play's produced.

DOROTHY: Heavens above...that's what we started to discuss. What have we been talking of since?

EDWARD: Dear Dorothy...I never do know what we talk of. I only know that by the time I've got it round to business it's time for you to go.

DOROTHY: Yes, I said I'd be back at the theatre by half-past twelve.

EDWARD: It's long after.

DOROTHY: I'm so glad. They'll finish the act without me and lunch. I never want food. Isn't it odd?

EDWARD: Do you decide to close the theatre after this next play?

DOROTHY: I decide not to ask man, woman, or devil for another penny.

EDWARD: Then you close.

DOROTHY: But if it's a success?

EDWARD: Then, when it's finished, you may have a few pounds more than four hundred a year.

DOROTHY: I don't want 'em.

EDWARD: But you'll close?

DOROTHY: I will. This time I really will and never, never open again. I want my Abbey. I want to sit in the sun and spoil my complexion and acquire virtue. Do you know I can have fourteen volumes at a time from the London Library?

EDWARD: Yes...don't spoil your complexion.

DOROTHY: Well...when it is really *my* complexion and no longer the dear Public's I may get to like it better. To acquire knowledge for its own sake! Do you never have that hunger on you? To sit and read long books about Byzantium. Not frothy foolish blank verse plays...but nice thick meaty books. To wonder where the Goths went when they vanished out of Italy. Knowledge and Beauty! It's only when you love them for their own sake that they yield their full virtue to you. And you can't deceive them...they always know.

EDWARD: I'm told that the secret of moneymaking's something like that.

DOROTHY: Oh, a deadlier one. Money's alive and strong. And when money loves *you*...look out.

EDWARD: It has never wooed me with real passion. Six and eightpences add up slowly.

DOROTHY: *(Throws herself back in her chair and her eyes up to the ceiling.)* You've never seen me asking for money and boasting about my art, have you?

EDWARD: That has been spared me.

DOROTHY: I'm sorry you've missed it forever. It is just as if the millionaire and I...

EDWARD: Though they weren't always millionaires.

DOROTHY: They were at heart. I always felt we were striking some weird bargain. For all I'd see at his desk was a rather apologetic little man...though the Giant Money was outlined round him like an aura. And he'd seem to be begging me as humbly as he dared to help save his little soul...You have made rather an arid world of it, haven't you, Edward...And you used to bite your pipe and talk nonsense to me about acting...about its necessarily debilitating effect, my dear Dorothy, upon the moral character! Edward, would I cast for a king or a judge or a duchess actors that couldn't believe more in reigning or judging or lawyering than you wretched amateurs do?

EDWARD: We "put it over," as you vulgar professionals say.

DOROTHY: Do you think so? Because your public can't tell the difference, as the voice of my business manager drones. I've fancied sometimes that poor actors, playing parts...but with real faith in their unreal...yet live those lives of yours more truly. Why...swiftly and keenly I've lived a hundred lives.

EDWARD: No...the trouble with my patients...

DOROTHY: Of course they are! That's why I've to be brought here by force. I never feel ill.

EDWARD: Never a pain in the pocket!

DOROTHY: I never *feel* it.

EDWARD: The trouble when most people do is that it's all they can feel or believe in. And I have to patch them up.

DOROTHY: Put a patch on the pocket... tonic the poor reputation.

EDWARD: What can I say to them? If they found out that the world as they've made it doesn't exist...or perhaps their next world as they've invented it either...

DOROTHY: Oh but I think Heaven exists... just about as much. And that you'll all be there...bustling among the clouds...making the best of things...beating your harps into coin...bargaining for eternity...and saying that of course what you go on in hope of is another and a better world.

EDWARD: Shall we meet?

DOROTHY: I think not. I flung my soul over the footlights before ever I was sure that I had one...well, I was never uncomfortably sure. As you warned me I should...biting your pipe. No, thanks, I don't want another. I have been given happier dreams. Do you remember that letter of your father's that I would read?

EDWARD: No...

DOROTHY: Oh yes! Think twice, my dear boy, think twice before you throw yourself away on this actress.

EDWARD: Old innocent! *You* were the cautious one.

DOROTHY: But you never knew, Edward, how tempted I was.

EDWARD: Dorothy, don't! The years haven't taught me to take that calmly.

DOROTHY: Every woman is what I was more or less...

EDWARD: Less.

DOROTHY: So they seem. And you won't pay the price of more.

EDWARD: What was it? I was ready... and ready to pay.

DOROTHY: The price to you of my freedom when you love me! Why...dear Edward...your jaw sets even now. And so...for your happiness...that your minds may be easy as you bustle through the world's work...so we must seem to choose the catlike comfort of the fireside, the shelter of your cheque-book and our well-mannered world. And, perhaps I should have chosen that if I could have had my choice.

EDWARD: Dorothy!

DOROTHY: Had not some ruthless windy power from beyond me...blown me free.

EDWARD: Dorothy...I've loved you... and I do...with a love I've never understood. But sometimes I've been glad you didn't marry me...prouder of you as you were. Because my love would seem a very little thing.

DOROTHY: It is.

EDWARD: I never boasted...never of that.

DOROTHY: But the more precious...a jewel. And if we're to choose and possess things...nothing finer. My dear...what woman wouldn't love you? You've not been flattered enough. Never mind...you lost no dignity on your knees. I had no choice though but to be possessed...of seven angels. Oh, my dear friend...could you ever have cast them out?

EDWARD: I've watched them wear you through...the seven angels of your art that kept you from me.

DOROTHY: Yes...I'm a weary woman.

(For a moment there is silence.)

EDWARD: But sometimes I've wondered...what we two together might have done. Dorothy, why didn't you try?

DOROTHY: Not with these silly self-conscious selves. Poor prisoners...born to an evil time. But visions do come...of better things than we are...of a theatre not tinselled...and an office not dusty with law...all rustling with quarrelsome papers. How wrong to tie up good lively quarrels with your inky tape! Oh, shut your eyes...it's easier to see then. Are they shut?

EDWARD: Close. And the grip of your hand is wonderful for the eyesight.

DOROTHY: Aren't you an artist, too, Edward...our fault if we forget it. For Law is a living thing. It must be, mustn't it?

EDWARD: Yes...I had forgotten.

DOROTHY: My dreams and the stories of them are worthless unless I've a living world to dream of? What are words and rules and names? Armour with nothing inside it. So our dreams are empty, too.

EDWARD: Dorothy, my dear, it may sound as silly as ever when I say it...but why, why didn't you marry me?

DOROTHY: Yes...I should have made a difference to this habitation, shouldn't I?

EDWARD: Would you have cared to come here then?

DOROTHY: Always...the spirit of me. And I do think you were a better match than the looking-glass.

EDWARD: I promise you should always have found yourself beautiful...in my eyes.

DOROTHY: But I'm widowed of my looking-glasses, Edward. Have you noticed that for fifteen years there's not been one in my house...except three folding ones in the bathrooms?

EDWARD: I remember my wife remarking it. She wondered how you studied your parts.

DOROTHY: I could have told her how I learnt not to...and it's rather interesting.

EDWARD: Tell me.

DOROTHY: This is perhaps the little bit of Truth I've found...my little scrap of gold. From its brightness shines back all the vision I have...and I add it proudly to the world's heap. Though it sounds the silliest thing...as silly as your loving me at fifty-seven, more babyishly than you did at seventeen.

EDWARD: Please heaven my clerks don't see me till...

DOROTHY: Till you're quite self-conscious again. Well, growing older, as we say...and self-conscious, Edward...I found that the number of my looking-glasses grew. Till one day I counted them...and big and small there were forty-nine. Yes...then I used to work out my parts in front of every mirror in turn. Now there was a woman used to come and sew for me. You know! I charitably gave her jobs...took an interest in her "case"...encouraged her to talk her troubles out for comfort's sake. I wasn't interested...I didn't care one bit...it didn't comfort her. She talked to me because she thought I liked it...because she thought I thought she liked it. But, oddly, it was just sewing she liked and she sewed well and sewing did her good...You remember my Lily Prince in "The Backwater"?

EDWARD: Yes.

DOROTHY: My first real failure.

EDWARD: I liked it.

DOROTHY: My first dead failure...dear Public. Do you know why? I hadn't found Lily Prince in the mirrors, I'd found her in that woman as she sewed.

EDWARD: I didn't think it a failure.

DOROTHY: Well...the dear Public wouldn't pay to see it...and we've found no other word. But I knew if that was failure now I meant to fail...and I never looked in a mirror again. I took the looking-glasses down...I turned their faces to the wall. For I had won free from that shadowed emptiness of self. But nobody understood. Do you?

EDWARD: If I can't...I'll never say that I love you again.

DOROTHY: What can we understand when we're all so prisoned in mirrors that whatever we see it's but ourselves...Truth lives where only other people are. That's the secret. Turn the mirror to the wall and there is no you...but the world of other people is a wonderful world.

EDWARD: We've called them your failures perhaps...when we wouldn't follow you there.

DOROTHY: And I that have, proudly, never bargained was so tempted to bargain for success...by giving you what your appetites wanted...that mirrored mannequin slightly oversize that bolsters up your self-conceit.

EDWARD: But you had meant our youth to us, Dorothy...

DOROTHY: I'd given you that...the flower of me. Had I grudged it?

EDWARD: I think we're frightened of the world of Lily Prince.

DOROTHY: Well you may be!

EDWARD: If we couldn't find ourselves there with our virtues and our vanity... the best and worst of what we know.

DOROTHY: So you all failed me, you see...Oh, my poor theatre! Keep it for a while then to patronise and play with. But one day it shall break you all in pieces. And now my last curtsey's made...

(The paper knife she has been playing with snaps.)

EDWARD: Dorothy...what an omen! Not your last visit here, too!

DOROTHY: A fine omen. I do not surrender my sword! But I shouldn't march off quite so proudly, Edward, if it weren't for a new voice from that somewhere in me where things are born saying...shall I tell you what it says?

EDWARD: Please.

DOROTHY: The scene is laid in Dorothy's soul. Characters...A voice...Dorothy. Dorothy discovered as the curtain rises in temper and tears. The voice: "Thirty-five years finding out your mistake! But that's a very short time." Dorothy: "Boohoo!...but now I'm going to die." The voice: "Who told you so?" Dorothy: "Oh...aren't I?...Or rather Am I not?" The voice: "Dorothy, my dear...what led you that November day to your ruined Abbey? What voice was it called to you so loud to make it yours? Yours! What are you beside the wisdom of its years? You must go sit, Dorothy, sit very patiently, in the sunshine under the old wall...where marigolds grow...and there's one foxglove...(hsh! I planted it!)

Did it trouble those builders...who built it not for themselves...not for you...but to the glory of God they built it...did it trouble them that they were going to die?" Dorothy: "If they'd known that the likes of me would one day buy it with good hard cash they'd have had heart failure on the spot. Besides they did die and their blessed Abbey's a ruin." Two thousand five hundred pounds it cost me to do it up!

EDWARD: Well?

DOROTHY: If I say anything like that, of course, the voice is silent. But if I sit there after sunset when the world's all still...I often sit to watch the swallows, and if you keep quiet they'll swoop quite close...then I can hear the voice say: "They built the best they could...they built their hearts into the walls...they mixed the mortar with their own heart's blood. They spoke the truth that was in them and then they were glad to die." "But was it true?" I ask. "And see how the wall is crumbling." And then the voice says, "What is Truth but the best that we can build?...And out of its crumbling other truth is built. I sit there till the stars shine and there are friendly spirits around me. Not the dead...never...but the unborn...waiting their heritage...my gift to them...That's the true length of life...the finished picture of his being that the artist signs and sells...gives...loses! It was his very soul and it is gone. But then he is glad to go...to be dust again...nothingness...air...for he knows most truly...

EDWARD: What?

DOROTHY: Why, I told you. That he was always nothingness called by some great name...that the world of other people is the only world there is. Edward...what's the time?

EDWARD: Past one.

DOROTHY: Well, I'm hungry. Take me out and give me lunch.

EDWARD: Bless you...I will.

(With three fine gestures she puts on her hat again. Time was when one would sit through forty minutes of a dull play just to see DOROTHY take off her hat and put it on again. Much less expressively he finds his and they go out together. The clerks all stare ecstatically as she passes.)

HARLEY GRANVILLE BARKER (1877–1946)

Harley Granville Barker was one of the most influential figures in the history of the modern theater. "We are all in debt to Granville Barker," wrote the *Guardian* in 2006, "His ideas were prophetic and extraordinary." He was an inspired actor and director, a visionary producer, and a brilliant playwright.

Harley Granville Barker's impact is still felt keenly, here and in England. His *Prefaces to Shakespeare* revolutionized the approach to staging the plays—in fact, some credit him with evolving the role of the modern director as unifier of the creative elements in drama and representative of the author.

In 1904, along with business partner J. E. Vedrenne, Barker began producing plays at the Royal Court Theatre. For three seasons—a "thousand performances," as they came to be known—Barker presided over one of the most influential theatrical enterprises, helping to give birth to a new drama. He became Shaw's champion, producing eight of his plays—and taking leading roles in several of them, including John Tanner in *Man and Superman* and Adolphus Cusins in *Major Barbara*. (The only other playwright to receive more than one production in these three years was St. John Hankin.) *The Voysey Inheritance* premiered at the Royal Court in 1905, with Barker in the role of Edward, but his 1907 play, *Waste*, was banned and did not receive a license until 1936.

Barker was the driving force behind the effort to see a national theater founded in England, and it was a bitter disappointment to him that his efforts were unsuccessful. In 1977, when the National Theatre finally had a home along the Thames, it produced *The Madras House* in tribute to Granville Barker, the first revival of that play since 1934.

To Hyphenate or Not to Hyphenate

Lillah McCarthey played opposite Barker in *Man and Superman* in 1904; two years later they married and they worked together on stage and as co-producers for nearly the next ten years. These years were filled with struggle, hardship, and frustration. In 1915 Barker accepted an invitation to travel to New York to direct; there he met and fell in love with a wealthy American, Helen Huntington, who was ten years his senior. Lillah resisted giving Barker the divorce he sought, and their parting was acrimonious. In 1918 Barker married Huntington, and he effectively retired from the professional theater, preferring the life of a writer and scholar to that of producer and director (he and Huntington translated a number of plays together). Apparently at his wife's insistence, he also rejected the socialism of Shaw and his old friends, and their bohemian lifestyle.

It was in 1918 that he added the hyphen to his name, and began using "Harley" for the first time. Richard Dietrich, author of *British Drama 1890–1950* writes:

> We all live separate public and private lives, but Barker made a point of it with his name change. He came to think the aristocratically hyphenated version his real self, long suppressed, but most of his old friends and colleagues thought the name change a sign of self-betrayal and even a betrayal of them and the cause of establishing an alternate theater.

Some scholars today refer to the author with either name, depending on the original publication date of the work they are discussing. For this volume, we have adopted the usage requested by the Society of Authors, which represents his estate; although this hybrid between the two names is not one he would recognize: he was first Granville Barker, and later Harley Granville-Barker.

MINT THEATER COMPANY

Established in 1992, Mint Theater Company exists to bring new vitality to lost or neglected plays. Mint excavates buried theatrical treasures, reclaiming them for our time through research, dramaturgy, production, publication, and a variety of enrichment programs and advocates for their ongoing life in theaters everywhere. Mint's 2001 Obie Grant recognized its success in combining "the excitement of discovery with the richness of tradition. When it comes to the library," the citation reads, "there's no theater more adventurous." Mint's Drama Desk Award (2002) recognizes the importance of Mint's mission of "unearthing, presenting, and preserving forgotten plays of merit."

Worthy But Neglected: Plays of the Mint Theater Company, an anthology of seven rediscoveries, is a lasting embodiment of Mint's mission and an important tool in the effort to broaden its reach. Other publications include two additional volumes in the *Reclaimed* series featuring playwrights who have received more than one production at the Mint. *Arthur Schnitzler Reclaimed* features new English-language versions of two masterworks from Austrian writer Arthur Schnitzler—both received their New York premieres at the Mint: *The Lonely Way* (*Der einsame Weg*) and *Far and Wide* (*Das weite Land*). *St. John Hankin Reclaimed* includes *The Charity that Began at Home* and *The Return of the Prodigal.*

Lost plays rediscovered by Mint include the world premiere of Dawn Powell's 1931 *Walking Down Broadway,* the New York Premiere of *Welcome to Our City* by novelist Thomas Wolfe; the first New York revivals of the Pulitzer Prize–winners *Alison's House* by Susan Glaspell and *Miss Lulu Bett* by Zona Gale as well as D. H. Lawrence's *The Daughter-in-Law,* John Galsworthy's *The Skin Game,* Rachel Crothers's *Susan and God*, St. John Ervine's *John Ferguson* and J. M. Barrie's *Echoes of the War.* Mint strives to expand the canon of plays considered worthy of production and study in theaters, schools, and libraries. In the last few years, Cecily Hamilton's *Diana of Dobson's,* Githa Sowerby's *Rutherford and Son,* and *The Voysey Inheritance*—all produced by Mint—have received productions at other theaters in the U.S. and Canada, bringing new vitality to plays that have lain fallow for years, some for nearly a century. Visit www.minttheater.org for more information.